THE *Archive Photographs* SERIES

RAMSGATE AND ST LAWRENCE

Mr Goatham, of Elliots the Stonemasons of St Peter's Park Road, Broadstairs, adds the finishing touches to the Borough of Ramsgate's Coat of Arms which would be proudly displayed near the main entrance of Hollicondane Primary School. The school's construction was started in 1939 but the Second World War interrupted its completion and it was not finally opened until April 1949, ten years later.

Compiled by
Don Dimond and Barrie Wootton

First published 1996

The Chalford Publishing Company
St Mary's Mill, Chalford,
Stroud, Gloucestershire, GL6 8NX

ISBN 0 7524 0035 5

Typesetting and origination by
The Chalford Publishing Company
Printed in Great Britain by
Redwood Books, Trowbridge

Contents

RAMSGATE'S HEYDAY HARBOUR PARADE, *c*. 1910.

Introduction

This book is a walk through the history of Ramsgate via the medium of the Victorian invention of photography. Never intended as a chronological history of the town – the late Charles Busson's book on Ramsgate cannot be equalled – it provides a peep at events and people of the last hundred years.

Starting at the village of St Lawrence, the original hamlet from which the town of Ramsgate was to emerge, the journey visits tumbledown buildings, majestic hotels, schools, colleges, and the narrow streets and parks surrounded by open fields which make up the urban sprawl called Ramsgate Town.

Revisit the Golden Sands packed with people, ice-cream stalls, Pierrots, concert parties and bathing machines. Gaze at the faces of former local personalities such as Dame Janet Stancomb Wills (Ramsgate's first Mayoress) and Lady Rose Weigall (the Duke of Wellington's niece). See local industries which are now no more, such as boat building yards, fishing smacks and breweries, and the crowded shops which filled the town centre and helped bring prosperity to its residents.

It is hoped these photographs will give the younger generation an insight into their town's former glories while bringing back many happy memories to its older residents.

One

Nethercourt and St Lawrence

NETHERCOURT TOLL HOUSE. This view greeted the traveller entering the village of St Lawrence. To the left was a small pond and on the right the Toll House, a single-storey building wherein lived the man who collected toll money paid by users of this private road for its upkeep.

SOUTHWOOD HOUSE, 1914. This imposing building was the home of Lady Rose Weigall, the niece of the Duke of Wellington. Her husband was half of a solicitors partnership called Weigall & Inch. During the First World War Lady Rose allowed Southwood House to be used as a convalescent home for the many wounded soldiers. Her daughter Rachel was a member of the Red Cross and helped to nurse the country's wounded at her mother's home. The house is now demolished but has been memorialized by naming the estate built on its grounds Southwood Gardens.

WEDDING GROUP. Among the guests in this photograph are Lady Rose Weigall and her husband, Henry Weigall DL, JP, an artist whose paintings were exhibited at the Royal Academy. Lady Rose and her husband are at the right hand end of the front row; the army officer in the back row, third from the left, is one of their sons.

ST LAWRENCE HIGH STREET. A Boy's Band marching past the Six Bells public house. During its existence it attained a notorious reputation and was eventually closed on the insistence of the Borough Police in August 1909.

ST LAWRENCE HIGH STREET A HUNDRED YEARS AGO. This bears little resemblance to today's busy thoroughfare. To the left, behind the thatched cottage, can be seen the imposing tower of St Lawrence church; in the distance is the Rose Inn, now sadly demolished.

ST LAWRENCE CHURCH, *c.* 1830. An old print showing St Lawrence church before any restoration work had been carried out. Note the absence of the church clock, and the small window which was later to be enlarged. The church was one of three main village churches in Thanet, the others being St Peter's and St John's. Canon Scott Robertson states that 'This church seems to have attained its present form about the year 1200, and there can be no doubt that a smaller church stood on the same site during the twelfth century.'

INTERIOR VIEW OF ST LAWRENCE CHURCH, 1920. This view shows the altar and the magnificent stained-glass window. In front of the altar stands a brass eagle lectern donated by Miss Astle during the church restoration year, 1890. Around the walls are memorial plaques to many local dignitaries and clergy; among those commemorated are Baroness Elizabeth Conyngham, Rear Admiral Fox, after whom the public house in Grange Road is named, and Thomas Garrett, who lived in Ellington House.

A HORSE-DRAWN HEARSE outside the main gates of St Lawrence church. The coffin being removed by the pall bearers is that of Lady Alice Harriet Seager Hunt Bt, who died on 27 August 1934.

ST LAWRENCE HIGH STREET as viewed from the Wheatsheaf, looking towards Ellington Park. The houses depicted on the right hand side have all been demolished and a road-widening scheme implemented. Sadly, this narrow tree-shaded thoroughfare has given way to today's traffic-laden and congested road.

ST LAWRENCE HIGH STREET. An old print of the High Street in 1851 (published by D.P. Fuller) shows the unmade road of the era. To the left can be seen the fine building which was the Deaf and Dumb Asylum, later called Uppercourt. Opposite, on the right, stands Wilton Croft, a Victorian mansion and home of the Wotton family. Ellington Infants' School replaced Uppercourt at a later date.

HIGH STREET, ST LAWRENCE, *c.* 1938. The change in this part of the village is readily apparent. All the old houses have been swept away to provide a wide thoroughfare for the horseless carriage to wend its way along, but now even this road is hard-pressed to cope with busy traffic. To the right is Ellington Infants' School.

ELLINGTON PARK, 1934. These ladies are elegantly dressed for the 1934 Ramsgate Pageant which celebrated fifty years since the Inception of Borough Status on the Town of Ramsgate. They are all teachers from Lillian Road Infants' School. The lady second from the right is Mrs Sparkes (née Smith); the lady in black in the centre of the group is Miss Nightingale, Headmistress of the Infants' School. Three of the ladies have long ringlets, which enhance their period costumes.

SOUTH EASTERN ROAD takes its name from the old South Eastern Railway, the first company to open a line, on Easter Monday, 13 April 1846. The only traffic is a horse and cart. Gone are the splendid trees.

ABERDEEN HOUSE, *c.* 1910, situated at the junction of Ellington Road and South Eastern Road. Once a Boys' School founded by the Reverend George Simmers MA in 1885, it later became a private boarding house under the management of Captain and Mrs L. Lanchester. In 1937 it became a Registry Office; today it is Thanet's only remaining one.

DUNCAN ROAD, *c.* 1916, once part of the vast Ellington Estate, photographed some time during the First World War. The third house on the left is a barbers shop, proprietor Mr J. Newman. Today it is a private residence.

Two

Town Centre

CANNON ROAD CAR PARK, MAY 1932. The municipal car park being constructed on the site of Ramsgate's Rope Walk, so-called because of the rope and cable work which was carried out on this site during the early days of Ramsgate's maritime history. The cost of the car park project was £7,149 10s 0d.

ST CATHERINE'S HOSPITAL. In 1901 a Mrs Ellis bought Conyngham House and two adjacent properties previously known as Conyngham House School for use as a hospital to be run by the Daughters of the Cross. During the First World War the hospital became a Convalescent Home for Wounded Soldiers, and after hostilities ceased it reverted to a Convent, and in due time became a Technical College. The grounds stood vacant for a period of time until, in 1995, a new school was built at a cost of £1,300,000, and named Priory Infants' School.

THIS INTERIOR VIEW OF S.R. PORT'S SHOP depicts a remarkable selection of building materials. The rolls of felt displayed in the foreground are priced at 5s 6d and 7s 6d respectively. There were branches of Ports at 68 Boundary Road and St Peter's Park Road, Broadstairs.

Opposite: S.R. PORT PREMISES, 66 HIGH STREET, RAMSGATE, previously the Isle of Thanet Cement and Drain-pipe Depot of Mr Brewer, established in 1852. S.R. Port were a well-known local builders' merchants who carried on well into the 1950s.

ST GEORGE'S CHURCH c. 1906. Built in the Gothic style on land purchased from Mr Townley for the sum of £900, the church took three years to build and cost £21,736 13s 2 Q w d. The architects were Mr Hemesley and Mr Kendall, the builders' were Jarman's of Ramsgate. The church was consecrated by the Archbishop of Canterbury in the presence of the Duchess of Kent and her daughter, Princess Victoria, later Queen Victoria, on 23 October 1827.

INTERIOR OF ST GEORGE'S CHURCH. This view depicts a spectacular painting called 'From Darkness to Light' executed by Mr Henry Weigall in 1885. It was restored in 1926. The painting shows three angels carrying a departed saint to Heaven.

J.C. LYNE, FAMILY BUTCHER. An incredible display of mutton and beef at J.C. Lyne's butchers, surmounted on each side by ornamental Victorian lamp standards which once graced Ramsgate's High Street. Lyne's was two doors away from Lord George Sangers Amphitheatre, now Gateways Grocers.

HIGH STREET, RAMSGATE, *c.* 1910. A superb view of the junction of Hardres Street and the High Street. The shop depicted on the right is a grocers, wine and spirit merchant owned by F.H. Welch. It is now the National Westminster Bank. The tranquillity of this Edwardian scene must bring back happy memories to those lucky enough to have been born in this era.

HIGH STREET, RAMSGATE, *c.* 1912, looking towards Chatham Street. On the right can be seen Marks & Spencers Ltd, Fuggles the Pawnbrokers, and H. Bourne & Son, ladies outfitters. On the left is the well-known Curry's cycle store, the Central Hotel, and the sign for the Granville Studio, later taken over by Samuel Carr & Son, photographers.

OLD POST OFFICE, *c.* 1900. Ramsgate's first postal service started at Burgess and Hunt's Library on the corner of the High Street and Queen Street around 1800 and later located further up the High Street, where it is depicted on this postcard.

THE TOWN HALL, RAMSGATE, 1912. A huge crowd gathers outside the old Town Hall to celebrate the visit to Ramsgate of 650 French people accompanied by the Calais Town Band. Before 1726 the site was occupied by a pond called 'The Sole'. In 1726 a Poor House was erected, which was replaced in 1785 by the Market House. The Town Hall, built on this same site in 1839, was demolished in 1955 and replaced by Burton's, the tailors.

THE RED LION HOTEL, *c.* 1908. Situated in King Street at the junction of Harbour Street and the High Street, this public house was established in 1717, making it one of the oldest in the town. The landlord in 1908 was Mr Arthur Wells and the brewer's were Fleet's of Broad Street, Ramsgate.

TOWN HALL, *c.* 1880s. Once the centre of Ramsgate's commercial life, regular markets were held here three days a week, on Tuesday, Thursday and Saturday, when market gardeners would attend from miles around. Standing in the centre of the picture with his left hand holding the lapel of his coat is Mr W.R. Martin, who had a greengrocery business in the plains of Waterloo. On Mr Martin's right is Mr Jack East, who once had a sailmakers' business in the town. Behind Mr Martin, wearing a cap, is Mr George Burbridge, who at one time ran a market garden near the synagogue. Seated on the horse in the foreground is Mr Weeks, a member of a firm of haulage contractors who carried on a business in Bethesda Street. The police officer on the right is thought to be PC Alfred Archer. The Town Hall was built in 1839 and demolished in 1955 to make way for Burtons the 30s Tailors, followed by 'Warehouse Club' premises now vacated.

YE OLDE HORSE AND GROOM. Situated in Charlotte Court behind the Stag's Head, Harbour Street, its claim to having been established in 1700 is erroneous as the Horse and Groom was first built as a dwelling house in 1830 and did not become a public house until 1840, when it traded under the name of The Royal Arms. Britain's once oldest brewery, Tomson and Wotton Ltd, bought it in 1865 and, because of the close proximity of Sacketts Livery Stables, renamed it the Horse and Groom. Its first landlord under Tomson and Wotton was Mr Stephen Fox.

ALDERMAN PAUL MAURICE UPRIGHT, 1888, the owner of Uprights Hotel in the High Street which later became Central Hotel, then Celebrations, then Quality Seconds. Paul Upright was one of Ramsgate's first Aldermen when the town became a borough on 21 March 1884, and he is depicted here in a drawing by the famous artist Frederick Waddy.

TOWN HALL INTERIOR. The above picture depicts a convened Special Meeting and Ceremony which took place in the Council Chambers on the afternoon of Thursday 27 February 1936, when the Mayor, Harry Stead, presented a framed Certificate of the Freedom of the Borough of Ramsgate to Alderman Mrs Florence Louisa Dunn, affectionately known as 'Auntie Flo'.

THE CENTRAL SUPPLY STORE, 1924. This quality grocery, wine and spirits store at 13 King Street was owned by John T. Winton and situated next to Abbots Hill. The store also stocked a large selection of china, glass and earthenware.

J. T. WINTON

(Late PILCHER PAGE & Co.),

The Central Supply Stores,

Telephone No. 17. Established 1799.

13 KING STREET,

Telegrams: "WINTON, RAMSGATE."

RAMSGATE.

Finest quality Groceries, Tea, Coffee, Provisions, Wines, Spirits, Bottled Beers, Mineral Waters, etc., at store prices.

CHINA, GLASS AND EARTHENWARE DEPARTMENT.

PROMPT DELIVERY IN TOWN AND COUNTRY.

The "CENTRAL SUPPLY STORES."

[P.T.O

ADVERTISEMENT FOR JOHN T. WINTON, SUPPLY STORES.

A.N. AUSTEN'S SHOP AT THE PLAINS OF WATERLOO. Mr Albert Austen's grocery provisions and tobacco shop was situated on the north-east side of the Plains of Waterloo which ends at the junction with King Street.

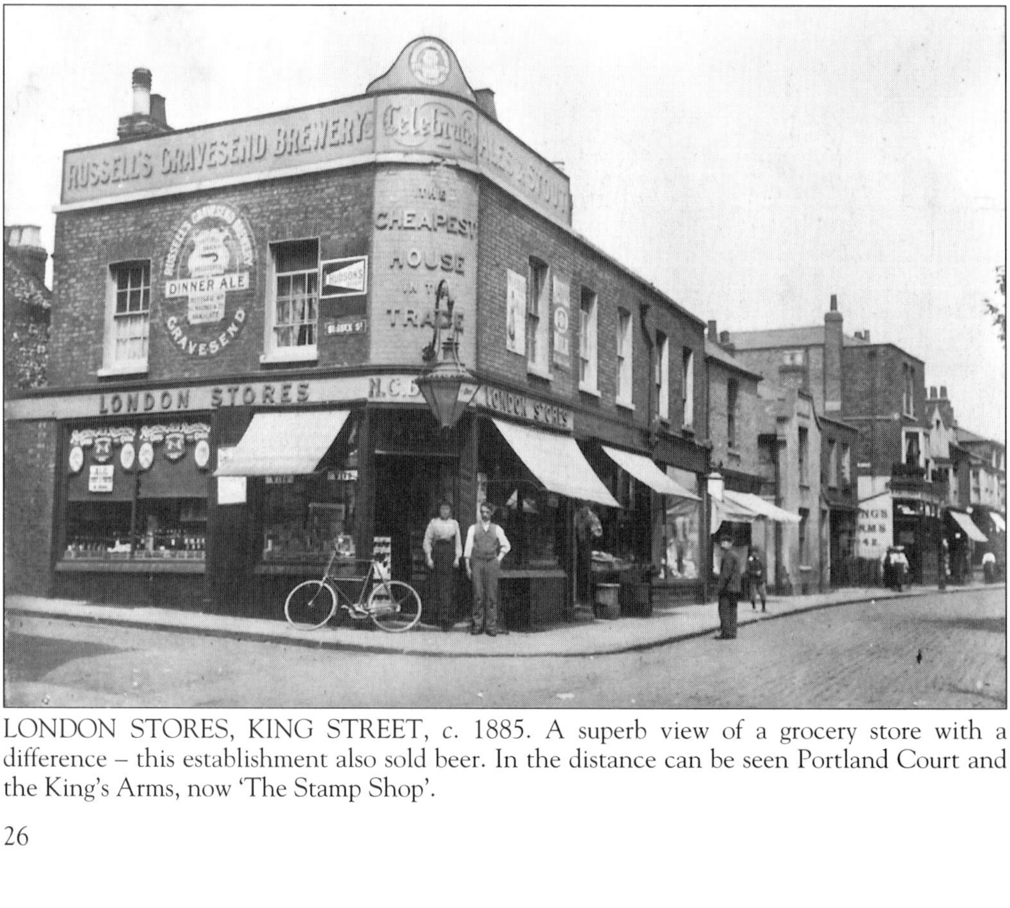

LONDON STORES, KING STREET, *c.* 1885. A superb view of a grocery store with a difference – this establishment also sold beer. In the distance can be seen Portland Court and the King's Arms, now 'The Stamp Shop'.

SS ETHELBERT AND GERTRUDE, ROMAN CATHOLIC CHURCH, *c.* 1919. A donation of £3,000 from a Miss Ellis, believed to have lived in Victory Villas, 18 Hereson Road, enabled the church to be built. The total cost was £3,300, the remainder coming from St Augustine's Abbey, Ramsgate. The foundation stone was laid by Bishop Francis on 15 June 1901.

MONTEFIORE DAIRY ON THE CORNER OF LILIAN ROAD AND HERESON ROAD, *c.* 1913. The proprietor of this dairy was Mr H. Denne. The photograph depicts some of the various means of transport once used to deliver one's pinta to the doorstep!

THE HONEYSUCKLE INN OFF HERESON ROAD, *c.* 1905. This old public house situated on the outskirts of the town offers a scene of great tranquillity in a sparsely populated area, all now totally changed by urban sprawl and the motor car.

OLD HOUSES, HERESON, *c.* 1902. These ancient houses situated to the right of the Honeysuckle Inn were demolished in the early 1920s. The site is now vacant. The photographer was Mr G.E. Hoile of Boundary Road, Ramsgate.

Three

East Cliff

EAST CLIFF LODGE, *c.* 1913. Originally built around 1794 as the home of Benjamin Bond Hopkins, the property changed hands many times before being sold to Sir Moses Montefiore for the princely sum of £5,500 in 1832. Among the many famous people who stayed at the house before its demolition on 7 July 1953 were Baron Rothchild, William Pitt, the Duke of Wellington, George IV, Queen Caroline, Princess Victoria, and her mother, the Duchess of Kent.

THE LADY JUDITH MONTEFIORE COLLEGE situated between Hereson Road and Dumpton Park Drive. The foundation stone was laid on 24 June 1865. The building cost £5,100 and was completed in 1869. Established for the study of Hebrew Law and Literature, it includes a Lecture Hall and Reception Hall, and a Library which contained a valuable collection of Hebrew books and manuscripts. Sadly the building was demolished in 1964.

The County Ball Room, Ramsgate.

Accommodation for 3,000. *Dancing Every Evening*

THE COUNTY BALLROOM, RAMSGATE, *c.* 1935, situated in Dumpton Park Drive, was built in 1910. Opened on Saturday 30 July, the ballroom measured 187ft 6in by 74ft 4in. One of the dance groups who played here was Alan Parson and his Band. Dancing was from 7.30 p.m. to 12 p.m., with entrance fee 1s. The ballroom was also used for roller-skating. Today it is a factory used by Hunton Ltd, Tool Manufacturers.

SAN CLU HOTEL, RAMSGATE, *c.* 1952. Built in 1833 and originally named St Cloud, the hotel was renamed San Clu in 1920. It was the scene of a disastrous fire on Thursday 25 October 1928 which resulted in part of the hotel being demolished. Mrs Robson, the owner of the hotel since 1935, was trapped on the top floor in another fire in 1973 but was successfully rescued by Ramsgate Fire Brigade and the building was saved.

THE GRANVILLE HOTEL, built in 1864, is a well-known landmark occupying one of the finest positions on the East Cliff. Designed by the famous Edward Welby Pugin, it is one of the finest examples of Pugin's Gothic style, and was used as a Canadian Hospital during the First World War. It also gave its name to the Granville Express, a train which ran London gentry to The Sands station for first-class summer holidays at the Granville Hotel.

THE FOUNDATION STONE of Holy Trinity church was laid by J.A. Warre Esq. on 29 March 1844. The architect was Mr W.E. Everard Henley LRIBA, of London, and the builder was M.W.E. Smith of Ramsgate. The total cost was £3,000. The first vicar was the Reverend Thomas Whitehead and the church was consecrated by the Archbishop of Canterbury on 11 June 1845.

THIS VIEW OF BELLEVUE ROAD in the early 1900s distinctly shows the tram lines of the Isle of Thanet Tramways which traversed this steep hill. Depicted in the left hand foreground is the magnificent ornate gas lamp which hung for many years outside the well-known Belle Vue Tavern.

EMPIRE BANDSTAND. This postcard was published by Arthur Narramore of the Post Office, 13 Bellevue Road. The bandstand was originally sited in front of the Granville Hotel but was dismantled in early 1914 and re-erected in the centre of Wellington Crescent. Sadly it has been replaced by a more modern structure.

WELLINGTON CRESCENT, *c.* 1930, built in 1819 and named after the famous Duke of Wellington, who often visited his brother, the Marquis of Wellesley, at East Cliff Lodge. During the Napoleonic Wars the grounds around this area were used for military purposes. The photograph depicts the old Truro Court building at the far side of the crescent which has since been demolished and replaced by flats.

ALBION PLACE. These properties built on Mount Albion in 1789 include Albion House, the residence of Princess Victoria in 1830, which is on the extreme right. Fronted by well-kept gardens, these houses were for many years the home of Ramsgate Borough Council until the advent of Thanet District Council.

KIRKALDIE OYSTER BAR, *c.* 1908, at the top of Kent Steps. Before the cliff was excavated a path and wooden steps gave access to Albion Place. Today stone steps give better access to the seafront. The Oyster Bar is now the Albion Café.

RAMSGATE TOWN WAR MEMORIAL. Dedicated to those sons and daughters who never returned, the sculpture, called 'Destiny', was unveiled on Wednesday 17 December 1920. Situated in Albion Gardens, the memorial was a gift to the townspeople by its wealthy benefactor Dame Janet Stancomb Wills; the sculptor and designer was the well-known Mr Gilbert Bays.

GROCERY STORE in Albion Hill, not Madeira Walk. This grocery store was first mentioned in 1883. It is believed that the owner, Mr Charles Foat, and his family are shown here.

HARBOUR PARADE, c. 1920s. This scene shows the changing mode of transport. A hand-cart is seen on the left hand side and a horse-drawn cart in the centre foreground; on the extreme right are the horse-drawn brakes and single-decker petrol-driven bus of the East Kent Road Car Company, all competing for the holiday visitors' custom.

Four

Ramsgate Harbour and Sands

THE HARBOUR PARADE, *c.* 1870, originally called Waterside. The most notable difference is the Albion Hotel in the centre of the picture which still had its left hand wing in place. This was later demolished to make way for Madeira Walk, built in 1892. The buildings on the side of the hotel have changed little but, sadly, the fishing smacks in the harbour have all disappeared. Smack R439 depicted right of centre is called *Young Tom* and was one of many smacks owned by Mr T. Hatton of Ramsgate.

RAMSGATE CUSTOM HOUSE, *c.* 1908. When it was built Ramsgate was a busy trading port. Next door is the Shipwright Arms, aptly named as it is almost facing Ramsgate's Pier Yard and slipway, once the home to Claxton's & Co., Ship Engineers.

THE REFECTORY when it was a Tomson and Wotton house, the local brewers of Elms Avenue. The pub achieved notoriety in the early 1950s as a favourite haunt of United States airmen stationed at Manston. It will be remembered by many who saw American 'Snowdrops' helping the servicemen out of the bar. Thought to have gained its name from a Refectory kept by a Mr Davidson in the area, the pub is a much quieter venue today!

RAILWAY STATION SEAFRONT, *c.* 1905. The first train to use this London Chatham & Dover Railway station on The Sands arrived on 5 October 1863. The line was to bring thousands of Londoners directly to Ramsgate's Golden Sands until 1 July 1926, when it closed and the town was served by the main station at St Lawrence and a smaller one at Dumpton.

RAILWAY ACCIDENT, 31 AUGUST 1891. Miraculously, only one person was killed in the first railway accident to occur in Ramsgate. A hawker, Mr Grainger, was killed while selling his fish, etc. by the turntable wall. The driver and mate jumped clear before the train smashed through the turntable wall and careered across the Promenade, stopping just short of falling into a sawpit.

THE MARINA. Built and developed by Mr Edmund Davis, the Granville Marina was opened on 5 July 1877 by Earl Sydney, Lord Lieutenant of Kent. Popularly named the 'Establishment', it was used for music and other entertainments. To enable the houses on the left of the photograph to be built, 80,000 tons of chalk had to be removed. The Marina Hall later became a cinema and is at present vacant premises.

THE MARINA GARDENS. Looking the other way, towards what was The Sands station, a typical 1920s view of an Englishman's holiday – overcast skies and overcoats!

EAST CLIFF BATHING STATION. Situated by the Eastern Undercliff, the station was opened on 24 June 1914. It was later to become the site of the Marina Swimming and Boating Pool. This view was taken in 1924.

MARINA SKATING RINK AND BATHING POOL replaced the Marina Bathing Station under the East Cliff. This former Ramsgate asset, with boating pool, cafés, sun-bathing terraces and skating rink, is sadly no more. Today it is a parking space!

RAMSGATE SANDS. This view of Ramsgate Sands was taken at the height of its popularity. The railway station to the left disgorged the discerning visitor directly onto the Golden Sands, where 'Lawrence', 'Taylor' and 'Mumfords' Bathing Machine proprietors vied for your custom. In the background can be seen the Iron Pier built by Head Wrighton and Company of Stockton-on-Tees which opened on 31 July 1881. It was finally demolished in 1930 after a number of mishaps including a fire and partial demolition by a First World War mine.

HARBOUR AREA, *c.* 1880s. Ramsgate Harbour Colonnade, on the left, consisting of lock-up shops, suffered severely during the gale of November 1877 which lasted for three days. On 25 September 1821 George IV sailed from Ramsgate to Hanover and on his return received such a warm welcome from the residents of Ramsgate that he decreed that the Harbour should be named 'Royal'. On both visits George IV was the guest of Sir W.M. Curtis of Cliff House. To celebrate the honour the people of Ramsgate raised £700 by subscription to pay for a granite obelisk to be erected in the Pier Yard. On 8 November 1822 the Earl of Liverpool, the Lord Warden, laid the first stone, which weighed eleven tons and contained new specimens of coins of the realm and one Coronation Medal sent by the King for that purpose. On 19 July 1823 the Obelisk, later known as the 'Royal Toothpick', was finally unveiled!

BITS OF OLD RAMSGATE. Two views showing old Ramsgate as a sea-faring port. The top view of the Western End of the Inner Harbour shows Jacob's Ladder, built in 1826, but no Sailors' Home or Church; therefore this photograph was taken prior to 1878 when these buildings were completed. The bottom picture shows the difference the new road made to Harbour Parade and the corner of York Street when it was built. The view clearly shows the inner basin was used by bigger vessels, as seen in the background.

THE LONDON BOAT ARRIVING AT RAMSGATE, *c.* 1905. One of the General Steam Navigation Company's paddle steamers about to come alongside Ramsgate's Victoria landing stage when this was one of the most popular ways to travel to Ramsgate for a day trip from the metropolis. Not always the most calm or comfortable, it was certainly the quickest until trains arrived on the scene in 1841.

RAMSGATE HARBOUR. This postcard, printed by Blinko's, the well-known Ramsgate stationer, shows, to the right, Shaw's Lighthouse built of Cornish granite which replaced an older building and was first lit in 1843. The fishing smack depicted heading for the open sea is R141 *Vie*. She was owned by G.T. Offen and built at Galmpton Creek, Devon in 1896. In the distance can be seen the old Town Bucket Dredger *Ramsgate*.

RAMSGATE INNER BASIN, *c*. 1885, showing the paddle steamer *Queen of Thanet* moored to the Harbour Parade. This vessel, weighing 93 tons, was originally the *Carham*, owned by the Ramsgate Steam Boat Company. In the background can be seen the old Fish Market building.

THE WRECK. This unknown vessel is depicted in Ramsgate's safe haven. Unfortunately nothing has come to light about this incident but the postcard clearly shows what befell sailing vessels which dared to sail near the notorious Goodwin Sands. This one could, no doubt, be repaired by skilled craftsmen in one of Ramsgate's many boat yards existing at the turn of the century.

THE *BOUNTY*. One of the most popular attractions in Ramsgate Harbour in the post-war years was the floating restaurant called the *Bounty*, previously named the *Alaston*. In 1951 it was the intention of the owners to tow *Bounty* to the Festival of Britain site on the Thames by the Watkins tug *Cervia*, but for financial reasons she was diverted to Columbia Wharf, Grays, where she was eventually broken up.

With all Good Wishes.

J. FARNELL,

Harbour Missionary.

Sailors' Church, Ramsgate.

Motto for 1912.

" My Times are in Thy Hand."

Psalm xxxi., 15.

Tho' times of trouble should arise,
Help me to understand;
They may be blessings in disguise,
Whose times are in Thy hand.

My times are in Thy hand,
Why should I doubt or fear?
My Father's hand will never cause
His child a needless tear.

HARBOUR MISSIONARY. J. Farnell was one of the many missionaries who worked at the Sailors' Church and Harbour Mission and concerned himself with the physical and spiritual needs of the seamen and smackboys. The Mission was founded by the Reverend J. Eustace Brenan MA of Christ Church, Ramsgate. J. Farnell lived at 142 Grange Road, Ramsgate and served the Mission from 1904 to 1913.

The Moss Rose, Ramsgate

THE *MOSS ROSE*, *c.* 1900. This 34 ton boat was built by John Legg of Penzance in 1878. She spent the summer months taking visitors on sea trips around the coast and Goodwin Sands. In 1899 she was sold and became a fishing smack, ending her days in Pegwell Bay after striking a submerged wreck. The pleasure yacht *Royal Sovereign* replaced the *Moss Rose* and, after thirteen months, changed her name to the *New Moss Rose*, preserving the name so familiar to visitors.

CHARLES AND SUSANNA STEPHENS. The launch of the Ramsgate lifeboat *Charles and Susanna Stephens* on 25 May 1905. Donated by Mrs Stephens of Reading in memory of her late husband Charles, the boat's cost was £1,635. The previous four lifeboats had all been donated by the City of Bradford, after whom they were all named. Sadly, this boat ended the link with the town of Bradford but served twenty-one years with the town and saved 294 lives from the seas around Ramsgate.

THE TUG *HIBERNIA*. This view of the *Hibernia* on the slipway at Ramsgate was taken by photographer James Bishop of George Street, Ramsgate. The *Hibernia* was one of many tugs owned by Watkins Tugs Ltd, the second oldest tug company in the country, which used to operate out of Ramsgate Harbour in the 1920s and '30s.

THE *GULL* LIGHTSHIP. The *Gull* lightship was rammed and sunk by liner SS *City of York* at 4 a.m. on 16 March 1929. Subsequently raised and beached at North Deal, she eventually came to Ramsgate for repairs and is seen here on the slipway. After a complete refit she returned to a new station on the Goodwins in 1930. (Photographer Carr & Son, Ramsgate)

FISH MARKET AT RAMSGATE. This photograph was taken during the heyday of Ramsgate's fishing industry. Standing in the centre of the boxes of fish is Mr Harold Gisby, while among the onlookers are well-known local people such as Penn, Strivens, Taylor, Todd and Jack Hawks. The man in the trilby hat is Fred Pullman, the fish salesman. The market building directly behind this gathering was built in 1881 and destroyed on 17 June 1917 by a direct hit from a bomb dropped from a Zepplin LZ42 The building was used at the time as an ammunition store and was totally destroyed.

EAGLE CAFE AND LANDING STAGE. The Victorian landing stage disappeared along with the paddle steamers and the new landing stage was built in 1948. Motor vessels *Queen of the Channel* and *Royal Daffodil* transported day-trippers to France for a return fare of 35s. – the lure of foreign travel had begun.

The pleasure of the Company of

Mr Jesse Wood Lifeboatman Ramsgate RNLI

is requested at the Opening of the new landing stage, East Pier, Royal Harbour, Ramsgate, by

HER ROYAL HIGHNESS THE DUCHESS OF KENT,

C.I., G.C.V.O., G.B.E.

ON WEDNESDAY, 19TH MAY, 1948.

It is requested that the directions on the reverse of this card be closely followed

ROYAL INVITATION. The official invitation to Mr Jesse Wood, one of the crew members of Ramsgate's lifeboat, to the Opening Ceremony of the new landing stage at the end of the East Pier by HRH Princess Marina, Duchess of Kent, on Wednesday 19 May 1948.

RAMSGATE'S ROYAL DAY. HRH The Duchess of Kent, escorted by Stanley Edward Austin, Mayor of Ramsgate, Town Sergeant Mr Henry Porter and dignitaries, make their way along the Eastern Pier to open the new landing stage.

RAMSGATE'S ROYAL HARBOUR, 1920s. The changing face of Ramsgate's fishing fleet. Steam trawlers outnumber those driven by sail. Among those vessels under steam are R212 *Olivae*, R219 *Liberty*, R246 *Loyal Star*, R243 *Ocean Pride*, names that recall the personal pride in the ownership of a fishing vessel that would be handed down from father to son.

VICTORIAN RAMSGATE HARBOUR before the new road was built. The chalk cliffs behind the small fishing smacks would be changed completely with the improvements to Ramsgate's road system.

Five
New Road to Newington

NEW ROAD AND ROYAL PARADE, *c.* 1900. The new road is supported on brick arches and has a gradient of 1:25 as far as a point opposite Addington Street. In the beginning the elegant ornamental arches to the right of the road contained stone busts of well-known local people. The idea did not meet with local approval and one night the busts mysteriously disappeared! I wonder where they are now? This view includes Sion Hill and, on its right, York Terrace and the Westcliff Arcade; opposite the steps to Sion Hill is the Royal Temple Yacht Club founded on 4 March 1857.

YORK STREET AND HARBOUR PARADE. The building in the centre of the photograph is the Old Admiral Harvey, pulled down in 1902 and replaced by the present public house. Next door is Holyer's, followed by the large double-fronted shop of W.T. Foster, and Seamans' General Outfitters and Drapers, who sold boots, watches, clocks and hosiery. W.T. Foster's windows are bare, suggesting that the shop was empty prior to its being pulled down, thus dating this photograph to 1902. As most locals will know, Foster's moved to the opposite side of York Street and stayed there until 1963. It was considered to be one of Ramsgate's finest fishing tackle shops.

LEOPOLD STREET, *c.* 1904. Named to commemorate King Leopold of Belgium, who landed in Ramsgate in 1838 to attend the Coronation of Queen Victoria, and again in 1841 for the christening of the Princess Royal, Leopold Street can be seen between the first and second houses to the left of this photo. Farley Place is seen between the third and fourth houses. It was named after Farley's, a notable old Ramsgate sea-faring and ship-building family, whose boat building yard was in Leopold Street. Also clearly seen is the back entrance to the Admiral Napier. Sadly, all these buildings have been demolished in a major redevelopment of this area.

STORM DAMAGE TO THE NEW ROAD, 1926. A terrific thunder storm occurred in the early hours of Tuesday morning, 17 August 1926, which brought havoc to the town. After nearly two inches of rain fell the retaining wall below Prospect Terrace collapsed. A large crack in the brickwork caused by the ammunition dump explosion in 1917 was thought to have been the reason for this calamity, which occurred without injury to anyone.

NELSON CRESCENT was named after Admiral Lord Nelson and built in 1798. The only way to reach these properties was a road from the town which afterwards became Addington Street. Nelson Crescent was so select that the residents once built a wall twelve feet high to obstruct the view of their neighbours in Prospect Terrace. The horse-drawn brake seen here ascending the new road was to disappear as the tram service took over the town routes.

TIDAL BALL, SION HILL. Prior to 1798 when it was first rated, the area was called South Cliff. Elizabeth Fry, the prison reformer, died in one of these houses in 1845. The Foy Boat Hotel on the left of the picture was a watch house during Napoleonic times. The old pub was destroyed in 1941 and the new Foy Boat Tavern built after the war.

PARAGON, *c.* 1927. Until 1816 this neighbourhood was known as St George's Fields. In 1817, at the far end of this row of houses, the Isabella Baths were built. The name was later changed to the Kent Baths. Not a good financial proposition, it was replaced in 1864 by a large new building known as the Paragon Private Hotel, proprietor Mr H.G. Rose. Shops later appearing on the ground floor included a restaurant and the Paragon Corner House. Note the large telescope on the left of the postcard.

ITALIAN GARDENS AND BANDSTAND, *c.* 1904. A small garden was known to have existed on this site as far back as the 1870s. With the passage of time, the gardens were enlarged and improved to accommodate a small bandstand. Royal Crescent (first rated in 1841) as a backdrop to this musical venue provided an air of late Georgian elegance. Sadly, the gardens and bandstand were demolished to make way for the Westcliff Hall built in 1914.

THE OPENING OF THE WESTCLIFF CONCERT HALL on 25 July 1914. The builder was Grummant Brothers of Grange Road, Ramsgate, and the cost £3,257, a mere pittance by today's standard. Among the stars to appear at the Concert Hall in later years were Billie Merrin and Freddie Hargreaves to name but two. Today the Concert Hall is home to Ramsgate Motor Museum.

SPENCER SQUARE, 1930s, named after the Spencer family, who owned a considerable amount of property in Ramsgate Town. The land stretching from Spencer Square to Adelaide Gardens was a parade ground for cavalry in Napoleonic times. The north side of Spencer Square and Townley Street were enclosed barracks, entry to which could be gained through large gates situated in Addington Street. The troops left in 1819, the barracks were converted to dwelling houses and the Square was completed in 1838. On 15 June 1912 a public bowls green and tennis courts were opened. Today Southern Water have installed a large storage tank below ground at this site.

ROYAL ROAD, *c.* 1930. In 1819 Royal Road was known as Royal Terrace. This view taken from St Augustine's Road shows a row of elegant Georgian houses, one of which (No. 6) was William Stokes' Private School. Vincent Van Gogh was a teacher here from 16 April to 12 June 1876.

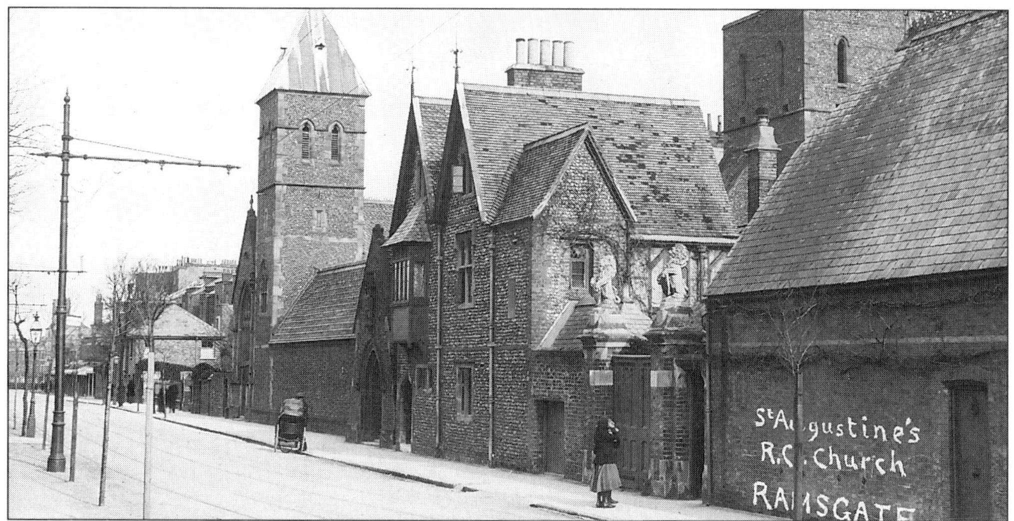

ST AUGUSTINE'S CHURCH AND THE GRANGE. Augustus Welby Pugin was the son of a French architect who fled to England at the time of the French Revolution. Born in 1812, he became one of England's best-known architects. He purchased land on Ramsgate West Cliff to build his own house and a church for the town's Roman Catholic congregation. Work started on the church in 1847 and was completed by 1851. The font was shown at the Great Exhibition at Crystal Palace in the same year. This view clearly shows the Grange to the right of the church. Pugin died in Ramsgate the year following the completion of the church at the early age of 40.

BANDSTAND AND TEA PAVILION in Royal Esplanade, part of the development of the St Lawrence Cliffs Estate which included a putting green, hard tennis courts, bowling green, shelters, and chine gardens. It was officially opened by the Mayor of Ramsgate, Alderman T.H. Prestedge CC, JP, on Friday 2 August 1927. The Mayor received the key from the architect, Mr Basil C. Deacon FRIBA, and unlocked the door to the magnificent Tea Pavilion. A fanfare of trumpets by the Band of the 14th/20th Hussars heralded the occasion. The cost of the Bandstand and Pavilion was £18,526, and the total cost of the scheme £160,519. Because of changing public demands, this area is now a boating pool.

THE WESTERN UNDERCLIFF, *c.* 1925. An unusual postcard, published by French company Enterprise Monnoyer, shows the sea wall nearing completion. On the right work is still being completed. Prince Edward Promenade and the Western Undercliff were officially opened by HRH The Prince of Wales on Wednesday 24 November 1926. The Undercliff Drive and sea wall cost £47,637.

THE WESTERN UNDERCLIFF AND LIFT, 1932. This view taken some six years later shows the finished scheme. The lift was completed and built by W.W. Martin at a cost of £3,328 in 1927. It is one of Ramsgate's most pleasant views.

WESTCLIFF TERRACE MANSIONS, *c.* 1904. Thought to have been built by Alderman James Wire in 1840, this magnificent row of houses commands views of the Channel and Pegwell Bay, once known as Greystone or Courtstairs Bay. The Mansions are now showing their age, but when this photograph was taken they were still in their heyday.

EDITH ROAD, RAMSGATE. This sedate scene was printed on a postcard for the owner of Grange Road Post Office, a Mr T. Roberts, and sent to Aunt Joe Millington of 5 Crawford Gardens, Margate, in May 1913. The sender was 'Kitty', who had rheumatic hands and feet and apologized for her handwriting.

THE VERY ORNATE MAIN ENTRANCE TO THE CONVENT OF THE ASSUMPTION in Goodwin Road, built in 1873 for the education of young ladies. This view also shows the Guest House. Sadly this is all that remains of this once large complex of school buildings.

CONVENT OF THE ASSUMPTION, c. 1902. Its extensive grounds were bordered by Goodwin Road, Downs Road, Pegwell Road and Pegwell Avenue. It was first occupied by Benedictine Nuns, who later sold this large estate to the Sisters of the Assumption who ran a Convent for young girls from 1878 to 1958. By 1960 the Convent of the Assumption became Assumption House, Abbey Junior School for Boys, until it was sold for development.

SOUTHWOOD TAVERN, SOUTHWOOD ROAD, *c*. 1900. Ramsgate ladies taking a ride under military escort in a horse-drawn wagonnette! The only identified person is the young girl in the middle of the front row: Ethel Florence Moody, whose grand-daughter, Doris May Dimond, found this postcard, produced by photographer C. Austen of 94 Southwood Road, Ramsgate, in the loft of her mother's house.

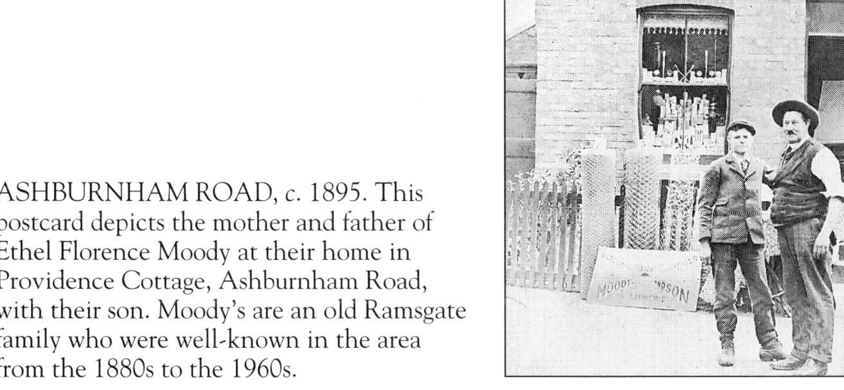

ASHBURNHAM ROAD, *c*. 1895. This postcard depicts the mother and father of Ethel Florence Moody at their home in Providence Cottage, Ashburnham Road, with their son. Moody's are an old Ramsgate family who were well-known in the area from the 1880s to the 1960s.

GRANGE ROAD. Named after The Grange situated next to St Augustine's Abbey, the site of the houses and shops shown here was once a large meadow belonging to Ellington Estate. The portion of Grange Road above Ellington Park was once called Lone Tree Lane because of a solitary tree by the footpath there which was thought to have been the site of a hanging; it was avoided after dark by locals.

THE FRANCES BARBER ALMSHOUSES, *c.* 1940, viewed from Ethelbert Road, were built in 1899 from money left in a will by Mrs Frances Barber to perpetuate the name of her husband, Francis Charles Barber, and her only son, William Charles Barber. The houses are within the boundary of St George's parish and are for parishioners only. They were officially opened on Friday 29 September 1899 by the Right Revd Lord Bishop of Dover Dr Walsh.

OLD HOUSE, QUEEN STREET. As far back as 1812 this pair of seventeenth-century cottages stood on the corner of Queen Street and Cornhill (now called St Michael's Alley), which leads to Albert Street. The name Cornhill is derived from the many farms in this area. The cottages were demolished in 1913 and on this site today stands Ramsgate's Model Shop owned by Mr Peter Hodgson.

QUEEN STREET FLOODS. On Friday 24 August 1923 a deluge of rain between 12 and 1 o'clock sent rivers of water cascading down Queen Street eventually to collect at the Market Place, where a miniature whirlpool occurred. Following this rainstorm came hailstones which added to the shopkeepers' misery.

RAMSGATE LIBRARY, 1904. Built on ground once belonging to Effingham House, this building was a gift from the American millionaire Andrew Carnegie and was the first purpose-built library in Ramsgate. It cost £7,000 and was opened on 13 October 1904 by Mayor Robert Dowling. The postcard was posted at Ramsgate on 22 December 1904, forty days after the library's official opening.

VALE SQUARE. This view of the spacious well-ordered Vale Square was taken in 1907. In the background is Christ Church, consecrated on 4 August 1847 by Archbishop Howley. The incumbent was Revd Edward Hoare, the architect George Gilbert Scott. In 1840 a Mr Eddles built the first house in this area but it was not long before more houses were built, eventually forming the Square.

Opposite: ST MARY'S CHURCH, CHAPEL PLACE. 'Ramsgate Chapel' was built in 1788 on ground provided by Mr John Fagg of Ramsgate. It was consecrated on Friday 8 July 1791 by Archbishop Moore of Canterbury. On 5 September 1866 it was renamed St Mary's church and was later damaged twice by German bombs during the Second World War. The damage finally led to its demolition in the summer of 1955.

CANADIAN HOSPITAL, CHATHAM HOUSE, CHATHAM STREET, first built as a private school between 1879 and 1882, was turned into a hospital for Canadian wounded in 1916 when this photograph was taken. In 1917 the hospital was bombed for the second time, the first bombing having been in 1915 when the schoolchildren then occupying these premises were evacuated to Gloucester. After the war, the building reverted to a private school, was purchased in 1919 for £22,000 by the Board of Education and became known as the County School. It later reverted to Chatham House. Among its most famous scholars is Sir Edward Heath, who first attended in 1926.

TOWNLEY HOUSE, *c.* 1911. Built in 1780, this elegant house was designed by and named after Mrs James Townley, who was born in 1753. Mrs Townley was a pupil of the famous Sir Joshua Reynolds, the great English portrait painter and very talented architect. Mrs Townley, a notable hostess, entertained prominent local society to balls and masquerades at her home, the most notable visitors being William IV and, during the 1820s, the Duchess of Kent together with the young Princess Victoria, soon to be Queen of England. Mrs Townley died on 19 March 1839. Her home is now well maintained by the local family of furnishers J.C. Farley Ltd.

GENERAL STORES, MARGATE ROAD. Situated on the corner of Kings Road and Margate Road, this shop was a general grocers store owned by Mr H. Colliass, who resided here for over twenty years. The collection of houses around his shop was known locally as 'The Blue Mountains'. This area's reputation was such that the Borough Police Force only patrolled in pairs!

HARE AND HOUNDS PUBLIC HOUSE, *c.* 1912. The view of this old Tomson and Wotton Inn shows how open and unpopulated the Ramsgate to Margate road was at the turn of the century. The Hare and Hounds once boasted a Tea Garden and was a half-way house for travellers along the road. It was also the local pub for the people in the Northwood area; what a contrast to today!

NEWINGTON SMOCK MILL, c. 1910, situated off Newington Road opposite Granville Avenue. Dating from 1819, the mill was owned by the Mascell family for over 100 years. The sails were in use until 1904, after which a gas-driven engine was used to power the mill. The gas used was produced at the mill by burning anthracite coal. On the mill site was a small bakery and the mill also produced corn fodder and flour which was retailed in its two shops in Ramsgate, one of which was at the bottom of Chatham Street.

Six

Schools

ST LAWRENCE SCHOOL, NEWINGTON ROAD. This 1912 postcard shows both boys and girls schools. The girls school is to the left and the boys to the right. The girls school was opened on 23 January 1841 and twice modernized in 1885 and 1895; the boys school opened in 1850. An infants section was transferred to the New Ellington Infants School in June 1939. Sadly, both these village schools were demolished in 1984 and replaced with a new single building on the old girls school site, which was opened by His Grace The Lord Revd Robert Runcie MC, DD, Archbishop of Canterbury, on Friday 14 June 1985.

ELLINGTON SCHOOL. This early school situated on the corner of Crescent Road and Grange Road was known as 'Ellington Iron School'. Erected in 1867, it was enlarged in 1897. When the new Ellington School was built in Ellington Place the old school was sold to the long-established Ramsgate firm of Grummant Brothers, who used the premises to store their building materials.

SOUTH EASTERN COLLEGE, 1907. The school was founded in 1879 by the South Eastern Clerical and Lay Alliance in Dane Park House, Ramsgate. The first headmaster was the Revd E.C. d'Auquier. It later transferred to its present position in College Road. On 17 March 1884 the foundation stone was laid and on 1 September 1884 the building was completed at a cost of £11,360. Today it is simply known as St Lawrence College.

CHATHAM HOUSE was first founded in 1797 as a private school by Dr William Humble. The boys attending the school were known by locals as Mr Humble's Bumble Bees! The buildings have now almost taken over one side of Chatham Street. Visited by Queen Victoria and the Prince Consort in 1842 while they were staying at Townley House, the school was destined to have an illustrious future. In 1921 it was taken under the wing of the Board of Education and became a breeding ground for the working-class academic. Among its hallowed names are, of course, Sir Edward Heath and Mr Frank Muir, the TV and radio script writer.

CLARENDON HOUSE GIRLS' GRAMMAR SCHOOL, 1910, which started life as a mixed school, was opened by John Henry Clutton, Mayor of Ramsgate, on 14 October 1909. It was then known as the New County Secondary School and its first headmistress was Miss Merryman. In later years the school became girls only, and later took the title of Clarendon House Grammar School for Girls.

ST LUKE'S SCHOOL was built on ground donated by Mr W. Farley of Victory Villa, Hereson Road. The Revd J.B. Whiting proceeded with the work of building, which was completed in 1875, nearly a year before completion of St Luke's church. The school was for girls and infants only and cost approximately £500.

HOLLICONDANE COUNTY PRIMARY SCHOOL, DUMPTON LANE, was officially opened on Wednesday 20 April 1949 by the Chairman of the Kent Education Committee, Sir William Nottidge. Construction began in 1939 under the former Education Committee of Ramsgate Town Council. By the outbreak of the Second World War, the walls and roof were completed but further development was interrupted in 1940. During the war the school was used to store furniture from blitzed Thanet homes. Slight damage by shrapnel to the roof and windows occurred during enemy raids. During 1946 the Kent Education Committee sought approval to complete the school which it eventually did at a cost of over £22,000. The first headmaster was a Mr H. Pinder.

DAME JANET SCHOOL, NEWINGTON ROAD, takes its name from one of Ramsgate's most generous and popular benefactors, Dame Janet Stancomb Wills. The school was opened by her close friend of many years, Mrs Florence Dunn, on 29 September 1933. The grounds, and Jackey Bakers playing fields, were a gift from the first Lady Mayor of Ramsgate. Sadly, Dame Janet never saw her good deed finished as she died on 22 August 1932.

ST ETHELBERT'S SCHOOL, seen here in Dane Park Road, replaced the old school in Artillery Road. The ground was a gift from a Miss Ellis. The Revd Peter Amigo, Bishop of Southwark, laid the foundation stone on Saturday 7 July 1928 with an inscribed silver trowel. In just under one year the new school building was completed, and on Monday 27 April 1929 the opening ceremony took place. It was presided over by the Right Revd Abbot Egan, and in front of a large gathering the school was declared open by the Right Revd Bishop Brown of Pella.

HERESON SCHOOL, LILLIAN ROAD. Officially opened by Councillor W. Coleman, Chairman of the Local Education Committee, on 10 September 1909, this school, whose first headmaster was Mr Percy Solly (nicknamed 'Pussa') started its life as Lillian Road Council School for Boys and Girls, and in later years became Hereson Road School for Boys. Renowned for its boxing prowess in the 1950s, the school produced a number of ABA Champions. One Champion teacher remembered by generations of schoolboys is Mr Victor Fox, who joined Hereson in 1931 and retired in 1975. The school colours were black and amber, which caused the boys to be nicknamed 'The Hornets'. In 1952 the school colours were changed to the present maroon blazer and silver badge.

HOLY TRINITY SCHOOL, erected in 1858, was once situated on the corner of Hereson Road and Thanet Road. The small flint-built Victorian School was for many years the seat of learning for most local children. Its pupils learnt reading, writing and arithmetic, the 3 Rs around which their world revolved. Sadly the school was demolished after it was damaged by fire in March 1987. A new school bearing the name Holy Trinity was built on a new site in Dumpton Park Drive and opened in June 1990.

ELLINGTON INFANTS' SCHOOL cost £17,628 to build and was formally opened by Willliam Joseph Jordan Esquire, High Commissioner for New Zealand, who was a native of Ramsgate and a Freeman of the Borough, on Friday 2 June 1939. A golden key was used to open the school during the ceremony. Its present whereabouts are unknown.

CHRIST CHURCH SCHOOL, ROYAL ROAD. Travelling along Royal Road it would be very difficult to miss this lovely and ancient school building, one of the earliest Church of England schools in Ramsgate. Its deeds date back to 1848. In 1898 the school was enlarged. During the Second World War (June 1940–February 1945) the children were evacuated to Hixon Church of England School and Stowe by Chartley, Staffordshire. The school was re-opened for those children not evacuated in February 1942.

ST AUGUSTINE'S COLLEGE, *c.* 1904. Built in 1816 for the Revd Alfred Luck, this building was named St Gregory's. In 1864 Alfred Luck died, leaving St Gregory's to St Augustine's Abbey to be used as a seat of learning. Records seem to have commenced in 1866. Permission was eventually granted to use St Gregory's as a boys school. Opening Day was 9 September 1867, when St Gregory's became St Augustine's College.

ST AUGUSTINE'S COLLEGE PLAYGROUND, early 1900s. All the boys have Eton collars and knickerbockers or long trousers. Then as now, football, played here under the watchful eye of one of the Fathers, was the nation's No. 1 game.

Seven

Services and Youth Organisations

RAMSGATE FIRE BRIGADE, 1921. Ramsgate Town firefighters pose outside their station in Effingham Street with their new Chief Officer, Captain F.C. West. The station is still used today but is now part of the Kent Fire Brigade. Officers present were, back row: W. Andrews, W. Wood, S. Wood, F. West. Middle row: T. Muir (Motorman), G. Knott, H. Rose, E. Attwell, S. Ellis, F. Nutty, F. Glenn, B. Bennett, A. Collard. Front row: C. Hammond, H. Holbrook, J. Palmer, F.C. West (Chief Officer), A. Attwell, S. Board, G. Waller. The fire station was built in 1905 on the site of a house called Effingham owned by Mrs Fox-Tomson. It replaced the earlier station situated on the left hand side of York Street.

THE REMAINS OF 139 GRANGE ROAD. A hairdressers and a tobacconists was devastated by fire on 13 February 1909. The three inhabitants, a Mr and Mrs Pino and their baby, were saved from death by their neighbour W.J. Sparkes (an unfortunate surname!) and Inspector Greedy of the Borough Police Force, whose quick actions enabled their escape. The family were given shelter by Mr J. Farnell, a Harbour Missionary (see page 47) who lived at 142 Grange Road.

UNKNOWN FIREMAN OF RAMSGATE BOROUGH, 1915, photographed by James Bishop of George Street, Ramsgate. The only clue to this man's identity is the No. 7 on his uniform. He is holding the remains of an incendiary bomb in his left hand. (Anyone who can enlighten me as to this man's identity is welcome to contact me at my home address.)

CAPTAIN CHARLES WEST'S FUNERAL, 1915. The funeral ceremony took place on Saturday 20 March 1915 of Ramsgate's respected Chief Fire Officer, Captain Charles West, who died on Wednesday 17 March 1915 aged 64 years. The funeral cortege is seen here just entering Hereson Road on its way to the Town Cemetery in Cecilia Road. Resting on the fire appliance is the oak coffin covered with the Union Jack. Ramsgate firemen acting as pall bearers reverently attended a Chief to whom they were devotedly attached. Fire brigades from all over the county sent representatives to pay their respects. The Mayor, Councillor J.W. Chapman, and other Borough officials, family and friends attended.

CREW AND APPLIANCE, 1930s. Chief Officer F.C. West with his full-time crew parade in front of a Leyland fire engine which cost £1,030 in 1930. The Ajax ladder seen above reached to a height of 30 ft when fully extended. The turbine pump was the latest of its kind and delivered up to 700 gallons of water per minute. Left to right are Firemen Kember, Pritchard, Chief Officer West, Station Officers Ellis and Muir.

GEORGE HENRY WATSON, whose nickname was 'Saint' because he was born on St George's Day. His rank in the Ramsgate Borough Fire Brigade was Second Officer. He is seen here proudly displaying two medals, one being the OBE, awarded to him for taking part in fighting the fire at the Ammunition Store at Ramsgate Harbour on 17 June 1917.

ALFRED WATSON, SON OF G.H. WATSON. Alfred Watson, part-time fireman of Ramsgate Borough Fire Brigade from 1926 to 1945. At the outbreak of the Second World War, Alfred, who was a Master Signwriter and Decorator, commenced full-time service in the NFS. He was given twenty-four hours in which to close down his business and find employment for the six members of his staff. After the war he returned to his peacetime occupation of signwriting.

RAMSGATE'S FIRE BRIGADE RESERVE BASE. Situated at the north end of Effingham Street, this building was the home of 'A' and 'B' Watch of the Auxiliary Fire Brigade. Once the premises of Ramsgate Motors Ltd, it became the Reserve Headquarters of the Fire Brigade in 1938. In the left background is Effingham House, now demolished and the site of an unkept piece of waste ground. Among those shown are the Chief Fire Officer of Ramsgate Fire Brigade, Frederick Charles West, standing third from left.

TOMPSON AND WOTTON'S BREWERY YARD, 1 SEPTEMBER 1939. Fireman Tom Wells stands proudly beside the converted lorry of F.J. Pike, Shopfitters. On the left is a Bedford trailer pump towed by the lorry which was driven by Tom, a member of 'B' Watch. The other crew members were Officer-in-Charge 'Siddy' Radford, E.H. Price and L.N. Dray.

FIRE AT BARNETT'S ELECTRICAL STORE on the corner of Queen Street and Cavendish Street, at 6.23 p.m. on Monday 7 July 1958. The first appliance to arrive was from Ramsgate Fire Station, Officer-in-Charge being Leading Fireman Alfred Challenger. The fire was contained to the rear of the premises and, with the help of public spirited people, the brigade was able to save a large amount of Joe Barnett's stock. Two officers are seen: on the extreme left is Leading Fireman Challenger, and in front of him is Leading Fireman Philpott. Fire appliances from Broadstairs and Margate backed up the Ramsgate crews and helped secure the premises. Mr Barnett, later Mayor of Ramsgate, paid tribute to the brigade's swift response and stated that they did a wonderful job in preventing what could have been the loss of his entire premises.

THE VISIT OF HRH DUCHESS OF TECK ON 21 APRIL 1897. Captain Charles West and the Ramsgate Borough Fire Brigade formed a triumphal arch with the aid of a pair of wheeled escape ladders decked with flags and a welcome sign in Honour of the Duchess of Teck. The visit was in aid of a local charity. HRH The Duchess of Teck was Mother of Queen Mary, wife of George V. (Photograph courtesy of Kent Fire Brigade Museum, Maidstone)

W.L. WELLBROOK'S FISH AND CHIP SHOP, c. 1968, the scene of a minor fire, seen here receiving the attention of Ramsgate Fire Brigade. The cause of the fire was thought to be an accumulation of fat at the rear of the fryer which ignited.

SUPERINTENDENT BUSS. Having started his career in the small village of Worth, Sandwich, this man became the first Chief Constable of Ramsgate Borough Police Force in May 1870. The strength of the Borough Force at this time was four sergeants and twenty-one constables, a far cry from today's stretched resources. He resigned in 1892 after twenty-two years service and died on 17 February 1904.

POLICEMAN ON POINT DUTY, 1920s. A Ramsgate Borough police constable on traffic duty at the busy junction of Harbour Street, Madeira Walk and Harbour Parade. The only traffic likely to cause this arm of the law any serious problem is the swift approach of a woman driver at the wheel of a pram!

A STEREOSCOPIC VIEW, WEST CLIFF ARCADE, showing Sergeant Port of the Ramsgate Borough Force on harbour duty. He spent twenty-six years with the Borough Force, retiring in 1908. His last fourteen years were spent on harbour duties.

WOMAN POLICE CONSTABLE KATHLEEN MARY PERRY at the rear of Ramsgate Police Station in October 1942. WPC Perry was a member of the well-known Ramsgate family of coal merchants. Born in 1904, she is seen here standing beside one of Ramsgate's five squad cars.

LIEUTENANT GENERAL SIR CHARLES WARREN, who spent his earlier years trying to catch the notorious Jack the Ripper. He retired from the Metropolitan Police only to enlist in the Army. On retiring he took up residence at Westbere near Canterbury, and in May 1908 was largely responsible for the formation of the 1st Ramsgate Scout Group which met in a Drill Room in York Street and became known as 'Sir Charles Warren's Own'.

FIRST RAMSGATE SCOUT BAND. On the reverse of this postcard is the message 'Wishes from 1st Ramsgate Band', commemorating the first rally held in Ramsgate. All the percussion instruments were loaned from Sir Charles Warren, the group's most ardent benefactor.

FIRST RAMSGATE SCOUT GROUP, *c.* 1918. Ramsgate's Scouting community included Sea Scouts and Cubs. The lady at the centre of the group is thought to be Sir Charles Warren's daughter, or Miss Young, the Cub Mistress. (Photograph by Barrett's of Ramsgate)

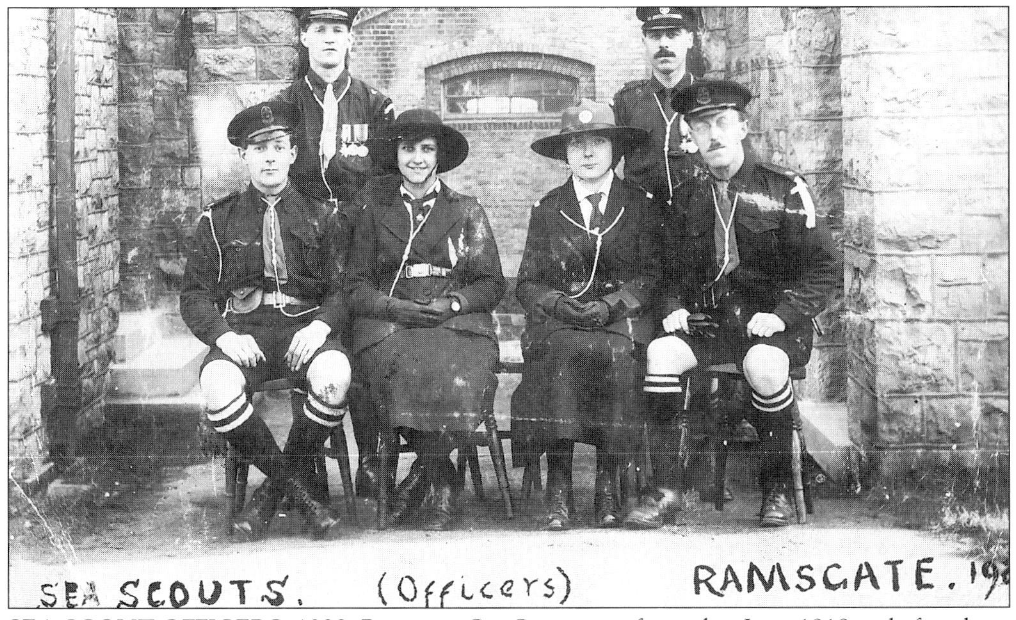

SEA SCOUT OFFICERS, 1922. Ramsgate Sea Scouts was formed in June 1918 and after three weeks the unit consisted of twelve patrols, each comprising seven scouts and a leader. The first Scout Master was Mr Greasley.

PATROL LEADER RAYMOND YOUNG, who joined the 1st Ramsgate Boy Scouts on 2 April 1914, is seen here proudly holding the pennant of Grey Wolf Patrol. Born in 1900, Mr Young was to become Assistant Scout Master in 1920 and play an important role in the development of many of Ramsgate's future residents.

SECOND BATTALION, ST GEORGE'S CHURCH LADS BRIGADE, outside St George's Church Hall in 1908. Their Captain, G.M. Willis, is at the centre of the front row; to his left is the Revd L.P. Crawford, their chaplain and vicar of Ramsgate and St George's church. Formed in 1892 by the then Mayor of Ramsgate, John Henry Glutton, the Church Lads Brigade was the forerunner of the Scout movement.

RAMSGATE SEAMEN'S GYM, 1914-18. This well-equipped gymnasium was at Farley Place between 9 York Terrace and Westcliff Arcade and was used by HM Forces during the Great War. Its hours of opening were 09.30 to 22.00 hours daily.

RAMSGATE FOOTBALL TEAM, 1923-24. Back row, left to right: Messrs Clay, Collyer, Brisley, Bowley, Hagerty. Front row: Turner, Hobby, Morris, Bourne and Bradshaw. Unfortunately 1923-24 was to be one of Ramsgate's worst ever seasons.

PRESS WANDERERS FOOTBALL CLUB, 1930-31. Back row, left to right: R. Trumpeter, A. Belsey, J. Bird (Captain), G. Long, R. Sheppard, C. Pedder, B. Cox, R. Collier, J. Ashby (Vice Captain), N. Ratcliff, E. Butcher (Hon. Secretary), W. Castle and L. Britcher. Front row: W. Groom, A. Marsh, T. Smith, D. Jauns and T. Collier. Eddie Butcher will be remembered by Ramsgatonians of the 1950s as the Mayor of the Town in 1954, 1955, 1959 and 1960. He was made a Freeman of the Borough in 1967. He was also a tireless worker on behalf of Ramsgate Town and its charities.

RAMSGATE ROVERS CRICKET TEAM, *c.* 1926 in the Warre Recreation Ground. Among the players seen here are: M. Sparkes, C.V. Stanner, J. Allright, C. Sparkes, J. Farley, T. Fortisque, M. Hooker, J.S. Sharman, W. Sharman, L. Darby, C. Stanner, C. Hurst, L.C. Austen and A. Talbot.

MONTEFIORE AVENUE leading to Thanet Bowls Club, which was formed in 1907. This postcard shows the new grounds, which were formally opened by Mrs Sebag-Montefiore on 12 June 1909. The grounds cover one and a half acres and originally housed six full size rinks, three tennis courts, one croquet lawn and one quoits pitch. They are now managed by Thanet District Council.

BOWLING GREEN, ELLINGTON PARK, 1932. This picture was on the reverse of a score card used by members of Ellington Park Bowls Club. To the right in the background can be seen a cone-shaped structure which was the Ellington Park Avery, now sadly demolished. The Bowls Club is still a thriving concern, however.

MEMBERS OF RAMSGATE ROLLER SKATING CLUB, which met at the Ramsgate Rink in Dumpton Park Drive in premises now occupied by Hunton's Ltd, tool makers. Members proudly display the club's badge, trophies and medals won during a season thought to be in the early 1900s.

RAMSGATE INDOOR HOCKEY TEAM pictured outside the Ramsgate Rink, Dumpton Park Drive. The poster in the background advertises Ramsgate vs Switzerland on Monday 17 November 1930, entrance fee sixpence.

Eight

Entertainers

RAMSGATE PIERROTS. These artists trod the Ramsgate Sands in the 1905 season. Pierrots were among the earliest entertainers. This troupe, under the control of Harry Gold, was later superseded by the Concert Party. Harry Gold also carried on the wardrobe dealers business at No. 48 King Street, Ramsgate, the proprietor being his wife.

ELLISON'S ENTERTAINERS, 1908, who later merged with Harry 'Golds Yachtsmen' to become 'Gold and Ellison's Entertainers', appeared for many years on Ramsgate Sands. Ellison was also the architect of a fold-away stage used all over the country by *alfresco* entertainers.

Jerry Hoey's Piccadillian Band, Royal Victoria Pavilion, Ramsgate, 1930

THE JERRY HOEY BAND appeared at the Royal Victoria Pavilion (now Grosvenor Casino) in the 1930s, playing to large crowds Saturday evenings on the Pavilion Promenade.

GOLD'S YACHTSMEN, 1911. Harry Gold formed this group of entertainers for his Ramsgate venue, and another concert party to perform on Margate Sands. Born Patrick Harry James Ricks, Harry Gold was born in Jersey in 1866 and died in Yeovil in 1946. One of his sons lived in Ramsgate and established a fancy goods shop in King Street, Ramsgate.

GOLD AND ELLISON'S, 1921, the amalgamation of the two principal concert parties then appearing on Ramsgate Sands. Sadly their names are not known.

WHITE STAR ENTERTAINERS. This Concert Party appeared at the Marina Gardens, Ramsgate, at the start of the Great War in 1914. They returned in 1919, showing that despite five years of hardship the show still went on. (Photograph Romney Studios, Ramsgate)

WILLAT'S AND GRANT'S WHITE STARS, 1923. These White Stars bear no resemblance to those in the previous photograph. Their humour was more earthy and their venue was Ramsgate Sands. (Photograph by Bennett & Son, 29 Addington Street, Ramsgate)

HOWARD FLYNN BAND. In 1927 Howard Flynn's Band appeared at the Royal Victoria Pavilion to packed audiences. Public taste was changing: the Big Band era had arrived.

VICTOR VORGANZER BAND, another well-known band which appeared at the Royal Victoria Pavilion during the 1920s and '30s.

AL TABOR AND BAND, 1936, another very popular band with the Ramsgate visitors. Al Tabor, who died in 1987, had a very unusual habit on pay day. He would draw the band's wages then take off, running the length of the building. The band, who were in the foyer, would chase him up the stairs and along the balcony to his room, only to find the door locked! Les Cripwell said 'It was the only time he saw musicians run for their wages'!

BILLY MERRIN'S BAND (1938) was formed at Nottingham Palais de Dance in March 1931. They came to Ramsgate in the early 1930s and stayed to the late 1940s. They played a sixteen-week summer season of at least two shows a day. Venues varied: West Cliff Theatre, Bandstands East and West, and the Royal Victoria Pavilion. Billy Merrin is in the back row, fourth from the left. On the front row is the only surviving member of the band, Les Cripwell, the bespectacled gentleman. The lady next to him is vocalist Rita Williams.

FREDDIE HARGRAVES BAND, 1939. Freddie and his Band had a sensational success at the Coronation Ballroom in the 1939 season, drawing as many as 500 people a night. Freddie Hargraves lived at 39 Grange Road, Ramsgate, and was a well-known personality.

DENE WILLIAM'S MARINA BAND, 1936. These musicians played in the Marina Ballroom. Dene Williams usually dressed in a white coat and top hat but is not portrayed on this picture. His band was known as the Marina Boys.

RAMSGATE CARNIVAL, 1939. The principal event during Carnival Week was a beauty competition in Ellington Park. The town's most famous mayor, A.B.C. Kemp, is about to introduce English film star Merle Oberon to a Ramsgate crowd numbering some 5,000. Miss Oberon chose 17-year-old Miss Joyce Allan of 68 Hardres Street as Carnival Queen, and her Maids of Honour were Miss Valerie Sly and Miss Marjorie Dawes. To the right of the picture is Billy Merrin with the baton and his band, the Commanders. Billy Merrin died in 1980.

Nine

Transport

HORSE-DRAWN CARRIAGES, *c.* 1900. Occupants of Nos 40, 42 and 44 Crescent Road, Ramsgate, gaze down on an elegant horse-drawn carriage with gentlemen in top hats. These carriages were drawn by smart horses and well-dressed grooms and are from a vanished era.

TRAM ACCIDENT, 7 AUGUST 1905. Crowds of sightseers surround Isle of Thanet tram No. 47 which has just run into the shop-front of Vyes Grocery Store on the corner of Plains of Waterloo and Bellevue Road. A 7-year-old girl standing in the doorway was seriously injured; others incurred superficial injuries.

TRAM CAR NO. 24 struggles up the steep Madeira Walk incline. On 3 August 1905 Madeira Walk was the scene of one of the tramway's best-known accidents, when a tram descending the Walk crashed through a parapet onto gardens 30 ft below, though without serious injury to the public or tramway personnel.

RAMSGATE GARAGE. Walter H. Barret, a local photographer whose address was 1 Clarendon Gardens, took this photograph of an unknown collection of local transport. Does anyone know the location?

A & B GARAGE. Two immaculate Rolls-Royce saloons for hire, for weddings, dances and even country drives, from the A & B Garage Ltd, Grange Road, Ramsgate, during the 1930s. This photograph was taken at the bottom of Nethercourt Hill where the large roundabout is situated today. Fare from Town to Station was 2s.

RAMSGATE CARNIVAL. F.A. Hollands' patriotically decorated lorry was among many entries for Ramsgate's Carnival in 1936. This entry is depicted in Harbour Parade with carnival crowds in the background. Hollands wholesale business was in Cannon Road.

CHARABANC OUTING. William Wallace Allen's charabanc of 49 Harbour Street, Ramsgate, at a country stop somewhere in Thanet. Seating twenty-four persons, these charabancs were the forerunners of today's bus transport, albeit without much protection from rainy weather.

ACCIDENT BELLEVUE ROAD-VICTORIA ROAD. J.C. Morrison's heavy breakdown lorry stands by ready to tow away the damaged vehicle which has been involved in an accident outside Holy Trinity church some time in the early 1950s. Two police constables endeavour to right the car while young teenagers watch. J.C. Morrison's Garage and Showrooms was for many years situated in St Lawrence High Street until it moved to the Broadway, Broadstairs, in the 1980s.

CONCORDE DE ELEGANCE, 1937-38. The years preceding the Second World War saw many parades on Ramsgate's West Cliff Promenade involving classic cars. Here an AA Patrolman stands guard over a beautiful Rolls-Royce saloon, behind which are a couple of immaculately turned out vehicles, while crowds throng the grass verges to gaze at these aristocratic wonders of twentieth-century British engineering.

ST LAWRENCE HALT was opened in October 1864 for travellers wishing to alight at the village of St Lawrence and also for those wishing to proceed to Pegwell Bay. It closed on 3 April 1916. On 1 July 1926 The Sands station and the Old Town station were closed, and on the following day the new Town station in Station Approach Road was opened.

BUILDING THE VIADUCT, 1925, showing the giant wooden formers used to erect the great brick arches of Ramsgate Viaduct across the Ramsgate–Margate Road built by McAlpine and Sons. This viaduct, the new Town station, thirty miles of new track and Dumpton station were completed in little over a year.

HERTFORD INN, 1907. A rather unusual advertising vehicle used by Worthington's the Brewers seen outside the Hertford Inn in Hertford Street, then a Tomson and Wotton House. Today there is a block of flats where the pub once stood. In 1840 the Hertford Inn had been called the Waterman Arms and kept by William Gurr and his wife Lydic.

MANSTON CROSSROADS, 1954. East Kent bus No. 65 bound for Manston struggles at the crossroads as another East Kent bus struggles up the hill from Manston. The snow in February 1954 was very deep and the roads almost impassable. Passengers are helping to push the bus onto the slippery roads. The thermometer reading during this period was 32 degrees Fahrenheit, freezing to say the least!

THE LORD WINTERSTOKE. Ramsgate's first motor fire appliance, was presented to Ramsgate town by Dame Janet Stancomb-Wills on Friday 1 October 1915. The demonstration and christening took place in Ellington Park. Chief Fire Officer Johnson and the town's brigade put the new engine through its paces to the amazement of onlookers and visiting Fire Chiefs. Other fire officers present were Chief Officer Hammond and Superintendent Bryant of Margate Fire Brigade and Chief Officer Jones of Folkestone. The gentleman in the bowler hat is none other than Mr Harry Jones, Messrs Merryweather and Co. Chief Mechanic. Merryweather were one of the world's leading fire appliance manufacturers for many years.

RAMSGATE TOWN STATION. Ramsgate's first railway station, situated at the top of Chatham Street opposite the Shakespeare public house, was opened on 13 April 1846 and owned by South Eastern and Chatham Railway (known by locals as the 'Slow, Easy and Comfortable' Railway). The station closed in July 1926 and demolition followed. The site is now occupied by flats called Chatham Court.

THE *CONQUEROR*, 1911. Built by J.T. Eltringham and Sons at South Shields in 1897 primarily as a tug, each summer she converted to a pleasure steamer and was run in the Thanet area by the Elliot Steam Tug Company. In early years she ran from Margate to Calais and Southend but later in 1909 started a daily return service between Margate and Folkestone calling at Ramsgate, Deal and Dover. During the First World War she became a tug by the name of HMS *Query*.

VIKING SHIP *HUGIN* entering Ramsgate Harbour on 29 July 1949. Her Danish crew had rowed her across the North Sea from Denmark firstly to Broadstairs and on the following day into Ramsgate. The venture was to commemorate the landing of Hengist and Horsa on the shores of Thanet in 449 AD, 1500 years earlier. The *Hugin* was bought by the *Daily Mail* newspaper and presented to both towns. Its final resting place was on the cliffs at Pegwell Bay, at one time overlooking the Hoverport, the home of the hovercraft, a much later mode of sea transport.

RAMSGATE AIRPORT. The Ramsgate Airport venture was started by a small committee of enthusiasts in 1932. Ramsgate, Broadstairs and Margate later formed a Joint Committee to investigate the possibility of a site at Rumfields for a municipal airport, but after some disagreement Broadstairs and Margate withdrew leaving Ramsgate to continue with the venture. Eventually, on Thursday 20 June 1935, Ramsgate Airport received its first official landing. The aircraft was a single-engined Miles Witney Straight flown by Mr Whitney Straight himself. The official opening of the airport on Saturday 3 July 1937 was performed by the Director General of Civil Aviation, Sir Francis Shelmarine; also present was the Mayor of Ramsgate, Alderman Nixon. Civil aviation returned to the airport after the war, and in the 1950s a company named 'Air Kruise' offered flights over Thanet at 12s 6d for adults and 7s 6d for children. One of the airport's last official uses was as a base for a civilian air-sea rescue site after the RAF Air Sea Rescue had left Manston. The service was run by BEA and the helicopter was marked up Civil Defence. Sadly, the airport closed in 1968 and the site is now the Pysons Road Industrial Estate and Bromstone Primary School. (Photograph courtesy of Mr Rex Austin)

Ten

Social Events

DEDICATION OF ST GEORGE'S CHURCH GATES. This photograph, taken by G.T. Allan of 14 Broad Street, shows the Dedication of the Church Gates at St George's, Ramsgate, by Archbishop Benson in 1890. The gates were presented by Francis Barber, whose generosity also provided the Alms Houses in Elms Avenue, Ramsgate. In 1992 these gates were restored to their former glory by local company Kayover, of Pyson's Road Industrial Estate.

A BOMB-DAMAGED BULL AND GEORGE HOTEL, once situated where Woolworths stands today. The damage was the result of an air raid by a German Zeppelin airship on the night of 17 May 1915. Miss Kate Moffatt, a barmaid at the hotel, had a remarkable escape. She had barely left her bed when a bomb passed through the centre of it! Apart from shock and bruises she was uninjured, although her eyebrows were singed!

GERMAN GUN, NELSON CRESCENT. This 88 mm gun was once part of the armament of submarine U48 which was trapped by three armed trawlers of Ramsgate's Armed Drifter Squadron, *Majesty*, *Paramount* and *Present Help*. The gun stood for many years on Nelson Crescent, a reminder of Ramsgate's part in the sea warfare of the First World War. The U-boat was finally scuttled on the Goodwin Sands and appears whenever the dreaded sands move to reveal this ghostly boat.

BELGIUM WOUNDED IN RAMSGATE'S SAILORS' HOME. During the early months of the First World War many Belgian wounded were brought to Ramsgate to recuperate. This photograph shows some of these men in the Sailors' Home. The nurse standing second from the left is none other than Lady Rose Weigall's daughter, Rachel, of Southwood House, St Lawrence. (See page 8.)

COKE RIOTS, 1920. Many Ramsgate residents felt very bitter about the use of German ships to export coke from Ramsgate so soon after hostilities. It was felt that British ships and labour should be used to export the coke from the gasworks in Boundary Road. On 14 August 1920 'The Old Comrades' formed up and marched down Madeira Walk to the Military Road to protest at coke being loaded on the Quay. There was a clash with police guarding the German ships and, for their safety, the captains moved their vessels to the Outer Harbour. The outcome was no more coke was exported.

ST GEORGE'S WAR MEMORIAL. On 7 October 1920 the Archbishop of Canterbury, Dr Randall Davidson, unveiled St George's War Memorial. His wife, Mrs Randall Davidson, performed the unveiling by lowering the Union Jack from the stone edifice. A large crowd gathered for this moving ceremony.

OPENING OF MARINA SWIMMING POOL by Mrs T. Wotton and Mr Martin Tomson (of the old Ramsgate brewery company Tomson and Wotton). Also shown are the Mayor of Ramsgate, Alderman Ernest E. Dye, and Mrs Martin Tompson and son. The cost of the pool was £30,000. After many years of use, this amenity was allowed to deteriorate and is now a car park on waste ground which does Ramsgate no justice whatsoever.

THE CELEBRATED ARCHWAY on the Western Promenade for the Prince of Wales' visit on 24 November 1926. The construction was by G.J. Attwood, a Ramsgate builder. The workman depicted on the second platform is the late Samuel Mathews of Ethelbert Road. The finished arch had the word 'Welcome' in large white letters across the top span between the two towers. The Prince later became Edward VIII.

HRH THE PRINCE OF WALES AT RAMSGATE HOSPITAL. Edward Prince of Wales is seen here shaking the hand of the Revd J.H. Askwith, Vicar of Christchurch and Honorary Chaplain of Ramsgate General Hospital, in the main entrance to the hospital. Behind the vicar is the local Doctor Hicks, after whom Hicks Ward is named.

THE OFFICIAL OPENING OF THE WINTERSTOKE UNDERCLIFF AND ROCK GARDENS by Alderman H. Stead JP, Mayor of Ramsgate, on 10 July 1936. On the Mayor's left is Captain W.T. Smith, Chairman of the Committee responsible for this project.

HOME GUARD. Tommies and Jerries pose for a photograph, but all is not what it seems. These men are all of the 6th Thanet Battalion Home Guard and are seen after an exercise laid on in early 1942 for the visit by the General Officer, Commanding Lt General Sir Edmund Schreiber. The only identified person is Maurice Leslie Eric Sparkes, third from the right in the back row. (Photograph courtesy of the late Mrs Sparkes)

EDWIN JESSE SMITH'S SHOP *c.* 1902. Edwin Smith was a baker, grocer and beer retailer whose shop was on the corner of Lorne Road and Bloomsbury Road. Mr Smith can be seen standing proudly in front of his premises. To the left of the shop is Melrose House, 12 Lorne Road; to the right is 14 Bloomsbury Road, which now appears to have taken over the shop premises which have reverted to a private dwelling.

ALEXANDRA ARMS. The Alexandra Arms may take its name from Alexandra Road upon whose corner it stands. During the First World War it was damaged by an enemy shell during a raid on the town on the night of 27 April 1917 by several enemy destroyers. This pub survived and is known today as The Blazing Donkey.

FORESTERS ARMS situated on the north side of Boundary Road between Finsbury Road and Alma Road. Note the Shrimp brand beers – quite an apt name for a seaside town! The brewers are Russells of West Street, Gravesend. This pub still survives, its outward appearance having changed little.

WHITE SWAN INN, *c.* 1905, once situated on the corner of Hardres Street and Boundary Road. To the left can clearly be seen the Recreation Ground and the Masonic Hall in St Luke Avenue; to the right are billboards advertising *Westward Ho*, Wills Tobacco and Peters Milk Chocolate, all echoes of an age now gone.

HOLLICONDANE ARMS PUBLIC HOUSE, c. 1900, on the corner of Holly Road and College Road. The building has changed little over ninety years, but the surrounding area has been fully developed. Russells of Gravesend held this and many other houses in Ramsgate at the turn of the century.

THE CANNON INN, ELLINGTON PLACE, 1974, in a photograph taken by Mr A. Horne. Originally the pride of a local company, the Cannon Brewery, it was owned by R.S. Cramp of Cannon Road, Ramsgate. Situated at the rear of this building was a fine beer garden. Many local organisations made use of this venue, two of them being the Antediluvian Order of the Buffaloes and the Isle of Thanet Philatelic Society. It was demolished during the mid-1970s to make way for improvements to Ellington County Secondary Modern School for Girls.

RAMSGATE BUSY HARBOUR PARADE. On the left is Tremains, the confectioners, while on the extreme right is the old Queens Head public house. In between these two buildings is a small grocers stall, and in the background is Madeira Walk. The two people standing on Madeira Walk are at the spot where an Isle of Thanet tram left the rails in 1905 and crashed into gardens below.

THE NEW QUEENS HEAD, HARBOUR PARADE, in 1910. Once a Tomson and Wotton house, this building replaced an older pub of the same name pulled down in the 1906-7 road-widening scheme which also saw the demolition of the Harbour Police Station opposite.

Eleven

Out of Town

BELLEVUE TEA GARDENS, PEGWELL. The Belle Vue Tavern was renowned in the 1760s for the sale of potted shrimps by its owner, John Cramp. In 1831 the Duchess of Kent and her daughter, Princess Victoria, honoured Mr Cramp with a visit to his humble establishment and were so impressed by his potted shrimp that when the young Princess Victoria became Queen he received the Royal Appointment as Purveyor of Essence of Shrimps in Ordinary to Her Majesty the Queen. Shrimps would undoubtedly have been on the menu when this photograph was taken.

THE WORKING MEN'S HOME, PEGWELL BAY. Formerly the Clifton Hotel, it was bought by Mr J. Passmore Edwards in 1894 as a convalescent home for the Working Men's Club and Institute Union. In 1896 the building was enlarged to include the tower which is today a well-known landmark. The top postcard includes two small inset photographs which are of Mr and Mrs Boyland, manager and matron of the home in the early 1920s.

PEGWELL BAY PIER, *c.* 1878. This was the second to be constructed in Pegwell Bay, an earlier pier of flimsy construction having been built by Daniel Curling in 1784 but destroyed by the elements. The new pier was part of a grandiose scheme which included a swimming pool to the right of the pier and the Conyngham Hotel, set back in the cliff face to the left of the pier entrance. None of this is left today. Even the swimming pool has disappeared under a carpet of weeds.

CHILTON FARM, 1904, seen here in isolation, not surrounded by the clutter of terraced houses which now line the roads leading to and running parallel with its barns. There was an earlier house here, but that shown was probably built by John Curling in the early eighteenth century. An unusual feature of the house is the subterranean passage leading from the cellars. Over 100 ft long, it ends in a dead end and is a puzzle to historians.

OZENGELL. This Victorian House is built on land that was once part of Ozengell Farm Estate. The old Ozengell farmhouse dating back to the Domesday Book is on the opposite side of the road leading from the Lord of the Manor to St Peter's. Once owned by a family called Judges, it is now the residence of television wrestler Mr Jacky Pallo.

CELEBRATING ST AUGUSTINE'S LANDING, 1897. The hierarchy of the Roman Catholic church gather around the Iona Cross which supposedly marks the spot where St Augustine landed in 597 AD. The cross was erected in 1884 by the Earl of Granville on the site of an ancient oak near a well said to be named after the saint. The event never made headlines in local newspapers as 1897 was also Queen Victoria's Diamond Jubilee.

THE SPORTSMAN, 1930, the last public house before you enter Ramsgate Borough. This pub dates back to 1750 and became a Tomson and Wotton house in 1872 when the local brewers bought the lease. This view has changed dramatically over the last sixty-five years.

PEGWELL BAY ROAD, 1930. Ramsgate's first unofficial camp site began here on the cliffs above Pegwell Bay on the road towards what was then Lord of the Manor crossroads. It is now the official resting place of Viking Ship *Hugin*. Teas were served to the weary travellers who owned this assortment of Romany caravans. (Photograph by Carr & Sons, Ramsgate)

VIKING SHIP *HUGIN*'s final resting place overlooking Pegwell Bay. It nestles proudly on its concrete cradle surrounded by its Viking Warriors and English Hordes. On 28 July 1950 the Mayor of Ramsgate, Mr Percy Turner JP, officially laid the *Hugin* 'to rest' at this ceremony. Bought by the *Daily Mail* newspaper, the *Hugin* was presented to the three major Thanet towns and placed at the point where it is thought the first Viking invasion started in 499 AD.

Acknowledgements

Mr Fred Lee, Miss Penny Ward and Mrs Pat Gardner of Ramsgate Library,
Mrs Leslie Stradling, Mr John William of Margate Museum,
Mrs Joyce Ware of Holy Trinity School, Mr Ross Palmer, Mrs Joyce Burlinson,
the late Mr A. Horne, the late Mrs Sparkes,
Mrs Marion Downer and Mr White of Kent Fire Brigade Museum,
Miss Dot Toft for typing the manuscript.

Sources

Cottons History and Antiquities of the Church and Parish of St Lawrence
Church of England Records Centre
C.T. Richardson: *Fragment of History Ramsgate*
John Heywood: *Illustrated Guide to Ramsgate*
Jas Simson: *Royal Ramsgate*
C.F. Dendy Marshall and R.W. Kidner: *History of Southern Railway*
East Kent Times
Thanet Advertiser and Echo
Kent Coast Times
Isle of Thanet Gazette

Montecatini

A Tuscan Murder Mystery

Justine Gilbert

So glad you enjoyed the murder mystery evening.

Best wishes
Justine Gilbert

3/10/24

MONTECATINI

A TUSCAN MURDER MYSTERY

Justine Gilbert
www.justinegilbertauthor.co.uk

Also by Justine Gilbert:

Daisy Chain, the story of the forgotten women who helped a disabled President.

Praise for Daisy Chain:

" ..a passionate and illuminating retelling of a seismic era from the perspective of 'the other women'.

Louise Dean, award-winning author and founder of The Novelry.

Store Link

Daisy Chain

DEDICATION

The location of this novel is based in Montecatini Val di Cecina, in Tuscany, but all the characters are fictitious and bear no resemblance to anyone alive or dead.
This novel is dedicated to the real women of the town, who are strong and kind and hard-working.
Roberta Sarperi, an intensive care nurse.
Stefania Falchi, owner of the cafe and restaurant, Il Buglione.

Epigraph

In the first four months of 2016, an estimated 5,200 unaccompanied minor refugees arrived in Italy. Overall, some 200,000 refugees went to Italy in that year.

Source: SOS Children's Villages

Prologue
Tuscany

In the winter months, the Italian seaside camping spots are closed like a clam. Even the street lamps are off. But tonight there is too much moon, and the light rippling to shore illuminates his every move. From the back of the van, he unzips the body bag. He is not long out of boyhood, friends with brutality, and clear about his instructions. *Dump the body, bring back the bag.* The former has no identification—not in this land and possibly not in any other—so there is no need to bury her. But the bag is trademarked and can be traced back to the source.

His mother complained the females in the village were worth less than the livestock. Now, as he lifts the little girl, he cannot help but think the child has the weight of a lamb to market; how ironic that her value in death became so great. His share needs to be bigger, he decides—much bigger than the amount the doctor is offering. He'll deal with that when he gets back, but for now the risk of discovery hurries his actions. He glances at the sky and damns the moon again. It will take one insomniac and his dog on a lonely night walk to bear witness, note the vehicle, and create a noise that requires another death. Slinging her over his shoulder, he determines there will be only one body here tonight, hidden just enough to give him a day's head start. Then he will be in a Belgian brothel without a care in the world.

Near a salt-mottled sign of Campeggio, he spies an upended wooden fishing boat and places the child by its side. Rolling the vessel over with a grunt, he moves the body to lie in the sandy depression. In a twitch of superstition, he presses her arms to her side and straightens her legs. Congealed blood dampens the shoulder of his jacket. He removes it, smacks his gloves together to rid the excess grit, and brushes the blood from his boots with a flyer he'd thrust in his pocket earlier. Then he turns the boat back to cover the body, forming a makeshift burial mound.

There. She is ready for her god. Whomever that may be.

It isn't until he has driven away that he realises he's dropped the printed Montecatini flyer, but it won't be important. No one has his fingerprints, and he'll be out of the country by the time someone finds the body.

Chapter One

The Tuscan Hills, Easter 2016

The enemy is at the gate.

In the bluish-grey of early morning, she can see he's exceptionally large. She flaps her arms and shouts. In response, he snorts and turns towards her, wet nostrils flared, catching his haunch on the wire. A harsh zap, and the wild boar's skin crinkles—more in shock than pain—but it has the desired effect. His tusks lower, and he trots away. Agata savours her victory. After a minute, she walks forward, cuts the electricity to the garden fence, and goes inside the perimeter of the vegetable plot to begin her daily watering.

None are immune to the sight of velvet darkness giving way to dawn over the Tuscan Hills, but neither is Agata in awe. This is the place where she was born. It is a place of hard physical farm work, where her father and mother died. A place to where she never wished to return. Florence is her preferred venue, and she had thought that she and Luca and the boys had lived happily there for the past twenty-five years.

Maybe not so happily. But that's an old story that circles

in her head. At least, it could be said they were content—until Luca shocked her with his midlife crisis.

'Let's move to the hills,' he said. 'That's what I need. Less stress. I want to connect with the soil, farm the land, touch the earth, feel at peace.'

Pah! The earth? Peace? He's a city boy, born and bred. What he knows about farming can be written on the back of a packet of pasta. She wanted to continue working in Florence as an *agenta di polizia*, and warned him country bugs are more relentless than city pickpockets.

But then her *Agenzia* shut down. And the *Polizia di Stato* offered him a transfer to the coast. Two more years of service, and he can retire. Sorted. So, at six in the morning, she stands over the embryonic vegetable plot—created not by him, but by her and her family, the ones with the skills—and thanks God that at least the air is cool now. Later on, the land and Agata will fry, and there will not be an air-conditioned office in sight.

She frowns at the upstairs window. Where is the would-be farmer?

A phone trills. Through open windows, she hears Luca's snores turn into an angry mumble.

'Too early! Go to hell!' After a deep cough, he regains his official voice. '*Pronto*—Commissario Agnello.'

A silence. Then a series of loud expletives that frighten small birds out of the fig tree. He emerges onto the balcony, scratching the grey curly hairs on his bare chest.

'Everything all right?' she asks.

He raises his eyebrows at her night clothes. 'Outside already?'

Her expression could probably slay a wild boar at five paces, but he yells 'No time!' before she can reply.

With a huff, she goes inside to grind coffee beans,

pressing the powder into the silver *machinetta*. A crime. A crisis. A reason for his blood pressure to shoot up, so it looks like they'll both need a strong morning cup. She drizzles olive oil inside a piece of focaccia and wraps it in a paper napkin for him.

Unshaven, he dashes into the kitchen and downs the espresso in one gulp.

'Bad?' She doesn't really have to ask.

'A murder at the beach, and Fabio's there before me.'

'The assistant who's no assistance?' she says lightly, neatening his tie. 'And yet you swore you'd have no trouble adjusting to the peasant police officers out here.'

'Must rush. He'll handle it all wrong,' is his reply as he stuffs the food parcel in his jacket pocket and stoops to pull on shoes.

'Back for lunch?'

A mumbled reply could be a yes or a no. A quick kiss and he's out the door. She watches his hunched shoulders, the searching movements of his fingers.

'House keys?' he roars.

'You don't need house keys,' she shouts back. Their new address is so far off the beaten track that even people who want to find them get lost.

He jumps in the car and fiddles with the GPS. She is about to remind him it won't work along this stretch but decides to leave him to it and return to the watering.

There's no doubt he'll dissect the case with her later. This has been their way. He—the Commissario, earning twice as much as she earns as a paid civilian investigator. Yet how she misses her work! The subterfuge, the occasional flirtations, the triumph of finding good information. The only drawback was Luca's interference. He's straight as a Roman road.

Arching her back, she turns off the tap. At least he'd never insisted on her being chained to the home. She loves her two boys, but that would have driven her mad. Thank God for younger sisters to babysit. Her eyes follow his 4x4 Fiat. Why can't she be the one spinning out the door instead of digging? She knows the answer: There is so little paid work here.

The tyres leave a fine dust lingering in the air between the olive trees.

* * *

The Tuscan Beach

In twenty minutes, Luca is on-site. He rubs the stubble on his chin and prepares himself. His stomach squeezes as he notes the insect trail to the overturned boat.

His assistant, Fabio, and a local Carabiniere grimace, lifting the wooden vessel from the prow end. Lying in the sand, the cadaver's flesh is wriggling with larvae. The victim's mouth is closed, but weevils ooze from eye sockets like black tears. Luca coughs and forces himself to inspect the naked body. The men are watching.

Despite the short hair, it is definitely female, and judging by the size—a child. African or Arab in origin. From the smell, he guesses she's been dead for many days. The sliced torso has been split from collarbone to navel. The cavity is almost empty, stripped white by maggots, ribs protruding from behind mottled flaps of chest skin. No heart, no lungs, just bloated intestines unraveling in the pelvic basin.

He shivers and crosses himself. Within a few seconds,

he can stand it no longer and waves a hand for the men to release the craft. There is a collective *oomph* of relief, and they retreat twenty paces, gulping the sea air.

'Has Gianni the Forensic been called?'

'Yes, but it's an undocumented migrant,' says Fabio with a snicker.

He reminds Luca of a police dog, quick to sniff and quick to move on.

'You don't know she's a migrant, Fabio.'

'I'm telling you, Commissario. Did you notice the calloused feet? I'll bet her death is connected to some voodoo thing.'

Luca's jaw tightens. 'Let's wait for more information. She could be a local.'

'Not a chance, Commissario. The campsite owner and the local shopkeepers know all the workers.' He jerks a thumb toward a corpulent man having a whispered but heated discussion with a reed-like male at his side. 'That's Enzo Bianchini and his eldest son. They say they've never seen her before.'

Luca grimaces, wanting to object to Fabio's lazy answers but knowing he must tread carefully where his junior assistant is concerned. The young man is the nephew of his boss, the Capo di Commissario, who, in turn, reports directly to the Minister of the Interior. Given free rein, Luca would shut down the boy's chatter, or clip him around the ear—something Agata would do with ease—but he has yet to test the extent of this workplace nepotism in his new job. He takes a long breath.

The upended boat fills him with disquiet. If the body had been that of a local child, there would be a sense of horror, a shout of urgency in the streets, eager citizens ready to lynch the perpetrator. Noise. Outrage. Even the local

Mafia wouldn't do something so barbaric as to slice up a young girl and leave her this way, without a sheet or a crucifix in her hands. They have standards.

The serenity of the blue sky and rippling waves defies the hidden horror. Bianchini and son stand under a bleached sign reading *Campeggio Bella Cecina*. They have stopped arguing, their eyes vigilant like field mice.

'The owner is a very unhappy man,' continues Fabio. 'The family came back this week to clear the beach in readiness for Easter, and they find this.'

Despite coming from a city office, Luca understands that tourism sustains this area even more than the city. Bianchini, like other campsite owners, is getting ready for the spring opening. His place will have been shut over winter, but now Easter is days away. Motorhomes and tents have probably been fully booked for months, and if the corpse forces a closure, far from cooperation, there will be curses and threats all round.

'It's murder, Fabio. She didn't crawl under there to annoy people.' Luca tries to keep his voice light.

Fabio runs fingers through his gelled fringe. 'This isn't Florence. Excuse me, Commissario, but you're new to the area.'

'But more experienced in police matters than you.'

'Didn't you see Rai TV news last night? One hundred thousand migrants have arrived in boats so far this year. What next? This government needs a kick up the arse.'

'Is this what you learned at that Lega Nord rally you attended last week? How to kick arse?'

Fabio lifts his chin. 'They're prepared to say what the government is too feeble to acknowledge! I'm telling you—you'll never get to the bottom of this death!'

Open wooden gates reveal the start of a row of planking

in the sand and a walkway to the toilet block. A smaller signpost shows the position of the cafe to the right. Luca has been to this beach once or twice in the past months to de-stress and enjoy the serenity of the empty Mediterranean. The area is a vacant canvas in winter.

The four co-opted Carabinieri are studiously ignoring the crime scene, standing next to a mound of winter detritus collated near the road. Water-scarred plastic bottles, metal caps, old flip-flops, and squashed drink cans await bagging and removal. A scattering of rocks and shells remains on the sand, but no proof of anyone carrying a body to the boat, unless Bianchini's movements obscured tracks.

'Looks like they killed her elsewhere and carried her here,' Luca says.

'It's the perfect spot to drop off a murder victim at night —no open shops, and the street lights aren't activated until next week. These smugglers know all the tricks.' Fabio moves to flag down a yellow and green car turning at the end of the road.

A tap on Luca's shoulder makes him turn.

'Enzo Bianchini, *dottore*.' The campsite owner has come over and holds out a hand with blackened fingernails.

Luca doesn't flinch, returning a firm handshake. 'We'll need your statement, Signor Bianchini.'

'When can the body be moved?'

'I'll do my best to get everything gone in twenty-four hours.'

The frown clears from Bianchini's brow. He is effusive with thanks. 'At first, we ignore the boat. It belongs to me and needs mending. Two, maybe three days, the body has been there and us working alongside.' He throws up his hands in horror. 'But the smell when the wind changed direction!'

'We're not in trouble, are we?' the son asks. 'We assumed it was a dead cat. Who knew?'

'Nothing to do with us.' The father gives an annoyed look at the son for this suggestion. 'This is the work of the devil. These migrants have strange practices.'

'Signor Bianchini,' says Luca, 'we don't know she's a migrant.'

'He said!' An accusing finger points at Fabio.

Luca perseveres. 'Are you sure the girl hasn't been with a local family? Perhaps her mother works for someone?'

The two of them are incensed at the suggestion. 'All the businesses along this stretch are family-owned. Respectable. Nieces, nephews, everyone helps in season. If we need extra, relatives are called over from Sicily. It's the only work we have.'

'Was she perhaps with one of the migrants selling umbrellas and plastic items along this stretch of beach?'

Again, they deny any possibility. '*Dottore*, none of the hawkers stay over winter. You know that. They arrive in summer only. Out of season, there are no tourists to buy things, so they move on.'

The son agrees with the father. 'Anyone from last year would be well gone by now.'

'I'm not an unfeeling man, Commissario. I have a daughter,' Bianchini insists. 'But will there be bad press? If people feel unsafe, it will cause cancellations. A disaster for us. We're only a small family business, with regular clients. If they're put off and find another site, they will expect refunds! They might not return next year!'

From the corner of his eye, Luca can see Fabio about to add his two euros' worth and interrupts, 'Signor Bianchini. Some coffee for my assistant and the Carabinieri would be welcome. They'll be standing here for a few hours more.'

'Gladly, Commissario!' The fat man almost bows in his effort to ingratiate himself. A friend in the local guard is always useful. Unless the local Mafia are stronger. Luca assumes this is not the case here, and the uniformed men acknowledge his request with grateful glances. A crunch of tyres heralds the ambulance crossing from road to sand.

'Must we wait? Gianni the Forensic takes forever on these morning calls.' Fabio cracks his knuckles. 'We'll not solve this. Migrant pimps don't talk.'

Luca stands tall. 'For God's sake, stop speculating. We need evidence, Fabio!'

'Evidence?' The chin juts out again. 'These people should be sent back to where they come from, not let loose in our society. Why should we deal with their problems? *Prima gli Italiani*!'

Luca swallows a pithy reply, unsure how sympathetic his Capo di Commissario is to the ultra-right wing Lega Nord group. Currently, Italy is so polarised, it's dangerous to assume political affiliations unless openly stated.

'Okay, young man. You say: Italy first. But I'm saying: Work first.'

Fabio looks ready to continue his political rant. Luca puts up a hand.

'She was just a kid, part of someone's family. Imagine if that was your child. Go through that pile of junk Bianchini assembled over there. A stray cigarette. A drink can. Something may give us a lead.'

Fabio holds his palms upwards in protest. 'Commissario! It's pointless.'

Ignoring him, Luca smacks his hands together, and the Carabinieri turn questioningly. 'Attention everyone. We're looking for clues about how the child got here. This isn't a place where the traffickers' vessels land, and she's too young to have travelled this far on her own. Someone must be missing a daughter. I want everyone to make enquiries door to door, cafe to cafe.' He slaps his assistant on the back with a false camaraderie. 'Come on, young Fabio. Politics second, humanity first. Let's do what we can.'

Luca looks back to where the body lies. The ambulance men are circling in masks and white gloves. Upside down, painted in faded lettering, there is a name visible on the sea-worn boat. *La Speranza*. Hope.

Chapter Two

Canary Wharf, London, May 2016

The luxury apartment is hermetically sealed, and the air conditioning is on full blast. Outside, birds wheel over the River Thames, a living tableau that stretches from Canary Wharf to the distinctive outline of Tower Bridge. But none of the occupants in the room are looking at the view. The three of them stand in a circle around the slumped body of a man, tied tightly to a chair. He's definitely dead. This wasn't supposed to happen.

Two of them are hired help, although all three had entered wearing plumbers' overalls and gloves. One of them gave the injection to the neck. A quick bee-sting stab. The victim was well acquainted with one of the band and wasn't expecting an assault, so there wasn't a struggle. And it's true, there was no serious violence on their mind. All that was needed was some information, delivered via a softener so they could have a little chat. Then they intended to leave, with Alessandro Verdi none the worse for it.

The men cross themselves and twitch, shouting at each other. When the Italian started to fit, they had thought he was teasing—so explains one of the goons. None of them recognised an allergic reaction. The victim talked in a staccato Italian, voice squeaking, chin jutting to his pocket. Searching, they prised out a page of an Italian newspaper.

The one in charge recognised it immediately and leaned forward. An article ringed in red. An article detailing the death of a migrant child on a beach. A shiver and a question. Why the hell did Alessandro Verdi have this in his pocket? Why keep the clipping? To the goons, it was all meaningless, and one of them stuffed the paper in the dying man's mouth to stop his increasingly wild spitting.

Now, the goons are muttering under their breath. A spreading dark patch indicates the body releasing urine, and the hired muscle shove each other, chattering in Polish before abandoning the boss and fleeing out of the apartment, down the back stairs. To hell with the money. They've had half up front. This is more than they bargained for.

The person responsible for the escapade stares desperately around the room. Is it necessary to extract the newspaper from the dead man's mouth? Would it be wise to untie him? No, the reluctant murderer decides. Alessandro Verdi is with the Syndicate, and they won't be fooled, no matter how the scene is laid out. Alessandro Verdi is—was—the banker to the Syndicate. When not frequenting expensive clubs, his elegant figure frequented the darkest corners of London and the blackest holes on the web. He could source fake passports and fake documents with a flourish worthy of a magician. He's valuable to the Syndicate. Rumour has it that he is a personal friend of the English Godfather.

And yet Verdi was prepared to do a side deal and cream

money from the Syndicate's coffers. The reluctant murderer's nerves twang. So again, the question. Why would he renege on their transaction? Is this all about the dead migrant child in Tuscany? Was that a move too far? Surely not. Alessandro knows the business of the Syndicate better than most, and no one could accuse him of having a conscience. Yet they have had an anonymous phone call warning them Alessandro is intending to tell the Syndicate about their side hustle. Rat them out! Why? That was the question. Not a Shakespearian to be or not to be. Why? Why would he do that? Did Alessandro consider his cut insufficient? They could have had a discussion.

But dead men don't talk. So, the reasons are buried in his cooling body.

The reluctant murderer moans. Verdi wasn't supposed to die. This wasn't supposed to happen. Now the Syndicate will hunt down those responsible and crucify them. And that may not be a metaphor.

A nervous check reassures him that no strand of hair or bead of sweat will leave a forensic trail. The flat, itself, is also devoid of personal details. There are no books, no feminine touches, no packets of salted nuts, no breadcrumbs on the marble kitchen work surfaces. One solitary picture stands in a silver frame on the coffee table. It might, or might not, be a wedding photograph. Judging by Alessandro's grey hair and his light grey suit, it is recent. Next to him, arm threaded through his elbow, stands a woman in a white suit. She has Chinese eyes. It could be photoshopped, knowing Alessandro.

While plucking out the mobile phone from Alessandro's pocket, the reluctant murderer's heart hammers like the bells of St. Paul's Cathedral. Time has run out. He and his partner must flee. And fast. A few loose ends to tie and then off to another continent. Birds on the wing.

* * *

Florence, Italy, the next day.

Tonight, Figaro Verdi, heir to the Verdi estates, has left Montecatini della Torre and driven through the hills, down into the bowl of Florence to his apartment. His city home is on the third floor of a nineteenth century building with tall windows and ornate stone arches overlooking the Arno. Upon arrival, he peels off his suit with a sigh. The day has been too long. As mayor of Montecatini, he has presided over petty local squabbles. A month ago, he sanctioned three Syrian refugees to live in one of the *comune* apartments. Two weeks later, the beach murder lit a bonfire under this decision. There is a paper trail that leads from the murder to the town, in the form of a leaflet advertising Montecatini's summer festival found beneath the body. *Madonna*! Such absurdity! Figgi's explanations about how he has followed government guidelines and why the Montecatini Council has an obligation to house a number of legal refugees goes unheard amid the angry voices. His observation that Syrians do not practice voodoo has appeased no one.

His Montecatini housekeeper, and long-term employee of the Verdis, has packed him off from Casa Verdi with a rough smile and a bowl of *Cucina Povera*. This is a soup-like mixture of Tuscan bread, chopped fresh tomatoes, olive oil, and basil, comfort food of the sort he and his siblings used to enjoy when young. Having checked the CCTV on the

Montecatini house, Figgi wanted a word with the housekeepers, but it will wait. He does not want more arguments. All he desires is a quiet evening before going into the Verdi corporation offices tomorrow.

Opening the terrace doors, he breathes in the Florentine spring and the petrol. Traffic honks below and couples walk entwined. As the sun goes down, the lights from the Ponte Vittoria have a perfect reflection in the river waters. This calms his restless spirit. He is alone and sets his table as if for a feast. A few slices of prosciutto crudo, fresh figs from the trees on his land, and a glass of his own red wine to accompany the bowl of *Cucina Povera*. Dante's Heaven.

No sooner has he sat down than his mobile rings. He can't abide those settings where the phone delivers a song. Songs are for concerts. Can he ignore the ringtone? The unknown number is from overseas, and the code suggests England. His nerves vibrate in time to the phone.

'*Pronto*.'

'Mr. Verdi? Mr. Figaro Verdi? This is the London Metropolitan Police. My name is Detective Inspector Vanessa Candle.'

There is a momentary silence at both ends as he rests the spoon in his hand.

'Sorry, sir. Do you speak English? At this hour, I couldn't find an Italian interpreter.'

Figgi's English is excellent—four years in London at UCL, as he quickly reassures the female voice. There is relief at the other end.

'Thank you, sir. Then may I ask, are you related to Alessandro Verdi?'

'Yes. He's my cousin.' His mood dips. 'I know he lives in London, but I haven't seen him for about four years.'

The voice dampens into a conciliatory murmur. 'I'm

sorry to be the bearer of bad news. We've phoned the Italian Police, a man called Captain or Commissioner Luke Agnello, and he suggested we phone you. The fact is, Alessandro Verdi was found dead in his apartment earlier today, and your card was in his wallet.'

There is another brief silence. Figgi wonders if he has misunderstood. The air is tight around him.

'Sorry, sir. There are more details, but in the first instance, can you help us? We have his wife, Susan Li Verdi, in custody. At this stage, she's not a suspect, but she's too distressed to identify the body. She's saying she doesn't know any of her husband's family, and there's no one we can call for her. We wondered if you might have any family locally who could help.'

Figgi's fingers press against the table's edge. 'A moment.' He rises, places one hand on his forehead, and clears his throat. Thoughts zigzag through his mind.

'Hello, sir. Are you there?'

'Yes.'

But no! Alessandro has a wife—Maria Giuliana (or Mariju, as she's called). They are separated, but Figgi knows her well, and Mariju knows Figgi well, and furthermore, Figgi is in contact with Mariju's parents, who live in London.

'Sir,' says the voice. 'We're treating it as a suspicious death. I am sorry to give you this news over the phone, but we're not sure where to send her. We collected Mrs. Verdi from her office at the Bond Street Auction House and took her to the station. The problem is her home is the crime scene. She can't go back. Is there anyone else in London who might help?'

His mouth opens and shuts. He sits and massages one knee, trying to process the information. They haven't mentioned a child. His nephew is four years old. Car lights streak white and red running down alongside the river.

'Who did you say was his wife?'

'Susan Li Verdi. Do you know her?'

'Susan who? Are you sure it's his wife and not a girlfriend?'

'Susan Li. That's L-I. Her middle name. She said they'd only been married for eight months, so perhaps...'

He senses her query. How close is this family that they don't know one of their kin has wed so recently?

'And you say she's not involved with his death?'

'No. Early signs are it was a robbery gone wrong. Although his wallet was untouched. The reason we rang the Italian Police is because a portion of a recent Italian newspaper was found in his mouth. I'm sorry. I'd rather give you more information face-to-face than over the phone. I'm phoning to ask if there is someone locally we can contact?'

Figgi's brain snaps. 'Yes. I have someone I can call.' The possibilities turn over like playing cards. The Verdis are close business associates of Mariju Mara's family. The implications hit him! But of course, the police know nothing about this.

Currently, the Verdi business is pushing to be first in line for millions of euros in a large government restoration project. With an election looming, if the swing goes right, rather than left, the contracts may be lost. But if Alessandro is involved in a British criminal scandal, they will definitely lose. There are certain Ministers who would gladly use any excuse to cancel Verdi business in favour of their own appointees.

The policewoman keeps talking. He struggles to concentrate. One fact emerges from the conversation: He must go to London on the next plane. In the past, he has dealt with a few females threatening to sue Alessandro. They all love him until they don't. But that is insignificant to this development.

'I will identify the body,' he says, making a sign of the cross. 'If I take the earliest plane to London tomorrow morning, I'll be with you by ten at the latest.' He asks her to repeat her name. 'Mrs...?'

'Detective Inspector Candle. London Met,' says the voice. The woman speaks with dry, flat consonants, and he collects a pen and paper to write the details. He thinks of Mariju's parents, Priya and Freddie Mara. They might want to spit on Alessandro, but he is sure they will help to avoid a scandal. Anything to protect their daughter.

'Our family lawyer will come to collect—um—Susan, and find her somewhere to stay.' He dictates the name of Priya Patel-Mara.

The detective seems pleased with this. It is only after Figgi finishes the call that he realises his hands are shaking, more with anger than sorrow. His stomach is empty, but the *Cucina Povera*, the meat and wine, will wait. He swills his mouth with water and pours an uncharacteristically large grappa. It looks like water, but the smell bites. He feels better and mulls over the details. There is no love lost between him and his cousin. He cannot pretend to cry.

He looks at his reflection in the ornate mirror over the fireplace. All his youth, his cousin had teased him. His cousin, a boy without a mother or father to check his excesses. The cousin that was an alternative brother and tormentor. 'Look who's here. It's Figaro. Figaro, Figaro, Figaroooooo.'

But four years ago, Figgi had the satisfaction of seeing Alessandro fall from favour when he slept with the eighteen-year-old Mariju. There is a medieval law about not impregnating your friend's daughter, isn't there? Even worse, finding their daughter pregnant, the Maras talked castration, and Figaro's father could not find the words to mitigate. To complicate things, Mariju insisted she loved him. The Sicilians talk about Omertà, the Tuscans have their own version, but no Verdi was going to kill their own. Family was family. So Figgi had negotiated a marriage.

'If you can't control yourself, Sandro, at least do the honourable thing. They're strict Catholics, and Freddie is the main importer of our best marble.' With some concessions, the wedding took place, only for the girl to leave him before the baby was born. Alessandro was already in other women's beds.

His father reacted by cutting Alessandro out of the will, and Figgi breathed. At last. No competition.

Figgi stands at the open French windows. The night air blows in inquisitive insects and questions: a mosquito for every unanswerable puzzle. What was his cousin doing? In his life, Sandro has sold artwork on the black market and broken a thousand hearts. Is this how it ends for a forty-eight-year-old man who lived to excess? And who is the woman claiming to be his wife? Susan Li.

Closing the terrace doors, his lungs heave with anger before sadness takes its place. The housekeeper of their Montecatini home will take it hard. Old Natale helped deliver Alessandro at birth and loves him like a son. The suggestion of a sob erupts from his chest. He finishes the grappa, pulls back his shoulders, and picks up his phone. There are so many calls to make.

A thought floats across his mind. The English rang Commissario Luca Agnello because of an article in the newspaper. There's only one newspaper that printed Luca's police contact details—a local paper only available in

Tuscany. And there was only one article that mentioned the migrant murder on Cecina beach. Why was this article in Alessandro's possession? Is it possible his cousin was involved? Did he witness something or instruct someone? Is this why he has died? With Alessandro, anything is possible.

Was possible.

Chapter Three

Montecatini della Torre

In the nether regions of the mortuary, the unclaimed lie abandoned in cold metal drawers: those with untraceable fingerprints and those without a strand of DNA to send them home. And the child with no heart or lungs. Luca decries the department's decision to dispatch his investigation to the back of a filing cabinet, but the Capo di Commissario refuses to upset the tourist market. 'It's that time of year, and her young life has ended,' he says, 'so the enquiry can wait for winter.'

Agata listens to his moaning with occasional comment. She will not cry over unknown children. Her tears are for those she knows, and if that makes her hard, so be it.

The phone rings, rescuing her from his diatribe about internal politics. An English detective with a strange name, Dee Eye Candle, has questions for Luca. There is a corpse in her English morgue, a man found with a piece of Tuscan newspaper stuffed in his mouth. The news article details Luca Agnello's name and contact details. And the dead man is Alessandro Verdi.

The blood in Agata's veins congeals.

Dinner also congeals, because Agata must translate with laborious correctness while Luca writes notes. When they finish the conversation, they look at each other. Luca shrugs and continues eating his cold *risotto alle vongole*. Agata gulps wine: The thought of seafood makes her nauseous. Luca knows Agata and Alessandro Verdi were once together—a long time ago in London—before he married her. If he notices her lack of appetite, he does not comment.

Within five minutes, the mayor, Figaro Verdi, phones for more information. Agata leaves Luca to discuss things and stumbles to the darkened vegetable plot. There she weeps, a hand over her mouth. The midges cling to her wet cheeks.

* * *

Hampstead, London, the same day

Sitting in her study, Priya is finishing some court papers. It's late, and when Freddie walks in, she turns in irritation until she sees his face. 'What's wrong?'

'Alessandro Verdi is dead.' His eyes are wide with shock.

She rises, a hand clutching the office chair for support. Then her lawyer training kicks in. 'Who told you? What happened? Where did he die? Why did the police ring us?'

'Not the police,' her husband says. 'Figgi. The police rang Figgi in Florence. They think there was a burglary at Alessandro's London flat.'

'Why on earth did they phone Figgi?'

'The police think Alessandro was in Italy a week or so ago, and there is some Italian connection.'

A thought strikes Priya. 'They're not going to involve us. Are they? Mariju and the little one?'

Freddie's lips have a green tinge, and he leans against the door jamb for support. 'A woman called Susan Li Verdi is in custody, claiming to be his wife.'

'Susan who?' She tugs at the spiral of her long hair, whipping it behind her shoulders and advancing toward her husband as if this is all his fault. 'What crap is this?'

'I'm just telling you what Figgi said. Susan Li. L-I. Sounds Pan-Asian?'

Her quick temper rises. 'Mariju rang me an hour ago, having tucked our grandson, little Matteo, into bed.' She emphasises the facts as she scrutinises her husband's face. 'Why don't you look as shocked as I feel? What do you know?' She is too familiar with his ways.

An hour later, Priya Patel-Mara, an experienced solicitor and enraged mother, is on her way to collect the fake wife from the police station and install her in a hotel of Figgi's choice. Yes—she has agreed to say nothing, but privately she thinks, *Bloody Verdi family*. They're more trouble than they're worth. Figaro is the best of them. An honest man, at least. But as for her daughter's lecherous husband—Alessandro Verdi, a bastard old enough to be her father, a bastard whom they used to consider a friend. Well! Mariju may stand at his grave and weep, but her parents will serve champagne at the wake.

Chapter Four

The week following the migrant murder, Agata discovered a small nest of tiny black scorpions near the house and closed the hole. With news of Alessandro's death fresh in her mind, she goes to check the nest. It is still there, the entrance reopened. With a deep thrust of her spade, she catches the lair in a chunk of earth, plops it into a bucket, and removes all to the edge of their land. Scorpions are harder to kill than memories. Best to put them out of sight. She works on the land, letting her tears fall silently until two surprise phone calls stop them. Alessandro's death has sent out shockwaves into the community, and the reverberations arrive at her door.

With this new turn of events, she knows an argument with Luca is inevitable. There's no avoiding it. Since Alessandro's death, they have hardly traded a word, but now she is ready to talk. Best to get all her news out in the open and deal with Luca's fireworks in one go.

When he returns at noon, he does not notice her mood, wallowing deeply in his own internal cloud. He launches into a rehash of his complaints about Fabio. Last week, when his assistant leaked biased opinions about the migrant murder to the press, Luca went on record to set things straight. Now his boss rebukes him.

'Me! Can you imagine? Not Fabio, the golden boy!'

But supplying a number for the public to phone has meant that the switchboard became blocked with a series of rabidly racist phone calls. It was surprising that the British detective got through by using the phone number in the paper. Nose in the air, Luca declares he never liked Alessandro, an egotist and art dealer, in that order. 'What did you see in him?' he asks. 'I told my boss the connection is coincidental. The muggers used some paper to stifle the man's cries. So what? Now if Fabio had been found dead with such an article in his mouth...'

As Luca scrapes bread around his lunch bowl to catch the last of the pesto, hostility creeps to Agata's fingertips. She drops her fork. She is sick of the running saga of Fabio. How can her husband chew and chew, at a time like this? Fabio is not important. If the stupid boy wants to have a beer with local reporters, Luca should turn a blind eye. If the press wishes to conclude that the child's death is evidence of migrant voodoo, let them.

The scorpion's lair is empty and so is her reservoir of sympathy. She notes the green pesto sauce on his chin, the blob elongating as Luca keeps talking. He continues, claiming he will drop nothing unless it is a clout on Fabio's head. Or a drop of sauce on his shirt, she thinks. Unaware that Agata simmers like a boiling pot, he drones on. Any minute now, she will bubble over and commit a murder of her own if he doesn't shut up. Her father's shotguns are locked away in the basement cabinet, but she has the key.

'You've done your best,' she says, giving up on any attempt to eat.

'All this prejudice about migrants. The murdered girl was a child. Just a child. We must at least find her name.'

Agata takes her half-eaten bowl to the sink. They've moved from Florence to the hills at Luca's request, and yet his anxieties and obsessions have followed him. He takes every murder so personally. She picks up the newly harvested peas from the basket. They are smooth beneath her fingers, but she treats them like the enemy, slashing the pods with a swift slice, dividing the green pearls from the chaff. A stab, and she sucks on a pinprick of blood that blossoms on her fingertip. She cannot fathom that Alessandro's life has ended this way. There was always the hope of a mythical future. Has it really been twenty-five years since they last lay in bed together? Twenty-five years of longing for a reunion. She curses her recalcitrant, illogical heart.

Luca finishes his glass of *aqua frizzante* and examines their mail. Agata turns to watch him. If she chooses her moment, he will accept her new job offer without argument. But regardless, she is more than ready for a fight.

The contents of some recent mail entrance him. 'My little Carlo! He's grown into such a wonderful young man! Look. He's sent an article he published in the University Science magazine. Can you believe it! Permaculture! This is the future of farming. I can't wait for him to come home from University and help me on the land.'

Their younger son is his father's favourite.

'Dino sent a postcard from Thailand last week.' She pokes him into remembering their eldest. Dino is named after her dead father, and he is Agata's favourite.

'Fine.'

'Fine,' she says, hearing the tap trickle. The flowing water draws her back to the River Arno and Florence, the clang of the tram on the streets, pavements sunny side up, even in the rain. And then further back to London and Alessandro. Long ago. Walks by the River Thames, that certain summer, red double-decker buses, Harrods window displays, concerts at the Round House, Hyde Park, and Alessandro's hand in hers as they strolled over Westminster Bridge.

What-ifs are dangerous. The radio pulls her into the present.

Radio Subassio: Breaking News. The Italian President, Sergio Mattarella, has paid a visit to the Rebibbia jail today. He is determined to push through his reforms.

'Finally!' Luca crows. At home, he likes to talk politics when he thinks no one will disagree with him. He expounds on the benefits of the president's move. But politics remind her of another yesterday, and the political sparring over drinks in a Knightsbridge bar. She can still see a young Alessandro laughing at the Spitting Image depiction of John Major. Not that he cared about politics. 'Money buys power, not elections,' he'd said, and he was right. In her role, working as a nanny for a wealthy London family, it was clear her boss, an English Lord, had far more power than any politician. But she was young and in love. It was a time when only the present and the man in front of her mattered. The rest of the world could go to hell.

She tells herself to leave these memories. What's the use of thinking of the summer of '91?

Because you have never let it go.

She sucks hard on her finger. She is in the Tuscan hills, and he is dead.

Luca pulls on his jacket as she dries her hands.

'Did your brother come back to mend the electrified fence?' he asks.

'Of course.'

'And the equipment promised from the Verdis?'

'Coming soon.'

Agata's family go way back with the Verdi family. When they found the property earlier this year, she contacted Figaro for advice on trusted artisans to help fix up the old stone house. And it was Figaro who haggled the price for them. After they moved in, Agata's family assisted when deer trampled the land. And every week, her brothers mend electrified fences when the wild boar trip the current. Each month, her cousins deliver fertiliser. Luca may earn the money, but she is the one with the know-how and nine siblings.

He's at the door when she tells the first of her three messages. Start with the good news.

'My sister phoned about a tractor.'

He whoops. 'Which sister? Bartolemia, Izabella, Yolanda, Giovanna? The hills are alive with your sisters.'

This is his running joke. Luca is an only child: Agata's family are everywhere. Like mushrooms, he often laughs.

'Izabella. Her husband has found a second hand one for sale.'

'The price? The condition?'

'They'll let us know.'

He pops one of the fresh peas in his mouth. 'Good!' he says. 'I also have some news. The Minister for Tourism wants us to close the migrant investigation by the end of the week. So, this morning I asked if I could hire an *agente di Polizia* to do some digging for us. I suggested this crime might be the work of a serial killer. What if we find more bodies at the beach? Very bad for tourism. Ha! That got their attention.'

Agata pours peas into freezer bags. 'Isn't there a local *agente* here?'

'No. But in any case, I can hire whom I want.' He stretches and tucks in his shirt. 'Unfortunately, they're only giving me a budget for one day's work, and it's not very exciting. You'll have to trawl through government asylum agencies and charities asking for missing children. But you said you wanted some work.'

'I want it,' she says. Being a wifely figure at the gate doesn't suit her.

He looks as though he expects a pat on the back, but she doesn't give him the satisfaction, so Luca speaks more to himself than to her. 'We're still waiting on the autopsy. Gianni says his initial impression is that the child is between eight and nine, according to the teeth.'

She studies the peas in the sink. Luca steps outside the kitchen, his eyes drawn to the smudge of deep blue sea between intersecting hills. 'My kingdom.' He thrusts out his chest.

'Yolanda said—'

He tuts and calls back into the kitchen. 'No more inaccurate information from your baby sister. She's a Montecatini gossip.'

'*Dio mio*!' Agata whacks the dishes into the dishwasher and slams the door. She comes to join him outside. 'I told you it was gossip. You asked if any local families in Montecatini had taken in migrants. My sister mentioned the new people who've just moved into the Montecatini Tower. They have an adopted Nigerian boy.'

'And,' said Luca, 'you said the new owner of the Tower used to work as a doctor on Lampedusa Island in the migrant camps.'

'That's what I heard! And what did you do?' Her voice rises in exasperation. 'You sent Fabio to question them at the Tower. The man is worse than a wild boar. The police car drove in with full lights!'

'I thought you wanted me to act on the information.'

'I didn't say I thought the boy or the doctor was involved in the beach murder. I just mentioned the coincidence, that you're looking for a migrant family missing a daughter, possibly from Montecatini, and here is a local family who have adopted an African son. Get it? So, what I actually said was that maybe the girl was adopted. As usual, you weren't listening. I wish you'd pay more attention.'

He straightens his tie with exaggerated dignity. 'Remember, you've only one day of paid work.' Then he turns back to the land, shading his eyes from the sun. Cypress trees stand thinly by the lower boundary of their acreage. He places his legs apart in his de-stressing position.

'Yes, a tractor will be good,' he says, with a deliberate change of conversation.

But Agata is not ready to be placated. 'Figgi phoned this morning and asked if I would investigate Alessandro's death from this end. A paid arrangement. So I've agreed.'

Luca spits. '*Mah*! Alessandro died in England. And you haven't seen him since before we married.' His eyes screw together. 'Have you?'

She ignores the barb. 'Figaro told me Alessandro married bigamously, and the so-called widow, this Susan Verdi, is coming to Tuscany. Now, isn't that interesting?'

Luca flicks his fingers in the air. 'The man was always an arsehole. Why investigate him now he's dead?'

'An investigation might help you,' Agata spits back. 'The British Police believe his death and the death of your migrant child are connected. Don't you want to know why?'

Picking a stone from the brick path, he jettisons it against an old stone shed. It cracks and splits. 'What's going on? I told the British they're crazy if they think an Italian newspaper article stuffed in his mouth is evidence of a forensic link.'

'And yet this Susan is arriving in Montecatini.'

He wags a finger at her. 'If you work as a private *agente* for Figgi, you can't work for me. There's a conflict of interest.'

'Don't be ridiculous. My enquiries are to help Figgi and the family. This year they've done us favours, now they call in the favour. And as for your case, one hand doesn't have to know what the other is doing. If I'm paid both ends, you can put the money into your tractor fund.'

That stops him. She almost adds that her intention is to exonerate Alessandro. But she holds back. 'And there's something else.'

'Oh?'

'My old boss, Bruno Collodini, has rung me. He also claims to know something about your dead migrant girl but will only talk to me. This girl passed through many hands, or so it seems. *Poverina*.'

Mention of her old boss in the Florentine *Agenzia* gets the predicted reaction. Luca's face flushes. 'Is this the week all your old boyfriends crawl back into your life?' Yanking open the car door, he growls. 'I never liked that Collodini. Fifteen years you worked for him, and I had to put up with it. You're retired now. Tell him to go to hell.'

Agata rises to his anger. 'Alessandro's dead and Bruno is dying, but you only have sympathy for an unknown child!'

Luca slams the car door. 'Alive or dead, they're sleazy bastards!'

'Bruno never laid a finger on me, and we used to supply you with good information. Anyway, the closure of his agency made it easier for us to move, so what the hell are you complaining about?'

'Come on, Agata, you know what I'm saying.' Joy for the tractor is extinguished. He starts the car's engine. 'I'll send you the details and phone numbers for my job—that's if you can find time.'

And he's gone. No Siesta, no kiss. *Bastardo.*

Silence is peace, but action beckons. Figgi's request is logical, given her history. Those months of dating Alessandro in London count for something—at least in the Verdi's eyes. But who is Susan Li?

Chapter Five

In the past twenty-four hours, Figaro has made some quick changes to his itinerary. He has flown to England and identified the body, meeting Susan Li Verdi. Detective Inspector Candle explained Mrs. Verdi has a solid alibi, although she has not been ruled out of the investigation completely.

Back at the hotel, the fake wife, unsmiling but without tears, shows him some texts sent just before Alessandro's time of death.

Urgent. You must go to Montecatini. Phone Figgi. Then wait for the package to arrive by courier. Don't speak to anyone else. Letter follows. Don't betray me. A x

It is definitely Alessandro's number, and Susan insists it doesn't make sense to her, either.

Don't betray me?

Figaro looks at this strange woman who claims to be his cousin's loving widow. She insists she must fulfil his last wishes. Figaro is as wary as he is curious. For a second time, he phones Freddie Mara, the father of the real wife. Freddie backs up Figgi's decision.

'If the Verdis don't want the police and media further involved, take her to Italy. On your territory, it will be your rules.'

Strangely, the day after his cousin's death, there is nothing in the British media. A death without a fanfare. Figgi sucks his teeth. How Alessandro would have hated that—an awkward demise, with little glamour. At the very least, Alessandro would have wished to die in the Bahamas in a shark attack. In the morgue, the police told him that initial findings suggest his cousin's death was caused by an allergic reaction to an administered injection. If he hadn't been tied up with an Italian newspaper stuffed in his mouth, they would not have phoned Italy.

'Stay in touch' is the parting shot from the British police when Figaro tells them they are both going to Tuscany. The vote for Brexit is in a month's time, and according to DI Candle, Britain and Italy are still one big, happy Union. They have all raised eyebrows at that comment.

At Pisa Airport, he collects his car, stashes her solitary bag in the back, and asks again to check her texts. Nothing new. If she is indulging in some form of fraud with Alessandro, he is at a loss to know the nature of the con. Nothing about her appearance suggests she was once married to his cousin. Alessandro wore clothes of impeccable taste: expensive silk suits to business meetings, smart casuals at the weekend, bespoke shoes. Susan Li's dress is smart but inexpensive, a chain store outfit, and her light sandals look cheap and unfit for walking in the countryside. But that is not the oddest part about her: She is daubed in layers of make-up.

As they speed down the motorway, he glances covertly at her for the hundredth time. She doesn't seem to notice.

Her gaze is on the pink hills that fringe the motorway, her deep vermillion lips, half-open, enraptured with the scenery. She has black glossy hair that whips in the wind. This is the one thing that resembles Alessandro's real wife. But in every other respect, Mariju is the more beautiful and younger woman. According to the marriage certificate, Susan is forty, and her maiden name was Watts. She is of mixed heritage, like Mariju Patel-Mara. But Susan's thick foundation reminds him of drag queens, the kind that pop up on bad Italian reality shows. Layers of kohl and false eyelashes redefine the shape of her eyes. She has told him her mother is Chinese, her father English, but it's hard to see her features under the artifice. The beige foundation alters her skin colour. Her hands are tan, yet her face is alabaster. She's a painted doll and definitely odd. But oddness does not make someone a murderer.

Figaro knows that Freddie Mara paid a private investigator to keep tabs on Alessandro. Apparently, Alessandro was leasing the Canary Wharf flat, although, unlike Susan Li, he had his own properties. The fake wife seems to own nothing and works in a lowly salaried job at the Art Auction House. Was that Alessandro's game? Art fraud? It's possible.

He has asked her more than once if she had any idea why Alessandro sent the text hours before his death. With a flutter of artificial lashes, she repeats that she has no inkling of any emergency or any package. Initially, she explained, she thought it a prank, hence made no answer. Figaro finds it interesting that the British Police neither found Alessandro's phone, nor checked Susan Li's. But faced with the dilemma of turning the fake wife over to the British Police, citing the text, or bringing her to Italy to collect the mysterious package, Figgi has chosen the latter. No self-respecting Verdi would trust the authorities over their own family. There's an unwritten, medieval law about it.

So here he is, with Susan Li, heading toward Montecatini in the hope that he can clear up the mystery of Alessandro's activities prior to death. Knowing his cousin's shady work in England, the package will probably be a stolen artefact. Figaro has already decided to return it quietly to its rightful owner. Anything to avoid unwelcome publicity. He has yet to discuss this with his father, but Figaro is poised to take over the family business, so it is his decision.

In his mind, Agata's early relationship with Alessandro makes her the perfect investigator. She promises to be discreet, and he trusts Agata. She will only share what's necessary with her husband. From the passenger seat, he hears Susan sniffle. Why did Alessandro have this effect on women? He was a bastard. Reluctantly, Figgi concludes women like bastards, especially rich bastards. And Alessandro was always a charming fraudster.

He takes in a large breath as he drives. Figaro must tell Susan The Truth, the whole Truth, and nothing short of the brutal Truth: There is and never has been a legal marriage. Susan is entitled to none of the Verdi estate, and she must accept that her relationship was nothing more than a statistic in Alessandro's catalogue of fraud.

Once again, he puzzles as to why Alessandro pretended to marry this woman. How did it benefit him? The connection must be to do with her job at the Auction House, and no doubt all will become clear once Agata questions her. A soft glove.

Behind the expensive Gucci sunglasses, the woman's

mood is unreadable. Her hair whirls in the wind as he speeds along the motorway in his soft top sports car, and she disentangles a long strand from her spiky eyelashes. He thinks it best to start by filling her in on some of Alessandro's earliest crimes. See how she reacts. Maybe she knows he is a con man, and this will make the information easier to accept.

'Alessandro hasn't been to Italy recently because four years ago, my father banished him from all the family properties. Alessandro insisted he wasn't interested in returning, anyway.'

'Banished?' she says. 'How very medieval.'

He omits to explain how perfectly the term describes the family punishment: The Prince refused entrance to the family castle.

'His first brush with the law was when he was at University. Did he tell you? He sold our family's *Mappamundi* by Fra Mauro on the black market.'

They pass a sign for the shopping centre at Navacchio. She seems more interested in the surroundings.

'Really? Those old maps are worth a fortune.' Her reply does not contain a hint of shock. As someone who works in a Bond Street Auction House, she would know the value of such things.

'That was just the start,' Figgi continues. 'We tried to get it back, but it was impossible. A Japanese buyer, and my father's refusal to take Alessandro to court for fear of causing a scandal, meant we lost it.'

'Proving ownership can be complicated. I suppose it was a family misunderstanding.'

Her comment doesn't begin to cover the shouting and swearing and punches that ensued at the time, but he's not going to elaborate.

'How did Alessandro know where to find a buyer back in the nineties?' she adds.

It's a good question, but he can tell she hasn't grasped that Alessandro was fundamentally a law breaker.

'Early days on the internet, perhaps?' says Figgi.

Susan kneads the voluminous brocade handbag on her lap. It reminds him of a smaller version of Mary Poppins' carpet bag in the film he saw as a child.

'The police asked me some odd questions. I told them all his sales were legal. He was a bona fide art dealer. It's my job to check the legality and ownership of artefacts, so if he'd been selling stolen art, I'd have known.' Her tone is firm. The facts, she seems to say, speak for themselves; therefore, Figaro's facts are wrong.

Merda.

A ping interrupts them, and she extracts her phone from the folds of the bag.

'*Welcome to Italy*,' she reads. 'It's my network. Is it expensive to receive and make calls here?'

Figgi's eyes fix ahead. Does she have money worries? Has she never travelled abroad? They know so little about her. At least she's going to their holiday home and not one of their main houses. If she is Sandro's sidekick in crime, valuables will disappear, but at Casa Verdi, there's nothing of any great value. You can't steal a pool.

'There's Wi-Fi at the house.'

If her concern is money, the news he's about to give her will not improve her finances.

A second text sounds. She looks at it, picking another black strand of hair from her mouth. Under the linen dress, he sees her shoulders rise.

'Anything to do with the earlier text? Read it to me.'

Her reluctance is obvious, but she reads out loud.

'Forgot to text earlier. Sorreee.' She spells the word. *'I used the special courier as requested. Wait for barcode. Must have passport to collect. A.'*

From the corner of his eye, he sees her push the phone deep into the bag and close the clasp.

'I've no idea who that is!' She licks her lips. 'The letter A is not for Alessandro. That's not his number or his way of signing off.'

He drives past blue and green road signs. Truth or lies? The text seems to have troubled her more than the rehearsed speech about Sandro being a bona fide art dealer.

'Ahhh. We'll ask Commissario Agnello to check the number. You understand, we're not going to my home in Florence, we're going to our family home in the hills.'

'The text specified Montecatini.'

'Yes, and I'm the mayor of Montecatini. I'll introduce you to the caretakers. They'll look after you while I go to my office to catch up on paperwork. And a friend will visit.'

'I don't need caretakers.'

He smiles at the assumption. 'Not you—the house. It's a large estate. Natale and Renzo have worked for us for forty years, and Natale's parents before them.'

Turning off the motorway, he shoots down a long road, racing past an acreage of symmetrically planted tall saplings, their barks bleached like driftwood.

'Trees for paper,' he says. Her dark glasses have come off, and she pushes herself up higher in the bucket seat, fixated on the landscape. 'Tourists always think every tree in Tuscany is an olive tree.' He's prevaricating, trying to squash the sense of an impending storm.

Oncoming cars throw up coppery dust, and pink mountains glow to the east with ragged lines jutting into the sky. 'Oh God!' she breathes as they pass heat-licked stone cafes nestling in village corners. 'I had no idea it was so beautiful.'

This is the most animated she's been since leaving the police station.

'The first time in Tuscany?'

'Yes. Although he promised to take me, one day.'

Her awe would be touching if she were on holiday. Every billboard fascinates her. *Fai-Da-Te* and *Co-operativa Supermercati*. She tries to pronounce the names on the signs, vermillion lips moving slowly—*Terricciola, La Sterza* —making typical English mistakes. Lost in the newness of her surroundings, there is no hint of a new widow's sorrow, even though the marriage certificate dates from eight months ago.

Clusters of plant and farm machinery shops remind Figgi of Luca's need. The detective is as ignorant about small farming as this woman is about the Verdis. Why don't people check things first? He is a man who researches everything carefully before making a move. And yet, here he is, driving this unknown woman into an unknown situation.

They dip between two hills spread with olive trees from end to end, branches pruned into the shape of a balloon. Normally, his heart rises when he sees a well-pruned olive grove, but he is filled with foreboding. Natale will not be happy to meet Susan. The old woman adored Alessandro, and to her, he could do no wrong. When Figgi told her of her beloved boy's death, she collapsed on the other end of the phone. He should have gone to deliver the message in person, but he detests weeping women.

'The olive trees are hundreds of years old. They existed earlier than the modern roads, so unlike the Romans, we build around them.' He tries to make a joke. 'How do you make a large fortune smaller? Run a business making artisanal olive oil. It doesn't pay, but we pretend, because tourists visit to relive Renaissance history.'

Her face remains deadpan. Perhaps the makeup freezes her muscles in place.

They drive alongside ploughed fields; early shoots rise from the ground. How to begin? It is a shame to spoil a good landscape with the truth.

The dark glasses are back on.

Porca miseria, he swears silently. Get on with it. 'Ahhh. I have bad news.'

'Alessandro is dead?'

Humour? He hadn't thought her capable.

'I'm going to be straight with you. We have some good family friends. Mr. and Mrs. Mara. You remember Priya? She was the solicitor who accompanied you out of the station. They live in London. Their daughter, Mariju, married Alessandro when she was eighteen. She's now twenty-two.'

The eyelashes blink.

'What I am saying is Alessandro was already married to Mariju when he pretended to marry you. Therefore, your marriage is bigamous. I think you knew about this? Yes?'

The eyelashes flutter. There is silence, with just the wind in their hair. The doll's face remains immobile. For a moment, he is convinced this news is no surprise to her. Of course, she knows. This journey is part of an elaborate plot to keep things from the British Police. That makes sense. They are all withholding information from someone.

'No,' she snaps. 'We had a small ceremony with two of his friends for witnesses. And he insisted I take out a passport in the Verdi name. You said you hadn't spoken to him in a number of years.'

Figgi slows down to take a bend. A glance, and he sees

her staring ahead, fingers welded to the handbag, her world in a lap.

'I was there when he married Mariju four years ago,' he says. 'It was a legal marriage.'

The hills are slices of ochre under the cobalt sky, not yet in full bloom. He heads forward and turns sharply right onto another twisting road. White cows chew placidly next to the verges.

'Obviously, he divorced and didn't tell you.'

Again, he silently curses. She is determined to make this more difficult than it should be. 'No. I've checked. His earlier marriage still stands, although they are separated.' He turns left, skimming another hillside worked by tractors. The machines look like beetles on the top ridge.

Silence. The eyelashes hover.

He clears his throat. Whether she accepts it or not, it's the truth. 'Priya told you we suspected him of forgery. That's right. Yes?' There is no response. 'He must have forged the papers for your wedding, possibly hacked into a database or two. It's the kind of thing he did.'

Silence. The eyelashes connect. The eyes close.

'I'm happy to introduce you as Mrs. Verdi when we get to Montecatini, if that avoids embarrassment.' He wishes she would say something. Anything.

In response to his prayer, a small moan breaks the silence, rising from low to high in a ghoulish crescendo. Her eyelashes open and then close in a vice. Since meeting her, he hasn't seen the suspicion of a tear, but now, the sunglasses are off, and her face is puckering. The stiff black lashes lattice together, and with a heave, she lets out a bellow of distress, akin to a cow giving birth.

The wheel slips from his grasp, and the car veers towards a side ditch before he yanks back control, fishtailing across the thin tarmac. Another louder bellow ensues. With one free hand, he clicks open the glove compartment and scrabbles for a small packet of tissues, tossing it onto her lap.

She grabs it and then weeps, each howl louder than the last. Since childhood, he can't remember anyone weeping so openly. She blows her nose, but the tears keep coming. Within a minute, every tissue is coated in gluey foundation and snot, and black tears line her cheeks like prison bars.

'I'm sorry,' she says, continuing to cry.

'I'm sorry,' he says, thinking: *What the fuck do I do*? He has no more tissues; any minute now, the oozing mass of makeup is going to wind up on his cream upholstery.

She wails. 'It's such a shock. I'm sorry. I'm sorry. I'm really sorry.'

Finding a narrow stopping point, he clicks on the hazards. He is in unchartered water—how to comfort her? After all, he is the victim's cousin; she may be involved in the crime. Should he be gathering her into his arms? That doesn't seem appropriate. A glimmer of realisation hits him —this cannot be fake. She might have faked ignorance in the police station, but she doesn't know about the bigamy. Either that or she belongs on a podium in Hollywood. Grabbing his jacket, he fumbles around for his phone, wondering who to call. He has never mastered the art of dealing with emotional women. Then he remembers Agata—a situation like this is exactly why he's opted to pay for her services.

Susan continues to cry. Agata picks up.

'I need you at my house. Now!' Speaking rapidly in Italian so Susan won't understand, he apprises Agata of the problem.

'I can hear,' she says.

'I know you said you'd come later, but I want you to come immediately!' He gabbles a further plea as Susan continues to cry and wipes her face. Then he spots a black mark on the inner door handle and gasps.

'Why didn't you have this conversation with her in London?' Agata is one of a very few people who still speaks to him as if they are still teenagers.

'She was desperate to come to Italy.' Such an excuse sounds pathetic even to his ears. 'I forwarded you the text. I didn't want to complicate things.'

'You're an idiot.'

'I know.' He doesn't care what she says so long as she comes.

Another bellow of distress. For a second, Figgi puts an awkward hand on Susan's shoulder. Someone in a cream camper van overtakes them, gesticulating at the inconvenience of his car causing an obstruction on the narrow country road.

'I have an appointment with an old colleague, but I'll re-route,' Agata says as Figgi watches Susan wipe her nose on her skirt. It's the most graceless thing he's ever seen in his life. The tissues lie in the car well.

'But what do I do now? At this moment?'

'For heaven's sake, Figgi! Distract her with the view. She's in Tuscany!'

The phone goes dead.

A string of phlegm attaches to Susan's clothes, and she sniffs loudly. 'I'm sorry,' she says. 'I'm sorry. It's such a shock.' She gulps. 'My mother left when I was young, and last year, my father died of cancer. Meeting Alessandro was a dream come true. I thought my luck had finally changed.'

This is news to him. He has absolutely no idea what to say next.

Tentatively, he raises a finger to the skyline. 'Look over

there. Do you see it? La Torre di Verdi. That's the historic tower of Montecatini. We're nearly at my home.'

'You live in a tower?' She sniffs, looking toward the top of the hill. A large stone cuboid appears to grow out of the tree canopy. Wiping hands on her skirt, she gives another shuddering gulp.

'No. We used to be the owners, but an ancestor lost the Tower in a game of cards. My grandfather built another house further down the hill. Much larger and more beautiful.'

He speeds upward along the narrow road. He can't wait to hand her over to someone else.

'I'm sorry,' she says again, collecting the discarded tissues into a ball. 'I don't usually cry, but it's like there's no hope left.'

'Ahh. I too am sorry.'

He sucks in his cheeks: *Here we are apologising to each other, and it's all Alessandro's fault.* Some things never change. But something puzzles him. Historically, Alessandro acted in his own best interests, yet Figgi cannot fathom why he would enter into this phony marriage. If she's not part of his criminal network, who is she? All he sees is a forty-year-old nonentity with a makeup fetish and no money.

Chapter Six

Montecatini della Torre

There are two Piazzas in Montecatini: a medieval one, built on the hill's ridge, nestling in the shade of the Tower, and a larger square, constructed more than a hundred years ago on lower, flatter land. The old Piazza is reached by a thin, twisting cobbled path. The newer one, Piazza Centrale, is cut through by a twentieth century tarmac road.

Long ago, medieval stalls deserted the upper Piazza in favour of the accessibility of the lower Piazza. Agata's youngest sister, Yolanda, owns the cafe on one corner of the square. She and her Dutch partner, Dana, have taken Verdi loans to revamp the premises.

La Pizzeria has a new white, red, and green sign hanging above the doors. Compared to the signs of the other shops, it gushes youth, serving freshly baked pizza from early until late.

Like Luca, Agata regards her youngest sibling as a gossip, or as Yolanda likes to say: *una signora amichevole.* But Yo-yo's friendliness and generous portions have made her popular with the townsfolk. As a member of a long-established Montecatini family, the townspeople feed her the inside line to local events. Too young to remember Alessandro as a boy, she and Dana have pored over old photographs and know the handsome Prince is viewed more favourably than his cousin, Figaro, who is regarded as a pen-pusher mayor. Agata considers the townsfolk's assessment of Figaro a little harsh, but Yolanda is quick to expand on Alessandro's smouldering charm from his last visit four years ago.

Agata stops to talk to Yolanda on her way to her old boss' place, which is in the nearby city of Volterra. She sits, watching her baby sister make pizza bases for the evening trade. There are few people in the Piazza Centrale at this hour, so the arrival of a thin Black teenager catches Agata's attention. He walks down the cobbled road from the Tower, coming into the square with a strangely cautious step. There is something deer-like about the way he moves: arms softly bent clutching an empty string bag, cropped head down, a careful tread of flip-flops on the cobbles. On the opposite side, the owner of the Trattoria della Torre comes out with three stacked aluminium chairs. The boy puts up a hand, halfway between a wave and a salute, but the grizzled man turns away. The boy quickens his pace across the pedestrianised centre.

'What's up with old Arturo?' she asks her sister.

Glancing up, Yolanda holds white floury hands aloft. 'Since the police visited the Tower, people have not been good to Edu. Honestly, did the men have to use lights?' She separates some pieces of dough. 'I feel sorry for Edu. Actually, I feel sorry for the whole family, but the boy is just eighteen, and he's a good kid. Very polite.'

'So that's the boy you told me about?'

'Yes. Umberto's adopted son. This is your fault, you know.'

'Not entirely.' Agata frowns. 'I passed on your information, but Luca wasn't listening properly. They also checked out the Syrian men in the *comune* apartments, and a few others. None were involved with the girl on the beach. They all had alibis. Fabio is a swine.'

'It's a mercy no one mentioned my name, or I would be mud with the D'Angelo family.'

'They're the ones who bought the Tower?' Agata picks a piece of dough from the mass and rolls it in her palm.

'Yes, and sadly Umberto isn't popular here.'

'Oh? You didn't tell me.' Agata comes to her sister's side and pulls a second tiny dough pellet from the pile, rolling it between finger and thumb. It sticks like elastic.

'I'm not a gossip.' Yolanda re-coats her hands in flour and makes a face as she squishes and pulls on the pizza base. 'It's been a combination of things. The paper ran that article about voodoo. Some people pointed at Edu just because he's from Africa. And then there's the doctor's nickname. *Il Macellaio*.' She spins the dough into an airy flatness.

Agata squashes her pellet on the granite surface. 'A butcher? So he's a surgeon?'

'Was. Was a surgeon, or a pathologist. Take your pick. The point is he used a knife to cut people.'

The boy is standing at the door of the *farmacia*. As the shopkeeper turns the sign from *Chiuso* to *Aperto*, he pokes his head in until all Agata can see is his body and the razored edge of his neck. Then he slips inside.

'It doesn't take much.' Agata sighs.

'In this town, Umberto and Naomi D'Angelo are *stranieri*. They're not Montecatinese.'

'I thought you said they were originally from Rome, not the other side of the planet.'

'*Stranieri*!'

Agata huffs. 'Ridiculous. The North-South divide!'

'Come on, I'm sure you city folk think the same. Florentines are better than Romans, *allora, allora*.' Yolanda finishes one pizza base and starts another, fingers working methodically. 'Anyway, Dr. D'Angelo was quite open about his work in the migrant detention centre in Lampedusa. Afterward, somebody remembered the scandal in the news about charity workers sexually abusing children and put two and two together and threw in the beach murder.'

Agata laughs. '*Madonna*! Two and two makes a hundred. That scandal had nothing to do with Lampedusa! Is there anything you haven't accused this family of doing?'

'Not me.' Yolanda spins another dough ball into a thin base and again places the circle on the wax paper. There are four stacked aluminium trays full of empty pizza bases, ready to be filled. She puts hands on hips with satisfaction, then turns and tuts at Agata. 'But nothing like the beach murder happened here until they came.'

'That's crazy logic!'

'Don't involve me.' She slaps her hands together, raising a fine white mist. 'I am Switzerland. I've a business to run.' With lowered voice she adds, 'Naomi, the doctor's wife, came to my Pizzeria after the police visited and wept over a Prosecco. She asked me to put out the word. Explain to everyone in Montecatini that these ideas are false news spread by the Lega Nord.'

'And you believe her?'

'Whatever makes money.' Yolanda grins for a second. 'But seriously, yes, I do believe her. Unfortunately, plenty do not. There was a meeting in Rome a week ago, and a speaker mentioned the beach migrant girl as an example of the government's inability to control our borders.'

Agata keeps eyes on the door to the *farmacia*. The boy leaves the shop with a small bag that has a green cross in a circle printed on it. 'Look at him. He's just a kid.' She catches herself sounding like Luca.

'Crystal said the same.'

'Who's Crystal?'

'An American lady who arrived a few weeks ago. Linda Jensen's niece. The Dutch people? You must know them. They've had a holiday home here for forty years. Anyway, last summer, Stefan said his wife had dementia. They're selling up their small holding. Very sad. This summer, according to their niece, is their last summer here.'

'I can't keep track of all the new residents in this town.' Agata makes a note on her phone while Yolanda takes more dough. 'I'm surprised anyone is Montecatinese anymore, what with the influx of new buyers.'

'Crystal says she's come to help for a month or so because she's a nurse. First thing she did was to hire migrant labour. After the incident with Edu, she came to speak to me. A bit like Naomi. She wanted me to tell everyone that the kids on her property are only here until her aunt gets into a hospice in Holland. They're part of a charity scheme, Migrants First, and they're all due to leave soon. Figaro Verdi checked it out.'

'I'll bet that's the charity I spoke to this morning. Yes. Migrants First. I've been in touch with them as part of Luca's investigation. God knows who funds them.' Agata watches Edu enter the bakery with another soft side shuffle. On her phone she taps in: *Linda and Stefan Jensen, holiday home owners. Migrants First, has Fabio spoken to niece, Crystal, or migrant workers?*

'The Jensens are not an *agriturismo*, so no one is really complaining. And Crystal and the family keep themselves to themselves.' Yolanda spins a final dough ball. 'In fact, Crystal orders a sack load of pizza for the worker kids. Pays cash. So I've no issues.'

'But free labour upsets people.' Agata watches Edu come out of the bakery with two loaves. He stands at the doorway to the *Allumentari*.

Yolanda flicks a spare dough pellet at Agata. 'Being nosy?'

Agata flicks a dough pellet back.

Yolanda laughs. '*Un cafe*?'

She checks her watch. '*Certo*,' but when she turns to the square, Edu has gone. She holds her breath as a delivery lorry brushes past her beloved Cinquecento. Geographically, Montecatini is the same as all small Tuscan hillside towns and has limited parking. The *comune* have widened one section of the square to accommodate larger cars, but even so, Agata has only found a vacant parking space because it is the tail end of Siesta.

As she sips her espresso, she watches the bank teller unlock the tiny branch of Banco di Sienna on the opposite corner to Yolanda's cafe. There is one bus stop, primarily for the school children who attend the senior school in Volterra. Two mothers wait for their offspring, chatting next to Yolanda's competition: the Bar Media.

Nearby, a man in overalls stands purchasing cigarettes from the vending machine outside the corner *Tabacchi*. Edu emerges with a bulging bag in one hand and long loaves of bread tucked under his other arm. As he crosses the road, the tip of a loaf touches the man's elbow, and Edu turns in apology. The workman jerks back.

'What are you doing?' he shouts. 'Go back to where you've come from.'

The mothers stare, then look away. Edu looks to stand his ground, one foot marginally forward. The man clenches his free fist, and Edu falters, turns, and sprints across the cobbles toward the Tower.

'*Madonna*!' Without hesitation, Agata flies down the four steps of La Pizzeria and crosses the square in four paces. 'Who do you think you are? That boy lives here! He wasn't doing anything.'

The man rebuts her with a fruity swear word that makes the mothers giggle. 'I live in Volterra, and I'll protect my family even if the police do nothing.'

Interrupting the exchange, the blue school bus wheezes in. It avoids the man's vehicle with a gap the thinness of beaten metal. Everyone steps back, and the workman spits on the ground. With a slam, he closes his cab door and drives off ahead of the bus, revving his engine.

Agata stamps back to Yolanda. 'Is this what goes on here?'

Her sister finishes her coffee with a mutinous glare. 'That man works with a team doing some building on the Hendersons' Airbnb house, the English people who live just over the hill. The workmen stop for food here, so again, Agata, leave me alone. I won't get involved. Can't you see? This murder has frightened everyone!'

'But Edu has done nothing wrong, and even that shit, Fabio, couldn't find a reason to arrest him.'

'That's the problem. People are angry because there have been no arrests.' Yolanda folds her arms. 'Don't look at me like that. I'm just a small business trying to survive.'

Agata raises her eyes to the gaudy metal sign over the bar and bites her lip. Her sister's pizzeria opened a few years ago with Verdi loans. Outside, there are railings with cushioned wooden seating. Agata knows the exterior alone will take her sister ten years to pay off. Thankfully, she has a business partner, a Danish woman called Dana. But the two of them must be up to their armpits in debt.

Agata shades her eyes and looks at the Tower. It casts a deep shadow on the northern side of the square. 'How has everyone taken the news of Alessandro's death? I assume it's public knowledge.'

'I'll say!' Yolanda clears the cups and walks stiffly back to the counter. 'The whole bloody town knows! Mayor Verdi told Natale, so what do you expect? The poor old woman came up to the piazza and wept in my cafe.' She goes behind the counter. 'We should charge for counselling. Everyone fussed over her, buying her drinks, giving her tissues and hugs. Renzo stood outside by the war memorial. You know how her husband is. But I tell you, we all had a tear in our eye, even though we haven't seen Alessandro for a few years.'

'Did she talk about his wife, Maria Giuliana?'

'No. Tell me she hasn't died as well?'

'No!'

Yolanda puts a hand on her ample chest. 'Poor Alessandro Verdi!' Her eyes become soft. 'Such a handsome man. Such a waste, to die so young, and Mariju loves him to this day.'

Agata has never made her affair with Alessandro known to her own family, so she feels free to ask questions. 'How do you know?'

'I'm on Mariju's Facebook. Nothing about his death so far. Perhaps she's in shock.'

'She still writes about Alessandro?'

'Sometimes.' Yolanda checks the pizza bases and spins

the parchment around, surveying her handiwork. 'Actually, she hasn't said anything about her private life in a while. Just pictures of food and drink in London. Nothing like as wonderful as Tuscany, but we privately message each other now and again. I'm closer in age to her than you.'

Agata ignores the jibe from her youngest sister. 'If you're in touch with Mariju, I'd better tell you something important.'

Her sister makes a face.

'Seriously, Yo-yo. This is between me and you. Figgi is bringing a woman to Casa Verdi this afternoon. He'll introduce her as Alessandro's second wife.'

Yolanda raises her eyebrows so high they disappear into her white regulation hairnet. Then she shakes her head. '*Figurati*! That can't be. They're not divorced. Mariju messaged me a few months back with a beautiful little photograph taken on their fourth anniversary. She said it was a secret, and I wasn't to share it publicly.'

'A secret. You!' Agata demands to see the picture.

Yolanda refuses, and for a moment Agata is tempted to wrestle her into compliance as she used to do when they were kids.

'I promised. She was worried her parents would find out they were back together again.'

Astonished by this news, she postpones the wrestling match. A member of Yolanda's staff arrives outside on her boyfriend's scooter and waves up to them. Agata wishes she had said nothing. 'Seriously, Yo-yo, who else knows about this?'

'Not sure. Dana, my partner, of course, but she won't say anything. So who's claiming to be his wife?'

Agata's phone rings. It's Figgi. She takes the call and listens to him pleading for help. 'Speak of the devil, this woman is arriving at Casa Verdi shortly.' Agata gives her sister a double kiss. 'Don't tell a soul. Promise?'

'Of course. But it's bound to come out.' Yolanda wipes her floury hands against her apron and follows Agata outside, passing the bar girl who bounces up the outer steps. They exchange a *buon giorno*. 'By the way, how's the search for a tractor going?' she asks.

Agata shrugs. 'Izzy is on the case.' She squeaks the key and jumps into the car.

Yolanda leans towards the window. 'Listen, Agata, do me a favour and make sure that Luca's assistant doesn't return. I know his sort—looks at his reflection in the cafe windows and keeps a comb in his back pocket.'

'I'll try,' she says, thinking of the morning argument. As if in sync with her thoughts, a text pings, and it is from her old boss, Bruno.

Looking forward to seeing you. B x

She sighs and texts back.

Running late. See u soon. A x

'Don't forget. You promised to help me at this weekend's Festa celebrations. You remember?'

'Yes, I'll be there.' Agata waves, impatient to be gone.

'Come early. Parking is a problem.'

'*Beh*! What's new?'

Yolanda pats the roof of the Cinquecento. 'You'll have to get rid of this now you're living here. Buy a Jeep or something. This car can't handle hill roads.'

'Get rid of the Cinquecento? Never!' She makes a rude gesture, and her sister laughs.

Chapter Seven

At school, she was Silly Sue Li. At work, her moniker is Strange Sue. She is on the outside, looking in. Her Chinese mother left when she was six. Her Anglo-Saxon father was an ex-soldier and full-time drunk. Are they to blame for her isolation? A teacher once told her she was unique, but unique is another word for an outsider.

Painting herself—her eyes, her face, her nails—became an early habit. Let the world stare as long as no one sees her true self. She has read some popular psychology paperbacks —*Learn to love yourself! How to gain happiness!* Amongst a plethora of advice mentioned, one quack has said: If your mother doesn't love you, you will believe you are unlovable. She tries hard to forget that. Alessandro loves her; that's all that matters. *Loved her.* He's dead. But did he really know her?

As the car ascends to Montecatini, she cannot shake an acute sense of mortification: She lost control. What she said was true; she rarely cries, and barely uttered a sob when she buried her father a year ago. But news of

Alessandro's subterfuge rips out all hope of a golden future with an Italian family. A future where she is *Mama* and taken into the bosom of a large, loving community. She glances at Figaro. His jaw muscles are tight as he drives at top speed. Perhaps he will crash on a bend. That might be a mercy.

Reflecting on Alessandro's text, she feels the message is clear.

Urgent. You must go to Montecatini. Phone Figgi. Then wait for the package to arrive by courier. Don't speak to anyone else. Letter follows. Don't betray me. A x

The instructions are simple. They denote trust. She—Sue Li—was trusted by him. So why the final sentence? *Don't betray me.*

The news that he has married her bigamously turns everything on its head. He has betrayed her.

The pain slices her afresh as they whip around a tight bend. She remembers reading the text in the office and assuming she should laugh. It had to be a prank. The logical thing was to ignore it until she knew more. She's never been one to make quick quips. *Text, emoji, lol, send.* That's not her. She tries hard to appear witty, but it doesn't come naturally.

When the police came to her place of work, she recognised instantly that the text implicated her in something sinister. She froze. Do nothing. Say nothing. Blink eyelashes. Her early training involved dealing with her father, a singing drunk, avuncular and loud. She has spent years surviving embarrassing moments by remaining silent. Because that was her primary emotion—not grief—but the embarrassment of being centre of attention.

Your husband has died? Oh, poor you? Your husband has died? Maybe you did it? No one spoke directly to her, but she saw the words in their eyes. *What has Strange Sue done now?*

The lawyer, Priya Patel-Mara, arrived. A plump, ill-tempered Indian woman who treated her like a worm. But Susan is used to condescension and so made the obligatory stutter of gratitude. Once outside the police station, she shared the text and was surprised at Mrs. Patel's reaction. It was almost as if this was to be expected. The woman explained how the Verdi family would agree to pay for her to go to Italy, provided she stayed with Figaro Verdi and spoke to no one else. It was an easy bargain. She has no one else to trust. *Money opens doors*, she tells herself. *You are joining their family*, she tells herself. *The Italians value family.*

But now—twenty-four hours later—the truth is revealed. She is once again Strange Sue. Nothing has changed. She may not be a suspect of the British Police, but is she a suspect of the Verdis? Is she—in fact—safe? For the past two nights, she has searched her memory about her husband. There is so little to remember. He was a firework in her life.

Her surroundings are beautiful. No photograph can do justice to the landscape. Figaro is trying to distract her by pointing out their destination on a far-off ridge. So much space and colour. So much sky, a summer blue. At the back of her mind, Silly Sue Li can hear the chanting in the playground: *Where's your Mama now?*

She wipes her face on her skirt. The grey and red cotton is a battlefield of foundation and mascara. Why didn't she flee when she had the opportunity in London? As they turn another corner, an even wider panorama opens out before her. Fields braided green stretch along the valley and touch the sky. In the distance, an ancient walled city sits on a ridge, a pallet of pink. She understands the medieval need to put up walls and wishes they were driving to the city, instead of hurtling upward, toward a canopy of trees surrounding the town of Montecatini. Before they reach the summit, Figaro turns right at a metal sign with gold lettering: *Casa Verdi*. The car bumps up a rocky path alongside a wire fence, and from nowhere, a large villa emerges. It is not so much a house as a mansion, hewn from the mountainside. The stone is too clean to be medieval. Rows of painted wooden shutters are half-closed under a terracotta roof, and wrought-iron railings run along the first floor terraces with Juliet balconies. Pots of red and white geraniums dot each balcony. On the ground floor, thick, pendulous grapevines hug the metal filigree of the pergola, stretching the length of a sun-baked patio.

'This is your holiday home?' She cannot hide her shock at the size.

'My family's. Not just mine. Although the others don't come here as often as they used to. But I'm the mayor, so I'm here most weeks.'

He gets out of the car and opens a barred metal gate before easing his Audi in front of a gnarled tree. Broad leaves glisten, and the branches bend with clumps of young figs.

With a fist full of soggy tissues, she wipes her nose, noticing the snail trails of phlegm glittering across her skirt. What must he think of her? She looks up and shades her eyes, stepping out to turn in a circle inhaling everything: rim to ridge. There are no shops or neighbours on the horizon, just the occasional house and the tip of the Tower. The valley dips below, sun-drenched and green. Figgi moves away to make a call on his mobile.

A flicker of sun in the far corner, and she sees floating

needle points of light, the shimmering of a pool. For a moment, her embarrassment fades. Why has Alessandro never spoken of this magical place? Tiny, bright green lizards dart in front of her, racing between perimeter rocks coated in purple blooms. It is impossible not to feel enchanted, and she wonders how her would-be, fraudulent husband tore himself away from such beauty to live in metal skyscrapers.

After a quick conversation, Figaro comes back to grab her suitcase. 'I've just rung Paolo at the local post office. No package has arrived for you, but I'll give you the internet code so you can check emails on your phone. If it's a courier, they'll give notification.'

With a jerk of his head, he asks her to follow. A large wooden door on the first floor seems to be the main entrance, located at the top of a grand external stone staircase, but he heads to the patio. Two slatted shutters are folded outward, revealing internal glass doors opening inward. Beyond is a modern kitchen. At the marble work surface, an old woman pushes thick fingers through pastry. Her hunched back and black clothes remind Susan of a wicked witch. Small currant eyes peer at her with suspicion. Only when the witch sees Figaro does her expression soften. Her floury hands imprint on his shoulders as she gives him a kiss on both cheeks. He fusses over her, gathering her into his arms and wiping the tears that spring to her eyes. For a moment, he cradles her like a child, then disentangling himself, makes introductions.

'Ahh. This is Natale,' he says. 'She's like family.'

'*Buona giornata*,' the old woman murmurs. There is no warmth in her voice, and she deliberately turns away to speak to Figaro in Italian, shutting Susan out. A long row of Sabatier knives gleam in a stripe of sunlight, magnetised against a metal strip on the stone wall. Heavy copper pans hang above them. Are these the witch's implements of harm? Susan looks outside, trying to quell a sense of panic.

Figaro's phone pings. He smiles with relief.

'Agata Agnello is coming to say hello. She speaks perfect English. I've called her to help you while I go into the council offices.'

'You're going? Now?'

'Unavoidable.' He ushers her to a marbleised downstairs washroom. 'Freshen up.'

Under the bright bulb, her face is worse than she imagined. The fake lashes have travelled out of kilter across her eyelids. Hastily she peels them off and wraps them in a fresh tissue, splashing water on her face. Her makeup is in the suitcase outside, and her handbag contains only lipstick and foundation. Wiping herself clean, she modifies her skin colour and clears the kohl tears. Her face has melted, along with her courage.

'Alessandro is the fraud. What am I afraid of?' She mouths the words to her reflection. But she knows the answer. She has omitted to divulge certain things. In particular, she has hidden the text received just before boarding the plane to Pisa.

Are you coming to collect the package? A x

This isn't from the mysterious *Sorreee A*. This is Alessandro—or at least it's his number. According to Figaro, the police have not found his phone, and it is Figaro who identified the body. Her choice is to trust him or disbelieve him. Fifty-fifty. Two people are texting about a package, of which she is totally ignorant. Not so much a quiz show, more a game of Cluedo. Alessandro is the body, the package is the weapon, and the witch in the kitchen is the murderer. *Deep breath, Sue Li, deep breath.*

Her fingers attempt to detangle her hair, and she re-enters the room of knives. Figaro is standing on the patio and points toward the hills, beckoning her to his side. A small red Fiat winds its way down the steep hill road.

'There's Agata,' he says as Natale places two tiny white cups of espresso on the wooden table outside. The aroma is bitter and makes her feel sick.

'Come on. I'll quickly introduce you to Natale's husband, Renzo, before I leave, so they both recognise you.'

She notices he has yet to use her name. In fact, he has spent their entire journey avoiding any direct reference to her. She is neither Silly Sue Li, nor Strange Sue, but summoned with an outstretched finger, or spoken to with vowels. 'Ahh...' Everyone around her has a name, whereas she has lost not only her husband, but also her identity.

Chapter Eight

This is a bad business, thinks Renzo as he watches the mayor's car, screwing up his eyes to get a better view of the woman. He and Natale have decided to say nothing. *Mah*! When he says he and Natale, it's his wife who has made the decision, and he has reluctantly agreed. Natale has always been loyal to Alessandro, and when he asked her to keep his recent visit secret, she was only too happy to oblige.

As for Renzo, his life has been spent working this land. His father was killed by looting German soldiers when he was a baby, and his grandmother brought him up on stories of Nazis and invading allied soldiers. Rome was the open city. Hitler blew up all the bridges in Florence except the Ponte Vecchio. In Montecatini, people starved protecting the Tuscan Verdi family's strongholds. Starvation was the norm. Renzo vaguely remembers the war, but whether it is the stories he's been told or what he actually saw, he isn't sure. He has lived the second wave of invasion: the tourists, Americans, Russians, Dutch, English—all buying houses, scattering their cash in bars, and declaring a love for *la dolce vita.* And as fast as they arrive, the younger Italian generation leaves, migrating to other countries, lured by higher earnings. Renzo has had a hard time hanging on to his sons. But Alessandro promised local jobs. His death is an injustice on many levels. Where does he get his money from? They don't care. Alessandro was the Prince of this town.

He shifts his pruning knife from one hand to the other and kicks the lopped olive branches at his feet. *Alessandro's death is a bad business*, he thinks again. Natale cries every hour. That's how it affects women when they act midwife and pluck a baby into the world. Alessandro is as dear to her as her own sons, and her heart will never let him go. But not Renzo. His expertise is pruning and making wine. He tries to concentrate on thinning the tree branches, aware that Figaro is approaching. Whoever this woman is, he wishes she would go away. This is not a day for guests. How typical of Figaro to be insensitive to his wife's feelings.

People can say what they like about Alessandro, but he was the man who brought life to the community. His infrequent arrivals always heralded the opening of a hundred Prosecco bottles and rich folk dancing until three in the morning in their glitzy finery. Those visits put happiness in the pockets of every bar and restaurant. Instead, after some family feud, the locals had to make do with Figaro, a man who prefers the company of bank balances to people.

Old Giorgio Verdi held fast to a brand of old-fashioned anti-Mussolini communism—back in the day when such things were normal. But the era of Berlusconi has beaten such notions out of the masses, and Figaro steps in tune to *Gli Americani.* The trouble is, at meeting after meeting, Figaro fails to take the temperature of the Montecatinese. First, he has forbidden a German hotel chain to develop land at a nearby ruined site called Buriano; then, he insists the locals help outsiders and the *comune* must house a handful of migrants. Government orders, he claims. *Porca miseria*! Jobs! That's what the local people need. Jobs! Not charity for strangers. Not seasonal menial work for the local boys. They need jobs with pensions. And a future. No wonder the Lega Nord gains ground.

Renzo shakes his head, thinking about two weeks ago and their unexpected meeting with Alessandro.

* * *

'I'm buying you and Natale your own house, so you can retire,' Alessandro said. 'It's a secret! Say nothing until I return. I'm also negotiating to buy the ghost village of Buriano.'

'No!' Natale hung on his words and on his shoulder. 'That will cost millions! How do you have this money?'

Two kilometres from the Tower, an empty medieval village lies in ruins, cocooned in red tape. Alessandro twisted his finger into his cheek with that wicked smile that always made her laugh.

'Don't worry, Mama Natale, I also intend to challenge Figgi for mayor, and when I am elected, I will pass an application to turn Buriano into a luxury spa. It will make millions for all of us. Your sons will be managers, and your nieces and nephews will have good employment at top wages. Trust me. Be patient until I return.'

Of course, they trusted him. The ghost village of Buriano is a beautiful place even though it's a faded lady, well past her prime. For years, people have wandered around the crumbling, exquisite chapel and along the walls of the large, beautifully crafted mansion with its rickety roof. But restoration is an expensive business. Only Buriano's land is maintained;

the vines and olive trees are subject to a local agreement. But not the buildings. Figaro and his father have consistently knocked back plans for re-development, although no one knows the real reason.

Alessandro's visit lasted barely an hour. Long enough for him to tell them how he intended to bring back Mariju and his little boy to the town. Natale wept joyful tears. She so wanted to see the little boy. With expansive gestures, Alessandro outlined a future where the town would be a jewel in Tuscany, but Renzo stopped him.

'I must warn you, Sandro,' he said, 'we don't have much time. The current political situation is tense.' He looked up the hill, as if he could see into the hearts and minds of the townsfolk, lit by the disc of the moon. 'That murder at the beach. Business confidence is low. I doubt outside agencies will give loans.'

Natale gave a tut. Alessandro frowned as Renzo thrust a newspaper into his hands. 'The details are on the inside page. If such things happen again, it might stop you raising the money you need. The camp sites have lost bookings.'

As Alessandro read, Natale let her fingers rest on the nape of his neck. 'When I was young,' she said, 'we watched for the Mafia from Sicily. We knew where we stood with them. This is different. One hundred thousand people arriving by boats is an army. And the illegals do strange things. How can you sort this, my boy? Are you in government?'

Alessandro frowned. 'I didn't realise,' he muttered at the paper. But then he laughs, although his eyes appear dark with anger. 'Government. In a way, you could say that. I know people, Mama Natale. Powerful people. More powerful than my family. Do not fear. I will sort this out.'

Renzo thought about the recent statement of the Pope

urging the government to act and avoid turning the Mediterranean into a graveyard. A poster in the nearby city pronounces the Bishops' party will stand against Lega Nord. The country teeters with indecision. But if the Bishops win, he doubts Alessandro will succeed. You can't fight the Catholic Church. But if Lega Nord wins...

As they waved him off, Natale insisted Renzo said nothing to the Verdis. Like a star, that night, she shone with hope.

Hope proved to be a candle, not a star, and how easily their brilliant shining future was snuffed. Now there is only a nagging at the base of Renzo's skull—not Natale's usual nagging, but a sense that their silence may have played a part in Alessandro's death. It's nonsense—or is it? Renzo is sleep-deprived with doubt. Their beloved Alessandro, murdered. If they had mentioned his visit to Verdi Senior, might this have been averted? He can't see any connection, and yet...

Renzo nods but doesn't smile as Figaro and the strange woman come toward him. Slicing the last olive branch with a flick of his knife, Renzo wipes the blade on his thick khaki trousers and hooks it to his belt. He folds his arms. The woman standing next to the mayor clasps her hands like a school child. She has a curious face, smudged with makeup. He's not seen anyone like her in town, and she's dressed in unsuitable sparkling sandals.

Figaro pushes her forward, mentioning Renzo's name, but not hers.

'*Piacere*.' He gives the habitual greeting for *pleased to meet you* but slides his hands in his pockets.

'Anything happening? Anything I should know?' Figgi asks.

'I grieve for the loss of Alessandro.'

'Of course.' Figgi pinches his nose. 'I told Natale that Alessandro's wife will stay with us for a few days. We're expecting a delivery that might help the investigation into his death.'

Renzo nods again. Two nights ago, Natale wept in the town square, the loud wailing of true sorrow. Everyone surrounded her, commiserating. Where is the outpouring of grief from the Verdi family at the loss of one of their own? And as for the woman standing next to him, she is as cold as the mayor: impassive, not a tear to be seen. But he's not surprised. They know she's a fake. When Alessandro spoke about returning with his wife, he mentioned Mariju. Now their only thought is whether this foreigner had a hand in his death.

They intend to watch her closely.

At a shout, all turn. A red Cinquecento is at the gate, and someone waves. Renzo sees Yolanda's older sister, Agata. The parents used to own a farm, nearby in Gello. A thought comes to him—should he entrust Signora Agata with his dilemma? Her family is old Montecatinese people, and her husband is in the police. Renzo watches Figgi and the woman descend the hill. The burden of his secret weighs him down. He is wrinkled as a walnut and as grumpy as the wild boar, so Natale tells him. But one thing's for sure; no man of his age should shelter a murderer.

Chapter Nine

Susan sees a short woman whom Figgi addresses as Agata. There is a sturdiness in her body and a confidence about the way she holds her head. Dressed in a white cotton shirt, Agata's tanned cleavage sports a small chain with a gold cross. Her dark, wiry hair is clipped back, a few grey threads escape to glitter like strands of paint. On each ear lobe, small gold hoops catch the sun. With corded sandals and clean, dark jeans, the overall effect is one of effortless chic. The woman's steady gaze assesses Susan's face. Susan looks down at her feet.

This is her childhood thing. When being admonished or embarrassed, always look at the feet. Susan has a deep familiarity with each of her painted toenails. Today, she sees the streaks of dust between her toes.

'I'm Agata. Pleased to meet you. What a pity it isn't under happier circumstances.' Like Figaro, her English is fluent, spoken with a light accent. No attempt is made to kiss her on either cheek. Instead, Agata turns and hugs Figaro like a long-lost relative, forcing him to bend to her shorter stature. 'Troubled times. How are you?'

Figaro extricates himself, pinches the top of his nose, and volleys a comment in Italian.

Agata returns the conversation to English. 'Look at her, Figgi. So thin! She probably hasn't eaten in days.'

'You see, her English is excellent,' says Figgi with a side shuffle.

'Thank you, Mr. Mayor.' Agata smiles at Susan. 'I used to work as a nanny in Knightsbridge, London. You English would call the family *posh*. They were so posh, I had to polish my accent before I spoke to the children.' She laughs.

Having grown up in the much poorer district of Bethnal Green, Susan isn't sure how to respond, but at least Agata sees her as English. Sometimes, as she hurries to work along Bond Street, Chinese tourists ask her for directions in Mandarin.

Figaro jingles a car key in hand. 'You can tell Agata anything. She's helping to find out what happened to Alessandro.'

'A private eye?'

Agata's eyes crinkle. 'Not exactly. So, you're a Londoner?' She doesn't wait for Susan's confirmation. 'I loved London. Ozzie Osbourne, Bon Jovi, Queen. London in the early nineties was such fun.'

Figaro continues his crab-like getaway. 'I'll be in my office for a couple of hours.'

'Hours? I told you I have an appointment, Mr. Mayor!' The tone is jocular, but there's a steeliness to the statement. 'You ought to stay with her.'

Figaro flaps a hand and removes himself without further conversation. Panic churns in Susan's empty stomach. Agata puts her hands on her hips as his car tyres crackle over the stone path.

'It's my fault,' Susan says. 'I embarrassed him by crying.'

Agata snorts. 'That one! He's made of metal.' She guides them to the house. 'But he told me about your situation.'

'I had no idea the marriage was invalid.' Susan risks a direct look at Agata. 'Please believe me. The Verdis must think I'm stupid.'

'I doubt that.' Her tone is dry. 'They knew Alessandro's ways. Although even for him...' Again, she takes open inventory of Susan, who responds by studying her toes.

'I don't understand why they agreed to my coming here if they knew.'

'Figgi said something about a package for you in transit?'

'I suppose they need my passport to collect it.'

A skinny, feral cat shoots out from behind a cypress tree, a flash of suspicion disappearing into the perimeter grasses. Susan stumbles, her sandals catching against the gravel that pricks at her heels.

'Tired? Do you need a Siesta?' Agata picks up Susan's small suitcase by the doorway and enters the house. 'You won't be alone. Natale is here.'

In the kitchen, the whole performance is repeated, only this time the witch is being comforted by Agata. Trying to zone out of the Italian conversation, Susan examines the small red blister on her injured foot. Her WhatsApp pings. This is odd because she's turned off the data as instructed and has yet to input the Wi-Fi code.

It is another message from Alessandro's phone.

Tell me when you get the package. Okay? It's important. A x

A sharp intake of breath and Agata stops her conversation to prise the phone from Susan's frozen fingers. '*Permesso*?' She reads it quickly.

'It's from Alessandro's phone, the one the police couldn't find,' says Susan.

'Well, at least we know it's not broken.' Agata proceeds to read out loud all the texts on Susan's phone.

Urgent. You must go to Montecatini. Phone Figgi. Then wait for the package to arrive by courier. Don't speak to anyone else. Letter follows. Don't betray me. A x

Forgot to text earlier. Sorreee. I used the special courier as requested. Wait for barcode. Must have passport to collect. A.

Tell me when you get the package. Okay? It's important. A x

'So, there is A with a kiss, and A without a kiss. Clumsy if someone is into fraud.' She forwards the texts to her phone. 'Don't worry. My husband is police. He'll trace the second call for you. It's just a question of time.' She returns the phone. 'Don't delete it! So what package are you expecting?'

They have a circular conversation in which Agata questions her and Susan is keen to reiterate her ignorance. Finally, Agata shrugs, says something to Natale, and motions for them to ascend a circular staircase at the back of the kitchen. They emerge into one end of a long corridor.

'Come on. Your room is along here.'

All the doors are shut, but a burst of light blazes from the far end.

'The living room is down here. Fantastic view if I remember correctly. I haven't been to Casa Verdi in years. Natale told me she's put you in Alessandro's old room. The largest guest room was last used for him and his wife, and it still has a crib in it.' Agata stops. 'You do know about all this, don't you?'

'A crib?'

Agata examines Susan's reaction and shakes her head. 'Mariju lived here for six months. About four years ago. She was pregnant. Sadly, there was a big argument, and she left just before the baby was born. Natale was very fond of her, and extremely upset at not seeing the baby, so she can't bear to clear the room. So sad.'

A hard pain forms in Susan's throat. She had longed for a baby, but now is not the time for desires. She needs to work out what's going on. Agata is opening and closing doors. Some are locked. Some are shuttered in gloom. 'Here it is.' She pushes against the heavy door, and they both gaze in.

Surrounded by white organza, a huge four-poster bed fills the room, a pastel impression of Renaissance art. At the foot of the bed is an intricately carved white crib with a sateen coverlet. The sole occupant is an old teddy bear whose button-eyes stare out in sorrow. Everything is clean. The small opening of one window allows a breeze to sift through the shutter's slats, puffing a smell of pine.

Susan can barely breathe under Agata's scrutiny.

'So you didn't know Alessandro had a child with his wife?'

She bites a knuckle as if to eat the bone, looks down, and shakes her head.

Agata sighs, closing the door, and pushes her across the corridor to another room. 'Here's your room.' This bedroom is smaller, although the ceiling is just as high. A fan whirrs over the masculine colours. Grey mosquito curtains surround the black-sheeted bed. Dark leather buttoned chairs sit in opposite corners, and worn hardbacked books of *Pinocchio, Dante's Divine Comedy*, and *Il Gattopardo* stand, well-thumbed, on a walnut dresser. A large walnut wardrobe shines with finely turned brass handles. Susan knows about wood. The auction house has sold many items of old furniture, and she recognises the value of each piece. Nothing is cheap or rustic. Everything is antique.

'Alessandro's childhood room.' Agata opens thick damask curtains, and Susan blinks at the vast terrain. The terrace looks directly across to the walled city on the opposite mountain ridge. From this height and angle, she can see the tip of a house below, its terracotta tiles half-hidden in a screen of overgrown fir trees. If things go badly, perhaps she can run there and claim sanctuary.

'I used to date him.' Agata runs a hand over the bed sheets in a way that makes Susan shiver. 'Before I married. A long time ago.'

'I didn't marry Alessandro for his money.' Susan twists the wedding ring on her finger. 'It was a Cinderella story. And no one ever accused Cinderella of being a gold digger, right?'

Agata gurgles. '*Cenerentolla*! Italian for Cinderella. A good point. But don't worry. I'm not one to judge you. Many women were gullible where Sandro was concerned.'

Blinking glue-laden lashes, Susan accepts the insult. 'That solicitor, Mrs. Patel-Mara—she said Alessandro was into fraud.'

'True, I'm afraid.' With practised hands, Agata opens the French windows and pushes the shutters further back to reveal a tiny terrace with table and chair.

'You mean nothing he said was real?'

The Italian woman shrugs.

'So why did he insist I get a passport in my married name?'

'I don't know.' Agata's smile is gentle. 'Come on. Sit down.' She points to the bed, pushing Susan gently, and picks up a clean comb from the dresser. From her back pocket, she withdraws some travel wipes. 'You've been through an ordeal. Let me help you.'

Fatigue makes Susan obedient. She allows her hair to be combed, wincing when the teeth hit a tangle. With careful strokes, the remainder of her makeup is removed. Agata wipes around Susan's eyes. It seems a faux sister act, but Susan is too scared to object.

'You're in the countryside here. You don't need a city look.' Agata steps back. 'There. Very pretty. I'm sure Alessandro found you attractive, whatever else was a lie. But I'm afraid no one has answers at this stage.'

'So why did his text insist I come here?'

'To get you out of the way? To make sure you were in the right place at the right time? What do you think?'

'Out of the way? Of what? Out of the way of his death?'

'No. He wouldn't have seen that coming. Not Alessandro.'

For a moment Susan sees genuine sadness nip the woman's brow and she is about to repeat her standard line that she knows nothing when a scrunch of tyres distracts them. To their right, a dusty grey van is just visible at the open gate. As they both move to the balcony for a clearer look, a strange projectile jumps from the car window. It plops onto the pebbles with a rubbery bounce and hurtles forward, ears flattened against skull.

A young girl waves up to them in agitation. 'Sorreee. Bad Ruby, bad! Hey, Susan—Susan Li Verdi—is that you?' Here accent is pure London.

Looking down, Susan sees a thick-set dog dance around the patio and dash after an invisible prey. From above, the girl's overly bleached blond hair shows a black badger stripe down the middle. The eyes are hidden behind heart-shaped pink sunglasses, and between the sawn-off shorts and the minuscule crop top, a belly button diamond winks in the sun against her ebony skin. The girl jigs on the spot in sparkly trainers. If Susan is overdressed for the country, this girl seems under-dressed for any place except a beach rave.

Agata goes out to greet her, while Susan slips on a clean skirt. The main door at the end of the corridor is now open, and Susan runs along and down the external staircase. Agata is attempting to catch the dog, hands lunging at the animal's collar.

Taking off her sunglasses, the girl reveals lurid blue eyeshadow thickly coated around dark eyes. 'So you're Susan Li. I recognise you from the pub. Remember me? Amy. Amy Joliffe!' The dog pounces around them, and Susan bats the animal away.

'The Duke of Wellington?' Amy says in exasperation at Susan's blank look. 'I work at your local, opposite the Auction House.' She laughs with a see-saw laugh.

Minus the heart-shaped glasses, the girl seems slightly familiar. She also looks very young. Ruby leaps onto the patio table, where Agata catches her and tries to fend off the licking tongue.

'Didn't Alessandro tell you I was coming?' Amy persists. 'Oh my days! He paid my ticket to get here. He said it was your idea, and you wanted proof of postage in Italy. Some art deal you're into! No border tax, he said. So, it had to be posted here. He gave me a letter to give to you.'

'I don't understand.' Susan cannot think of a reason for a bar person to be in Alessandro's pay.

Amy pouts in disappointment. 'You crazy? Don't deny it! He knew I needed a deposit to rent a flat with friends, so he paid me half, and said you'd agreed to pay me the balance.' She puts up garishly polished fingers and ticks her tasks off, one by one. 'One. Post a package by special courier at Pisa. Two, go wait at the Hendersons' Airbnb until you got here. Three, hand over this letter in person. Four, you give me the 3,000 quid.' She frowns at Susan. 'Actually, I think he said I could also hand it to his cousin if you weren't here, but it's addressed to you.'

'I don't know what you're talking about.'

There's a shriek from Natale as the dog breaks free from Agata and races into the kitchen.

Amy folds her arms. 'Don't tell me you know nothing.' Her face scrunches in anger. 'I've done what I was asked to do. I sent the package, but I'm not handing over the letter 'til I get the rest of my money. And he told me it was very, very important.' Her silver-ringed fingers clink together. 'You're rich. I grew up in care. I know about people like you, and nobody's going to cheat me.' Leaning against the van, she slings a jeans jacket over her arm and pats a pocket. The tip of an envelope shows stark white against the blue.

Having retrieved the dog, Agata attempts to tie it to one of the pergola's poles with a rope while shouting: 'Hey, you. Don't you know Alessandro is dead?'

The blue eyelids flutter, and the girl bites her lip. Shock shines from her eyes. 'Fuck. What happened?'

'He was murdered three days ago in London,' says Agata.

'Oh my days!' Amy flutters her jacket like a matador's cape. 'Nothing to do with me! I've been staying with Carl Henderson and his mother in their Airbnb over the hill. They'll tell you, I've not been in London all week!'

'What was in the package?' asks Agata, continuing to work hard to restrain the dog.

'I dunno!' Amy's forehead wrinkles in thought. 'It was all a bit weird, like, but he said I didn't need to know and it wasn't something I could get arrested for. It was a small parcel, wrapped good and proper. It went through security at the airport. No probs. He swore to me it wasn't drugs. He said it was an artwork. My instructions were to tick the box for a gift when I handed it to the Italian courier in Pisa. But as for the letter...' She jams the sunglasses back over her eyes. 'I need the money. I can't pay the Hendersons' bill and pay a deposit on a rented flat without it.' She taps the van door. 'This is Carl's, in case you're wondering. Mrs. Henderson's son. And just look at your house.' She waves toward the expanse of Casa Verdi. 'You're bloody loaded. That's certain. So, I'll be back tomorrow and I expect to get paid. A deal's a deal. No money, no letter. And then I'm off, 'cuz I ain't done nothing wrong.'

The dog barks, trying to reach tiny lizards creeping around rocks.

Amy turns with an afterthought. 'And according to Mrs. Henderson, even though that dog is an English bull terrier, it belongs to the mayor. Carl says he only looks after Ruby when the mayor's away, so we're bringing her back today. Mad dog.' Amy starts the engine. 'I'm not gonna lie. I'm sad about Alessandro, he's a gent. Never made a move on me. But fuck! Not my problem.'

Ignoring Agata's calls, she rattles off in a cloud of dust, crunching gears.

'You knew about this, didn't you!' Agata is fighting the dog and glaring at Susan. 'Two of the texts are from Alessandro's phone, but the other was from her, wasn't it? What was her name? Amy?'

Susan's tongue feels thick in her mouth. She denies everything, desperate to prove her innocence, but Agata looks unconvinced. Another thought comes to Susan. 'Why would Alessandro, a computer expert, send me a handwritten letter? He could have handed it to me himself, or he could have texted! Or emailed!'

'Did Alessandro ever mention anything about a beach murder near Montecatini?'

Susan stares at her. 'Murder on an Italian beach? No. What's that about? He's been in London with me for the past year.'

Agata shrugs. 'There's a connection, but I'll let you know when I find out.'

The dog wriggles out of the makeshift rope collar and dances away from her would-be captor. For the moment, both dog and answers evade them.

Chapter Ten

Pontiginori Quastura, the police station at Ponteginori

Luca waits for Gianni the Forensic. Thin lines of sun creep through the half-closed blinds, forming prison stripes on his desk. He huffs; Gianni is habitually late. The office faces the inner courtyard, a patch of scrubby grass and a smoker's paradise. He looks with disinterest at a few colleagues sharing Marlboro cigarettes. In the past, he considered smoking, but he's never liked the taste. Through the frosting of his internal window, Luca sees Fabio's shadow. His assistant is leaning back, feet on desk, chatting on the phone. Judging by the muffled laughter, it is a personal call.

At the end of the corridor, the balding man arrives and hovers around the reception desk. Luca surmises he is trying to make a clumsy play at the female officer. All the women in the *Quastura* know Gianni too well. Although she appears to respond with a smile, Luca is aware that behind Gianni's back, she has complained—as do they all—of the formaldehyde that permeates the medic's clothes. In typical Gianni style, he moves with heavenly slowness, a genteel saunter, his briefcase bumping against his thigh. Luca cannot imagine him quickening his gait even if a bomb dropped. It is just as well that he works with the dead. When anyone complains, Gianni shrugs and says, 'Corpses don't rush.'

Gianni knocks on the open door. 'Commissario.' He looks more sombre than usual. His moist eyes bulge with sadness. Luca thinks when God was handing out physical attributes, he stubbed his toe on Gianni, but at least the man is apolitical. They shake hands, and the odour of chemicals attaches to Luca's palm.

'I hope you have more precise information about our little victim. London has sent me preliminary details of the autopsy on our murdered Italian citizen. That took them three days. This poor girl was found a couple of weeks ago.'

Gianni takes Luca's rebuke without rancour. 'I am a precise man, Commissario. The dead remain dead. I cannot raise them to life, so I seek accurate knowledge. Perhaps the British are less meticulous.' He puts his head on one side. 'Or perhaps they have a larger team?'

Fabio joins them and adds his support to Gianni. The Italian methods require the greatest rigour, he agrees. The Italian doctors are superior. Then he backtracks.

'But Commissario, do we need to bother so much? I thought the Minister for the Interior phoned you and insisted we drop the case. Aren't we supposed to be organising the rota for the upcoming protest marches?'

Gianni stares blankly at the assistant. 'The autopsy is done. Don't you want it?'

'Fabio!' Luca feels a rise in his blood pressure. 'This child's body remains in the morgue, so let's hear what our learned pathologist has to say.'

'No family is yet to claim her!' says Fabio with evident distaste.

'Commissario.' Gianni takes a ring-bound sheaf of papers from his briefcase and places it slowly on Luca's desk. 'Whether you regard her small life as important or not, I do my job well.' He crosses one long leg over the other knee and settles back in the chair.

Before even reading it, Luca knows the academic prose will be impenetrable. He opens to page one and sees the contents page. 'Translate?'

'I will put it in layman's terms for you,' says Gianni with a hint of superiority.

Fabio leans forward, in his usual sniffer dog pose: eager to dispute, refute, or seize upon facts.

'She was operated on by someone with medical training. There's no doubt about that. The cuts, incisions, and needle markings. The child has undergone a surgical procedure.'

'Will we find her listed in a hospital?' asks Luca.

'But we've checked!' says Fabio. 'And nothing! No fingerprint matches. Nothing. She's an illegal!'

'She's a *child*,' Gianni says, emphasising her status as a minor, 'who is about eight or nine years old, judging by the baby teeth remaining, and her height. Not as malnourished as you might think. Her muscle mass indicates a poor diet recently, but bones show she had sound nutrition under five.'

'Economic migrant!' says Fabio.

Luca wraps his knuckles on the desk. 'Fabio, let the man finish!'

The assistant simmers.

Gianni continues, 'What's particularly interesting is her blood type. I made small mention of this to you before, but I didn't have the full picture. She has what's known as Golden Blood. It's so rare that only about a hundred people in the world are documented with this. It has neither Rhesus positive nor negative markers. R-Null we call it. The intention of the operation was obviously to remove the heart and lungs, and the child was alive when they were removed. There are the usual signs of the circulatory system being re-routed in order to ensure the organs remained healthy.'

Fabio sits up excitedly. Luca holds up a hand to stop the racist traffic. If he hears one more speech about voodoo, he will create a doll of Fabio and stick pins in it himself.

'But there are two more points of interest. Her stomach retained evidence of a final meal. Not much, principally bread, but she had eaten.'

'And so?' Luca frowns.

'So, it was an emergency operation. There was no time for the proper preparation. That's what I would assume, and this is borne out by my second point.' He hesitates. 'Let me put it simply for you—she had appendicitis. Yet the organ was ligatured, not removed. I imagine the intention was to prevent further bacteria getting into the bloodstream, and as there was no trace of sepsis in her limbs or the pectoral muscles in her chest cavity...' He pulls his lips into a downward curve.

'You are saying?' The nerves in the back of Luca's neck kink, and pain runs along his collar bones. 'You are saying she had appendicitis, but there was no attempt to remove the appendix.'

'Exactly. The surgeon wanted to stop the infection spreading, but the main purpose of the operation was to remove the heart and lungs. That is my conjecture.'

'To eat?' says Fabio, unable to contain his outrage. He points a finger in triumph at Luca. 'I told you it was voodoo.'

'*Va fancullo.*' Luca rarely swears, but he's making an exception.

Gianni gives Fabio a sad smile. 'No, not at all. I think it was used for transplantation purposes. The cuts, the way the vessels have been arranged. She's had an operation. With her blood type, the organs would be worth a fortune on the black market.'

Luca watches Fabio subside.

'Is there such a thing as a black market in organs? In Italy?' Even as he speaks, he knows it is possible.

Gianni raises his sandy eyebrows. 'Commonly it is the poor in undeveloped countries who donate a kidney or an eye, because they need the money. It goes without saying that you can survive such an operation. But in this case, I suspect someone identified her blood group and sold her for her organs. The heart and lungs. It's possible that a surgeon flew in specifically to perform an operation on her. An outside agency on Italian soil. And a purchaser with sufficient money.'

No one speaks for a moment. The sounds of the outer office give a surreal background to the sense of horror pressing down on Luca's own internal organs. He takes a pen but is at a loss to know what to put on his pad. 'Can I clarify,' he says. 'You think the child would have survived the operation for her appendix, so she was operated on purely to remove vital organs?'

'Given the forensic evidence. Quite possibly. Although with her blood type...'

'You're guessing,' says Fabio.

Gianni closes his eyes for a brief moment. 'Yes. I am a pathologist. My clues lie with the dead. So I make an educated guess. I believe the operation was for the removal of the heart and lungs. The need to perform the appendectomy would have been necessary, but it was not the main reason the child was sedated. There are puncture points that bear witness to this.'

'But no one is missing a child,' says Fabio. There is a touch of petulance in his voice. 'Perhaps, a migrant parent has butchered one child to save another. Or—' His eyes widen with a new idea. 'Perhaps you're missing another possibility, and perhaps her body was packed with drugs. This is a thing and—'

'Drugs, no!' Gianni interrupts.

'How can you be so sure?'

'The incisions were made while the girl lived. Drugs are packed in corpses.' Gianni smiles thinly. 'According to a recent course I attended.'

Fabio makes a face. 'So? Body parts? Who wants a migrant's body parts?'

'As I explained. Someone who has a tissue match and needs a new heart, and crucially has plenty of money. This sort of operation is expensive, and in the case of R-Null, the donors would be sought far and wide.'

'Where do I go to find out about such a black market?' asks Luca.

Gianni spreads his hands. 'Most surgeons are aware of such practices, and many have been approached to do private operations. Of course, it is illegal in Europe, and I'm not sure where you would start. You could try getting a list of all the private Tuscan surgical clinics licensed with overseas money. Clearly, this operation took place nearby.'

'Commissario.' Fabio's raises a finger again. 'I know of such a clinic.' He turns to Gianni. 'It's true. This rally I attended in Pisa—one of the speakers was talking about such clinics and how they do terrible things to those little African girls.' He makes the gesture of scissors between his legs. 'They say that is the reason the migrants seek to come to our country. And the current government is doing nothing—'

Luca smacks the pen point on his desk. 'Fabio, you make no sense. You're trying to tell me rich people in other countries can't afford operations in their homeland?'

'They don't have the doctors!'

As Luca goes to protest, Gianni puts out a hand to both men. 'A moment, gentlemen. Please. Our girl has not been the victim of genital mutilation, although it is hard to tell if she had been sexually abused. The flesh was too deteriorated.' He allows Luca to make a note. 'But I know of this private clinic in Cecina, near where the body was found. It's one of a handful throughout the country, doing Botox and plastic surgery for wealthy foreign clientele. State-of-the-art operating suite. They specialise in enlarging things.'

Luca stares. Fabio lets out a guffaw.

'What?' says Gianni, before a small flush spreads across his pale cheeks. 'Not me, personally! I had a girlfriend who was into enlarging things. Breasts. Lips. She told me about this clinic, and wanted me to investigate, but...' He breaks off, nodding his head like a bird. 'Never mind. I think you will find the clinic is run with Russian money. The point is they have the facilities to do extensive operations. I'm not saying they break the law, but it's possible. Especially as they guard their clientele's identity rigorously. You would have to go through the courts. It's harder to get information from these businesses than to get hold of Berlusconi's tax records.' He uncrosses one leg to cross the other. 'And of course, there are many such places. The Cecina clinic is only one, but the location fits.'

'I see,' says Luca. His stomach curdles at the image that springs into his mind.

'What happens to the bodies?' says Fabio.

'I imagine it's very rare that a client dies from such an operation. But in the case of a tragedy, their families claim them.'

Luca clicks his tongue. An idea occurs to him. 'We need to approach this from the other side. Can you tell me where I could find a black-market list for organs? Where would it be posted on the internet? If we could locate a person who needed a new heart and lungs, then perhaps... Fabio, can you do this?'

Fabio shrugs. 'I can try, but looking for body parts on the dark web, I'll probably hit porn, and I don't want my reputation ruined. There's a computer division that deals with this in Rome.'

Luca thinks about the time it would take to put in an official request. He doesn't have time. His investigation is being shelved. What they need is someone local, available immediately, and prepared to hack into websites. Agata is a good researcher, but she's not a computer hacker.

'Maybe you know someone in Florence?' says Gianni.

'I used to know someone in London.'

Fabio looks at Luca in disbelief.

'Unfortunately, he's just died.'

Chapter Eleven

An East London police station

Police stations are not known for their beautiful decor. Detective Inspector Vanessa Candle sits in her drab office, surrounded by paperwork, sipping a watery coffee, and looking across at the large industrial fans attached to the back of a takeaway shop. But the view doesn't bother her. She is mulling over her fresh case, finding the whole situation unsatisfactory. Why did Priya Patel-Mara come to the aid of Susan Li Verdi? She's a solicitor more commonly associated with asylum claims than murder. What is the connection with the Verdi family? Vanessa crumbles a biscuit and looks at its broken parts. She cannot see the whole picture of this man's death. In fact, the team is unsure if Alessandro Verdi's death is a murder. It could be manslaughter. Or aggravated burglary. Or even an accidental death.

Soco has puzzled over this. Yes, the victim was tied up and his mouth stuffed with an Italian newspaper, but the man clearly died from an allergic reaction to an administered drug. Flunitrazepam. Also known as Rohypnol. CCTV records three men going into the building, faces hidden by caps, bodies covered in grey plumbing overalls. Twenty minutes later, two of them run down the stairs and out of the building through a fire escape door. The third leaves by an unknown exit and disappears onto the crowded streets. He must have whipped off his clothes and stuffed them into a backpack, because no external CCTV picks up overalls. Everyone is wearing a suit.

To Vanessa, the most puzzling of all is why Mrs. Verdi headed off to Italy with her in-laws. Both parties claim they have never met before, so the move seems strange, and the inconsistencies bug Vanessa.

'Are we being played?' she wonders out loud. Her team have already found out that Verdi was renting Canary Wharf and owned one fast car. Yet they cannot find a money trail, and even his office is no more than a paid address. She can smell the links to organised crime, but there is no flag on the database for him or his wife or the address. No one is watching them. Is this a grudge match, between rival gangs? She grinds her teeth. Too many questions and not enough bloody information.

In a small press slot, Vanessa has urged witnesses to come forward, but the crime does not excite the level of attention she had expected. The Verdi man may have been good looking, but he's not famous, and there's a lack of gore. Grittier things are happening in the world, and Matt Damon has visited a pub in England, leaving a seventy-pound tip to each of the bar staff. How can she compete with that on the front page of The Daily Mail?

She is about to have her weekly chat with Superintendent Levenson when her Sergeant, Brian Blunt, knocks on the door. They call him *old-school*, and he has three months left before retirement. She can't wait. He's been metaphorically putting two fingers up to her ever since she was promoted. He lumbers in like a Macbeth stooge.

'News, Ma'am. From uniform. They've caught two of the men. Drunk and babbling. They're in the cells at Snaresbrook nick, but Hickock has arrived to defend them.'

'Hickock!' A well-known criminal lawyer showing up is an unwelcome surprise. 'So we can discount murder?' She laughs. Hickock's claim to fame is that he can prove the Kray twins and Adolf Hitler were misunderstood innocents.

'They're Polish, and scared,' says Blunt. 'They won't say a flying fart about the third man. He's still missing.'

Dismissing him, she casts a fresh eye over her emails. The men will be incarcerated until they are sober enough to interview. But before she can check the time scale, there's a phone call from Superintendent Levenson.

'I've told your DCI, and now I'm telling you. You're to hand over the remaining files to an Organised Crime Unit operating near Harwich,' he says.

'What!' Vanessa doesn't bother to hide her outrage. 'What reason did they give, sir? They didn't contact us the day we found the victim!'

'An ongoing case, apparently. Something involving Border Force and smuggling. DCI Baker is the contact at the OCU. He says we can keep the collar for the thugs as a robbery, but any other intel goes to them.'

'We've only just pulled these guys in. How did DCI Baker in Harwich know we've got suspects in a London cell?' Vanessa feels the pricking of her thumbs: Mrs. Verdi's silence and two mismatched solicitors and now an Organised Crime Unit report that they've never seen.

'There's a tail on Hickock, apparently,' he says. 'Sorry, Vanessa.'

'But sir, the victim, Alessandro Verdi, hasn't featured on any of the databases we've searched, not even the Police National Database. We looked, and we should have seen a flag to indicate he was a person of interest, especially if he was involved in smuggling. And sir, why didn't they want to speak to Mrs. Verdi? I don't get it, sir.'

'Vanessa, you know as much as I know. I'll ring and ask a few more questions.'

Inspector Candle swears out loud to the dingy walls. She has another four cases on her books, and shutting the files with a result will tick a box. But there are glaring anomalies. One possibility is that big shit is going down, and she's about to miss out on the glory. It wouldn't be the first time that those in power took the credit. She's a Black woman in a White man's world, and she knows the realities of police politics.

The arrest information pops up online. Two sparse recounts; one from Traffic Division and another from local Uniformed police. Two tattooed men were arrested trying to buy vodka at eight in the morning at a corner newsagent. The owner of the shop alerted the police not just because the men had parked their car on a double yellow outside, but also because they were aggressive at the till. Initially, the duo boasted about the ease with which they accessed a luxury block of flats, but when local police mentioned Verdi's death, they insisted they were innocent muscle up for hire, and the victim was alive and well when they left.

Drunk babbling is not admissible evidence. When expensive defence solicitors like Hickock appear, it's common for villains to change their story. Vanessa is familiar with the pattern, but crucially, Alessandro Verdi's missing mobile is not in their possession. So where is the third man?

Vanessa looks up DCI Baker on the database and is in the middle of reading when another email comes through. Hickock's papers are posted. His clients will plead guilty and own up to several previous burglaries in return for a more lenient sentence and bail.

Her phone rings. It is DCI Baker. Vanessa snaps her pen as she takes the call.

'Good afternoon, Detective Inspector Candle.' His tone is smooth and confident. 'I'm sure you've heard we're taking over the Verdi case. Our operation is at a delicate point and Verdi was a known associate of certain gangs. We've been monitoring them for the past three months. So we want all your information on the victim, immediately. It's important you don't jeopardise our work.'

Vanessa wipes biro ink from her fingers. 'None of this was flagged on the database. And I'm reading your file on the computer. You're listed as Border Force, DCI Baker. You're not Organised Crime.' Then she adds *sir*, as an afterthought.

DCI Baker clears his throat. 'Undercover. Your Super will confirm that. There should have been a *Restricted Information* tag on Verdi. I'll find out who's to blame and roast them. All right, Candle?' He rings off.

The sarcastic twinge in his voice reminds Vanessa she has met this DCI Baker once, several years ago, at a police liaison event. He's a ginger-haired man with a chewing gum habit and bitten fingernails. Unfortunately, if her Superintendent insists she gives him the files, there's nothing she can do. They outrank her. She sits, thoroughly disgruntled. What's really happening? Would they be requesting this manoeuvre if she were a White man in the Masons?

The landline phone rings again. 'What?' she shouts.

'It's the IT department. Is that DI Candle?' says a

youthful male voice. 'We thought you'd like to know. The missing phone from the Verdi murder? Well, you're in luck. It's been switched on, and we've located it.'

Vanessa punches the air. 'Tell me more.'

'Someone has redirected it through a VPN, but it's definitely the victim's phone. Whoever has it sent two texts. Do you want us to keep tracking it?'

'Fuck—yes! Where is it?'

'In Italy. Tuscany. It's gone on and off twice, and a message has been sent to the number you've given us for Susan Li Verdi's phone.'

She pulls out a few scribbled notes from under a pile on her desk and finds Figaro Verdi's address in Montecatini. 'How close can you pin it? Is it switched on now?'

'No. And we can't read the message yet, but we've put in a request to the provider.'

Vanessa exhales. 'Shit, we shouldn't have let her go. Shit!' She thumps her desk with a fist. 'Sorry. Ignore that. Can you leave it with me? Don't give anyone else this information. Okay?'

'Okay,' the voice says breezily. 'As far as I'm concerned, my instructions are to tell the head of the enquiry, and that's you.'

'That's right. I'm leading the case! Just me. Don't put it on the system until the end of the week? Can you do that?' She thinks, *I'll shove it up the Organised Crime Squad's arse later.*

'No probs. Anything else happens, and we'll let you know, ma'am.'

With a jackal trot out of the office, she ignores the enquiring eyes of her team and leaps up the stairs to the Superintendent's office. The elevator isn't fast enough for this, and she doesn't want to phone in case the call is recorded.

Superintendent Levenson listens, staring out of the window, then turns, with a smile. 'I'll share a little-known fact with you, Vanessa. A few years back, the Home Secretary's office had a right shout at DCI Baker's team. He was in an Organised Crime Unit that had info on a lorry load of illegals coming in at Liverpool docks. They were supposed to have stopped it at the port, but it got through. Instead, the poor buggers were found dead at a motorway service station. Fifty of them. Word was some of our members were in the pocket of the traffickers, but nothing could be proved.'

'I remember the incident. But it was outside our jurisdiction.'

'People move about, Vanessa. Baker's moved to liaising with the Border Force in Essex.'

'So, you think he's in league with someone in Organised Crime and they're running a racket? How does this involve our dead man, sir?'

'I don't know, but I'd like nothing better than to pin something on DCI Baker. He compromised a friend of mine. Old scores to settle. Know what I mean?'

Indeed she does. Vanessa has a mantra: *Don't get mad—get even.* Speaking of which, she would like to see Sergeant Blunt get his comeuppance for the many times he has mimicked her behind her back. A plan pops into her head.

'I've got some funds that would pay for us to re-interview the widow. I'm aware she's in Italy,' says Levenson.

'Just to check. We're keeping this between us, sir?'

'Absolutely, Vanessa. Need-to-know basis.' Unusually, he grins. 'So do you want to go to Tuscany?'

She hesitates. 'Let me get this clear. We want someone

to talk to Mrs. Verdi off the record and check if any person of interest has shown up to console her. That about it?'

'That's it.'

'What about Sergeant Blunt? When I took over the team, you told you me he was useless on the computer systems, but sharp-eyed and good for surveillance.'

The Super wags a finger at her. 'I know what you're thinking.'

Vanessa doubts that.

'Send a Brexiteer to Italy? Someone who won't be lured by the Italian coast! Why not? He's experienced enough. And a ladies' man, I've been told.'

Ladies' man? She spits on her way down the stairs. But she's happy with the thought of two birds, one stone. Her team will perform better without Blunt and his daily innuendos. She asks a fresh-faced colleague to put through a call to Commissioner Agnello, alerting him that a Met Police detective is coming from London to re-question Mrs. Verdi. Next, she checks if there are any football matches organised near Pisa for the next few days. If Juventus are playing a British team in Tuscany, her sergeant will be less than diligent, but Fate smiles on her.

In reality, she doesn't want to be the one to flag up internal corruption. There's always blow-back from colleagues. In addition, she has no intention of telling Blunt of their Superintendent's suspicions. Let Blunt stumble over the shit. After all, he's about to retire, so he has less to lose. She calls him into the office, thinking the faster he goes, the better.

Chapter Twelve
The walled city of Volterra

While Sergeant Blunt is en route to Pisa, Agata is on her way to see her old boss, Bruno Collodini, who has moved into his daughter's apartment.

Bruno's daughter lives just outside the Volterra walls, which is fortunate. Only residents can drive inside the walls. Outside, a mix of eclectic housing clusters along the slopes. Her car is small, but still the Cinquecento struggles to find a parking spot. With a dog's whisker between vehicles, Agata slips into a space and steps out. Flanked by modern apartment blocks, the oldest apartment building stands elegantly retro on the street, four stories of regal stonework. It overlooks the western slope, allowing the afternoon sun to reach across the road and slink up the windows. The entrance to the flats is through an elaborate arch. Satellite dishes cling like carbuncles, but otherwise the building recalls a turn of last-century splendour.

Although she denies it, Agata knows why Luca doesn't like Bruno Collodini. But Bruno's agency afforded her the chance to work in an environment she enjoyed, in a city she loved. She has enjoyed every single one of the last fifteen years as an *agenta di polizia.* Many of their clients were Americans requesting help to navigate Italian bureaucracy, and therefore, her English came in useful. Most were grateful and provided large tips. Local work, liaising with police was less lucrative, but regular. Everyone knew her, and she knew everyone. Added to which, there was the perennial compensation of walking and looking in the Florentine shops. Such beautiful things in their windows, with a cash discount to La Signora Agnello, especially after catching a pickpocket or two. Volterra is smaller, but at least it's a city. She breathes in the mix of modern and medieval civilisation.

The battered intercom buzzes, and she waits. Another buzz. As she pushes on the huge carved door, she hears a rumble and a shuffle and sees Bruno stands in the hallway in crumpled pyjamas attached to an oxygen cylinder. He takes off his face mask and delivers two kisses on her cheeks with purple lips. She smiles to hide her dismay at his deteriorated condition.

'Why are you up?' she chides him.

'Don't sound like my daughter! I wanted to greet you standing.' He wheezes and wheels the cylinder like a dog toward the ground-floor apartment. 'It's terrible to be an invalid.'

She follows him in, admiring the high ceilings with the ornate cornices and the artwork on the doors. Better to look at the surroundings than to look at him.

'No mosquito screens at the window,' he grumbles. 'I scratch all night.'

She eases him into a high-backed chair in the *salotto.* The junk of illness surrounds him; newspapers, a glass of water, tablets and an old-fashioned radio are scattered on a side table.

'Good to see you, Bruno.'

He moistens his mouth with a sip of water. '*Pah.* But I don't look good. I'm sinking, don't deny it. How's your retirement?'

'Harder than working with you, my friend. The land is a fearsome enemy.'

He chuckles and coughs. He used to be gregarious. This isolation must torture him, she thinks.

'Espresso?' He waves to the kitchen.

'I'll make it,' she says, and he doesn't argue. The Bruno of old would have insisted on making coffee for both of them with suggestive flourishes. Even the smallest errands were punctuated with sexual innuendo. Now his hands are clamped on the oxygen mask.

She chats about her new home as she makes the coffee, trotting out inconsequential details of hacking at thick brambles and her battle with the wild boar that cross the land. He listens. His formerly plump frame currently resembles the consistency of an ancient pillow: rolls of empty skin in a chair. His neck is a mass of strings. From the kitchen, she sees him grip the armrest for support, trying to sit higher as he emits a hawking cough to clear phlegm, and then wiping his face with a linen handkerchief. She puts the coffee beside him, flapping away a lazy fly.

'We had good times, didn't we?' His eyes are sad. 'I'm sorry, Agata. I should say that before I die. Before I tell you what I must.'

She gives his desiccated hand a small slap. 'Die! Not yet! Anyway—why have you asked me to visit? You said it was about the child's death on the beach at Cecina.'

He looks at the wrinkles in his pyjama knees and tries to

smooth the material. 'What I really want is to tell you the reason I hired you.'

Agata laughs. 'You want to confess you hired me for my shapely legs? I knew it the day I met you!'

He chuckles and coughs. 'Yes. But no. Although I'd hoped you were going to wear a skirt today, rather than jeans.'

'Who do you think you are? Berlusconi having a Bunga Bunga party?' She wags a finger amiably. 'You haven't changed.'

'They've been in touch with me.'

'They?' Agata sits with her cup poised. The fly stirs at the window.

'The people who suggested I hire you.'

'I don't understand. I was married to Luca, a police officer, and I spoke English. Wasn't I perfect for the job of *agente*?'

Eyes closing, Bruno takes a sip of espresso. 'I was to tell your former employer if you ever came back to England.'

'Sir John? That's nothing new. He wrote my reference.' She remembers the aristocratic family she worked for with mixed emotions. 'I'm grateful for the opportunities they gave me, but it was a long time ago.'

'Opportunities? Something happened there, Agata. I always thought you'd tell me one day.'

'There's nothing to tell.'

Bruno sighs into his plastic mouthpiece. A suck, and he removes the mask. 'Anyway, things have changed. He died.'

'Sir John died six years ago.' Of course she knows. She's always checked in the papers, and his children still send her the occasional card. 'I didn't go to the funeral, though. It was too grand for me!' And there were people she wanted to avoid.

Bruno reads her mind. 'The stepson has taken up the reins, or at least he was the one who got hold of the names.'

Her fingers close on the cup. 'Jett?'

'Would you recognise him if you saw him again?'

The fly surges back, and Agata bats it away. 'You don't forget Jett Parminter. The nannies used to say he'd either be a prime minister or a drug dealer. Something in the eyes. But this was twenty years ago.'

'He took his stepfather's black book. Apparently, the eldest son was disinterested. And a fool.'

She thinks for a moment. 'It's possible. Sir John's children were never interested in government.' She remembers the small leather book that was always on his desk in Knightsbridge. 'Is Jett working in government?'

'Not exactly. But I had a phone call asking after you six years ago. Just a politeness, he said. And then two days ago... Apparently, you're to drop it.'

'Drop what?'

'Don't be innocent. It's me you're talking to. Alessandro's death. The word is you wouldn't want Mr. Parminter to disclose what he knows about you.'

An old fear clutches her, but she's had years to learn how to hide it. Her next thought is that Figgi has reconnected with Jett. But she cannot imagine him in league with any of Alessandro's friends, least of all Jett.

'He wants you to leave the questions to the British Police.' Bruno breaks into her thoughts. 'That sounds reasonable, given Alessandro's death was in London.'

The fly buzzes again, landing on the low marble table. Agata watches as it crawls over some crumbs. 'I thought this was about the beach murder.'

'They're connected.'

Agata leans forward. 'How? Tell me!'

'I don't know the details, but it's all part of the English Syndicate. As I understand it, Jett Parminter is the Godfather to the upper classes.' He moistens his lips with his water glass. 'I want you to live, Agata. Pay attention.'

The fly buzzes. 'Since when have you worked for the English?'

He sucks, and the oxygen hisses. 'Even before Sir John's death, the Syndicate offered to feed me information when I needed it. In the past six years, the Syndicate has increased its operations from London to the boot of Italy. Smuggling.'

'And you never shared that with me?'

'You wanted to be a provincial housewife.'

'*Dio mio*! I lived in Florence, and I was working for you!'

'I gave you the smaller crimes. Tourist muggings, insurance fraud. That was you. I took the bigger cases, and I walked the tightrope between police, our Mafia, and theirs.'

Agata clenches her hands. The fly lifts itself, circles, and rests again. 'Don't make fun of me! I knew how to sidestep the local Mafia!'

'The Albanians, maybe, but the English Mafia are different.' He coughs. 'They're connected. It's big business, and this Syndicate dips between the Italian Mafia's toes. They're after unaccompanied children. Nameless, faceless. I was given a phone number and told whenever the police noticed their operations on Tuscan soil, it was my job to feed false information to the authorities. In return, we were rewarded.' He inhales and coughs as if his guts would spill.

Outrage overtakes her. 'You were giving me bullshit to feed to Luca's department!' Buzzing on the table, a sudden swipe sees the fly meet its death against Agata's fist.

Bruno sucks on the oxygen under her angry glare. 'The

Doctor Albina case. That's when they began to increase their demands.'

'I remember that case. An American boy died in a car crash, and they released his organs for donation without the correct paperwork. The family hired us to investigate. Nothing to do with Mafia. A hospital error.' She rubs the fly's blood from the side of her hand.

Bruno smiles thinly. 'You always had good recall. So you know that despite the parents shouting 'Mafia', they buried their son without kidneys, and the case against Doctor Albina dissolved.'

'The paperwork showed up belatedly, and nothing was ever proven. What has this to do with a migrant child found dead on the beach?'

'The Syndicate paid for Doctor Albina's legal fees. He was one of many in their pay.'

She stands, recollecting that the beach child had no heart or lungs. '*Dio Mio.* Dr. Albina was a surgeon.' Then she shakes her head. 'If this is true, why tell me now?'

'I meant to tell you when the time was right.'

'And now?'

He coughs. 'What happened to the smart clothes and the high heels? Look at you. Grey in your hair.'

She's not to be put off by his wandering eyes. 'Don't change the subject.' She has a flash of memory: Alessandro and Jett, laughing outside a pub in Sloane Square.

'Parminter rang recently because...' Bruno coughs harder and points to the newspaper on the table. 'The paragraph on page five mentions your husband as leading the murder investigation into that girl's death.' He leans forward with effort and taps the page.

'The newspaper in Alessandro's mouth!' She puts a hand over her mouth.

'The child's death has Syndicate written all over it. Sick as I am, I can connect the dots.'

'No! Alessandro's and this girl's death are completely different.' She moves to crouch by his side, searching his face as if the thread veins will map the way to the truth. 'I don't believe Alessandro would be involved in child trafficking. Do you hear me?'

'Perhaps you are right.'

'So why mess with my head?'

'Luca doesn't deserve you.' He puts a hand on hers.

She yanks it away. 'I'm furious you haven't told me about Jett before. I know him better than you do. You should have told me. You should have trusted me.' Inflamed with the news, she is also desperate to take something useful from the conversation.

Bruno wipes his forehead. His cheeks hollow as he inhales again to cough. 'I'm guessing there are problems within the Syndicate. Usual power plays in organised crime.' He rumbles and beats his chest with a feeble fist. 'Alessandro and this man, the stepson of Sir John—perhaps they fell out. I don't know, but stay away, Agata. Alessandro is dead. There's nothing you can do for him.'

She presses one fingertip to Bruno's forehead in the pose of a gun. His fingers catch at hers with a weak grasp.

'I cared about Alessandro,' she says, and as the words leave her, she feels the familiar pain. 'But Jett has always been a little shit. If Jett contacts you, tell him I've gone to fight vegetables and brambles. Tell him I will discover nothing. Lie. It seems you're better at that than I gave you credit for.'

'But he remembers you with Alessandro. He knows it will be personal.'

'So remind him it was quarter of a century ago.'

Bruno strokes her hand, and she slaps him.

'Come on, I'm on your side. But I know you, Agata. You like digging. I had to work hard to put you off Dr. Albina's trail.'

Her finger gun clicks at his temple. 'I want that doctor's name and number. If he's connected to the murder at the beach, I want to know. Let me worry about my safety. You worry about yours.'

He shrugs and points to the drawers in the old dresser by the window. 'All my files are there. If you must, take them. There's a hard drive and a box of paper scribblings. Take it. Take it. But for God's sake, don't get yourself killed.' He grimaces. 'I wanted to protect you. I wanted to make love to you.'

'Pfft.' She begins searching.

'You're more sexy than Claudia Cardinale. All the men wanted you.'

'You're a stupid arse.' Her tone is gentler than she wants, because he looks so frail. 'Too late for this now.'

His hand goes to his heart. 'So hurtful! Am I too old and sick? Not even a sympathy fuck?'

One drawer spills out elastic bands. She snorts. 'It might kill you prematurely. Although you deserve death for such treachery.'

'That's the way to go! Die in glory!'

'But what if it's a whimper and not a blast? The saints will laugh at you when you get to the gates of Heaven.'

'Or Hell.'

'Even worse, to have the devil sniggering. Can you take that chance?' She gives every syllable an acidic touch. All those years of putting up with his sexual innuendos so she could do a job she loved, and now she finds he did more than gawp. He treated her like a second-hand investigator. She keeps searching.

'Get stuffed!' he says grudgingly, but she ignores him.

Then she exclaims in satisfaction. The box and hard drive are there.

'You should have slept with me. I might have told you everything. Pillow talk.'

'Go fuck yourself.'

'I was hoping you'd do it for me.'

The shoe box is crammed with paper of all sizes, a small black hard drive perched on top. Pushing it into her bag, she looks at him. He has the sour smell of approaching death, so she gives him a quick goodbye kiss on the top of his head.

'I'd rather have known the truth, you stupid old fool. We should have played this differently. Instead, Jett's used you, and you've used me.' For a moment, her anger abates, and she runs a finger down his cheek.

'*Vai, vai,*' he says. 'Such tenderness. You'll give me a hard-on, and I won't know what to do with it.' His eyes moisten as she gathers her things to leave. 'Agata. You will come back? Another visit to let me know you're safe?'

He has never begged for anything, not even when a disgruntled client marched into the office with a farmer's shotgun.

'You don't deserve it. If you're keeping anything else back from me, I swear, I'll come back to cut off your oxygen.'

'Promises, promises.' He spasms with coughing.

She waits for him to finish, then sweeps to the door. 'Tell your daughter I said hello.'

Outside, a small tear escapes, whether in fury or sorrow, she isn't sure, but everything Bruno has said changes her past perceptions. Has she really been so stupid? Was she given her job—a job of which she was so proud—as a means for Jett to keep tabs on her? Perhaps signing the official secrets act with Sir John wasn't enough. They were a powerful family, and she was only a nanny. Who respects the nanny? Yet the nanny hears all.

Shadows have elongated along the hills. She clutches the bag. She must talk to Dr. Albina, shake a tree, and see what falls.

Then she thinks of Amy. It's a shock to realise that if the girl has been working for Alessandro, she could be part of the Syndicate. Despite her youth, is Amy capable of doing harm to Susan? And how is Susan involved? And where does the dead migrant child fit in? The last vestiges of stubbornness flood through her: She cannot believe Alessandro was a murderer. But if he is involved with an English Mafia, the connection must be there. She has to write down all the details and see them in front of her. She'll do that tonight.

Sitting in the Cinquecento with a box on her lap, she realises: There is an enemy at the gate, not a wild boar, but a man or group of men, and no one has identified them.

Chapter Thirteen

Unable to sleep, Susan wanders to the brick patio in the late afternoon heat. She watches Renzo close the gate. He steps into a three-wheeler scooter on the stony path, revs the tiny engine, and waits while Natale squashes next to him. The old woman heaves a large bag onto their combined laps, and they bump down the road, motor going like a zipper. Figaro has not returned. The dog, Ruby, has exhausted herself chasing lizards and is now stretched out in a patch of shade, paws twitching in a dream of murder.

Washed, changed, and redefined by makeup, Susan feels ready to meet people. She scans the horizon and tries to prioritise her next move. Uppermost in her mind is whether she needs to source 3,000 pounds. Does Montecatini have a local branch of an Italian bank? And if so, does it keep large amounts of cash? And what about the exchange rate? Perhaps she doesn't have to bother, now that Alessandro is—gone. Her red lips twitch at the callousness of the thought.

For a flicker of time, in England, she thought she lived

on terra firma. With a rich husband, she could meet colleagues' derision with increased confidence. But there is no breath of strong wind in the valley and she is back to being Sue Li, the girl who is afraid. Closing her eyes against the sun's glare, she imagines snatching her suitcase, dashing down the drive, and fleeing. Maybe someone in the house below will know how to order a taxi to the airport. Her home is a crime scene, but her boss, Elliot, will help her sort out the mess that is her current life. He's always been approachable.

With a start, she realises someone is walking towards the house: a blond, athletic looking woman, not just walking but power-walking up the drive, dressed in cargo shorts and a brilliant white T-shirt. The woman gives a friendly wave before vaulting the gate, and Ruby dashes to meet her, barking at full volume. Susan rises awkwardly. Does this stranger speak English? How should she introduce herself?

'Stay,' the woman commands in an American accent. The dog freezes. She holds a biscuit in her outstretched arm, and they both remain still for several seconds. 'Okay, take it.'

A snap of jaws, and Ruby melts from a statue into an adoring audience, wagging her tail so violently that her whole body shifts from side to side.

Susan relaxes a fraction. Language won't be a problem.

'Hiya!' The stranger comes over and shakes her hand with a hard grip. She is without a crease of spare flesh. 'I'm Crystal, Linda Jensen's niece. You know—Linda and Stefan—they live down there? We're neighbours. And you are...?'

'Susan.' She hesitates. 'Susan Li. A guest.'

Crystal smiles with teeth as white as her T-shirt. There is something about her eyes, an unnatural hazel colour, flecked and shiny.

'I wasn't sure you were in. No cars around the house. Are you with Figaro?' The woman's head twists. 'I had a one-night stand with him when I arrived a couple of weeks ago. Just thought I'd put that out there in case he mentioned me. Helluva nice guy.'

Susan looks down at her spangled, cleaned feet. One hand touches the wedding rings on her finger. Should she take them off? 'I am—that is—I was Alessandro's wife.'

As if discovering a prize, the woman rattles a phone and keys in her cargo shorts pocket. 'Huh! So it's you! I wondered. Sorry to hear about his death, but everyone is talking about you in the Piazza.' She comes closer and stares. 'Hey. I'm sorry. I don't mean to be insensitive. You're widowed, and you must be upset.'

Susan takes a step back from the inspection.

Crystal puts out a hand and touches Susan's wrist. 'Do you know me? Or are you staring at my eyes?'

'They're unusual.'

'Contact lenses. It's all the rage in Florida, but it unnerves some locals here.' She barks a laugh. 'Anything new unnerves them. You'll soon find out. You'll scare the hell out of them with your model style get-up. You a Brit?'

Susan nods, trying to accept Crystal's scrutiny of her face. It's as if she is trying to read some internal computer programming.

Embarrassed, Susan looks down. 'I don't think we've met.'

'Huh.' Crystal draws another biscuit from the cargo shorts, throwing it farther across the patio. Ruby bounds after it. 'So, what about some coffee? Or tea? Do you drink coffee? Natale's is the best. I don't know where she buys it. Not at the *supermercato*!'

With familiarity, Crystal steps into the kitchen and

fetches a silver coffee machine from the cupboard. Dismantling the coffeepot into three parts, she gives a commentary about its workings while Susan stands silently. 'First time at Casa Verdi?' she asks as she fetches ground coffee from another cupboard and packs it into the internal colander.

'Yes.'

'Huh! Figaro asked me up here. He wanted to know about the kids working my aunt's land after that dreadful murder. I can tell you, there are all sorts of rumours going around. It's as bad as American politics. Loads of fake news. Typical fear of migrants taking over. Anyway, one thing led to another.' She turns on the hob and leans against the work surface. 'I'm being insensitive again.' She puts her head to one side. 'Such a shame about his cousin. His death must have hit you both like shit. By the way, what exactly happened? No one knows the details. It's all gozz.'

'Gozz? You mean a burglary?'

'Gozz? Gossip! Oh, but you think he was robbed! Huh!'

Susan feels they are speaking two different languages. 'What?'

'Did they steal much? If you live in London, that's gotta be an occupational hazard. Being robbed, I mean.'

'I don't know any details. I wasn't there, and they wouldn't let me back into the flat.' Susan focuses on the hissing coffeepot. She doesn't want to answer questions, but Crystal's penetrating gaze is unnerving.

'So, what do you do? I'm a nurse—here for a few months to help. My aunt has Alzheimer's. Really tough.' She sniffs the rising steam with a smile of satisfaction. 'I don't know anyone here, but hey—I'm an American, and you're a Brit—what about uniting against the locals? Especially now I hear there's likely to be this Brexit thing! England detaching from Europe? I guess that means you'll not be a European anymore! Closer to the Yanks than the Franks.' She gives a raucous laugh.

'Are the local people against you?'

The coffee completes its bubbling, filling the kitchen with a powerful aroma.

'Sure! I'm broke and stran-year-i. Heard about that?'

'You're what?'

'That's the Italian word for an outsider. Mind you, an American is better than most. They usually have plenty of dollars to spend. That's according to my Aunt Linda. She's Dutch, but she's been holidaying here for forty years.'

'You're Dutch?'

'Nah. Do I sound Dutch?' She laughs. 'My father is Dutch. Auntie Linda is his sister. My parents separated when I was a kid, so I grew up in Florida with my mom.'

They are interrupted by Ruby, who has returned to beg. Crystal pulls another dog biscuit from her cargo shorts and throws it out the door. Then she picks up the coffeepot. 'Want one?'

One more coffee and Susan thinks her brain will explode. She's hardly eaten any lunch, which has given rise to more witchy stares from Natale. When she shakes her head, Crystal pours the entire contents into a small porcelain bowl and leads the way outside to the terrace, plunking herself on a wooden bench. Susan follows and tucks her feet under a canvas chair.

'Well look at that. You can hardly see our house from here. I've only been here in the evenings.' She holds the bowl firmly in two hands as she expands on what she's learnt since coming to Montecatini. 'Gotta spend money to earn points in these parts. *Porca miseria*! Nobody likes a mean tourist. *Va fancullo*! Only eat Italian food, don't ask for burgers. *Dio Mio*! Learn the language, even if you don't know what the hell you're saying. And swear in Italian.' She roars with laughter before taking a mouthful of coffee. 'I thought Figaro and I could hang out on weekends when he was here, improve my Italian, but, no. The mayor is an uptight, upholder of morals. I had to get him drunk to even get near him.'

To Susan, the image of a drunk Figaro requires considerable imagination, and she squirms as Crystal pulls a long face and mimics his Italian accent.

'*La famiglia, la famiglia e tutto*! Jeez. He's like something out of The Godfather, isn't he? What do you reckon—Mafia or mayor? Or both? I mean, who knows?' She holds the coffee bowl aloft, in a toast to the countryside, then downs the rest in one and smacks her lips. 'Darn good! I am eighty percent caffeine.' She laughs. 'Anyway, what are you doing here? Don't you have kids or something back in the UK?'

Tiny lizards dart furtively between large rocks, and Susan wishes she could follow them into the dry cracks as she admits to being childless. Why do those questions always make her feel inadequate? 'His family said they're bringing his body here for a funeral.' It's the best excuse she can think of.

'Yeah, right. Sure.' Leaning forward, Crystal crosses her long, tanned legs. 'Who inherits this pile?'

'This? Figaro said it was a family home.'

Crystal frowns. 'Is that right? My aunt's house will be sold at the end of the year. They've acres and acres, and it all needs to be mown and the weeds cut. I couldn't manage without the migrants. They're supplied by a charity that finds work for teenagers about to get their papers. But the locals want me to pay for Italian labour, so they spread rumours. So prejudiced. My money is on the Verdis stirring things. They say old Signor Verdi funds the far right. Y'know, Italy for the Italians party. And I hear the African boy up at the Tower was given the third degree after they found the dead kid at the beach. Honestly, it's ridiculous. Africa is a continent, not a country.' She spreads her hands wide. 'And the beach is miles away. But the police scared the living daylights outta the D'Angelos. That's Umberto and Naomi who own the Tower. I expect you'll meet them. They're Italian, but not from here. They speak English fluently, though.'

It's too many names and too much information all recounted at lightning speed. Susan's head aches, but she feels compelled to say something in order to appear polite. 'Will you be here long?'

'Nah.' Crystal wrinkles her nose in scorn. 'Too boring. Give me a city any day. I'm just waiting for a place in a hospice for Auntie Linda. Then we'll leave and take her back to Holland and I'll see Dad and return to the ol' U.S. of A. I told all this to that Yolanda girl at the pizzeria. By the way, Yo's English is a bit weird, so speak slowly. And I told Mayor Figaro all this, because Uncle Stefan said keep in with the Verdi family. But as for who friggin' owns the town—let me tell you—my family have as much right to say what goes on here as anyone. They've been coming here for forty years.' She flaps a hand impatiently. 'Oh, listen to me! Talking too much, as usual. And another thing—the Wi-Fi's bad.' She pulls a phone out of her back pocket and checks the bars before resting her flecked eyes on Susan. 'It's good to talk to someone of a similar age. Why don't we swap phone numbers, yeah? Go for a glass of vino? The way Italian bureaucracy works, you could be stuck here some time.'

Finding no reason to refuse, Susan agrees.

After inputting the number, Crystal smiles, then gives a huge yawn. 'Sorry, Auntie had me up in the night. Anyway, must go. Got things to do.' Standing, she pulls out another biscuit and throws it as far as she can. It lands down in a clump of bushes on the other side of the pool. The dog races off. 'Beautiful here, isn't it? Real paradise. Sort of hides what's going on.'

'What is going on?' Susan rises with alarm.

'Aw. Nothing. Dead bodies washing up on Italian shores.' The American squeezes Susan's shoulder. 'I feel for you, girl. Horrible things have happened to you and you're in a strange place. So listen. I'm just across the road, and as we're both newbies here, call on me anytime. I'm telling you what my family told me: Never trust the Verdis. Maybe you weren't married to Alessandro long enough to find out. Good old-fashioned Mafia. Remember the fishes?'

Her hand does a mock wiggle of fish swimming, and she laughs. With rapid strides, she vaults the gate again, walking down the path. Ruby runs after her, pushing a sad muzzle through the bars. Susan stares after her, finding it impossible to picture Crystal and Figgi having sex. Actually, she can't imagine Figgi having sex at all, or even being drunk.

Surrounded by miles of hills and woodland, Susan tilts her head to the skies. At the furthest summit, the miniature white form of windmills can be seen slowly wheeling, but the pine forest looks dense. There's no escape that way, and when she scans the valley and the winding roads carving up the land, she knows it would take hours to reach the medieval city on foot.

Her phone pings. She picks it up, drops it, picks it up. Reads.

Il tuo pacco è stato spedito e verrà consegnato a breve.

Non c'è tracciabilità disponibile per questo articolo.

It takes several minutes of wrestling with Google Translate and predictive text to get the message.

Your parcel has been dispatched and will be delivered in short. There's no tracking available for this item.

Should she tell Figaro? She thinks about Crystal's warning and wonders what the Verdis will do to her when she has the package in her hand? Sever a finger? Even the thought makes her hyperventilate. The speed and angle of descent from rich wife to murder suspect are making her nauseous. She is forty. She is someone who has looked after her sick father and held down a secure office job and paid her rent on time. There is nothing in her past that equips her for dealing with this current situation.

She thinks back to the last time she and Alessandro were together. It had none of the hallmarks of an ending. A soft spring evening and a seat together on the expensive sofa in the Canary Wharf flat. As electric lights pricked across the skyscrapers touching the Thames, they shared a glass of wine and a laptop between them, while he gave her instructions and told her how much he loved her. Why do young girls believe in the Cinderella myth?

Chapter Fourteen

Agata stops at the pizzeria. Bruno's revelations burn, and she must cool her temperature before speaking to anyone. The bar girl says Yolanda and Dana are getting provisions, so she sits alone at a table outside, chewing a fingernail, and examines a yellow slip of paper. It contains the contact details of Dr. Albina and a note about the case, written six years ago.

David Alan Wycker car crash; brain stem dead; kidneys missing;

Dr. Albina surgeon; no next of kin consent.

Case closed April 2010

She re-examines the case with a painful sense of inadequacy. The parents of the dead boy raged in the office, demanding help to investigate, yet when the paperwork showed up belatedly, they were forced to drop the charges. But none of this should be laid at her door. It's not her fault.

Is it? Principally, it was Bruno's case, and for some reason—she cannot remember why—she was the *agente* dispatched to speak with the doctor prior to the retrieval of paperwork. He protested his innocence, and she believed him: a surgeon caught up in a bureaucratic disaster. Now she wonders. There's no reason to suspect a connection between Alessandro's death and this case or even the murdered child on the beach, but with mention of the Syndicate, there is potentially a link. It's like picking shelled peas from a kitchen sink full of water; they bob around, unconnected, but they're all part of the same harvest. Agata introduced Alessandro to Jett, in the summer of '91. She tries to fit the puzzle pieces together. If Jett runs the British Syndicate, then Alessandro might be involved. They were firm friends. But where does the girl on the beach fit in? Why the news article in Alessandro's mouth?

Two vehicles pull up and park in the piazza. They take the space designated for the bus, but no bus will come for an hour. Amy Joliffe gets out of the battered van. It's been over two hours since she was at Casa Verdi. Why hasn't the girl gone back to the Hendersons' Airbnb? A thickset man emerges from the other vehicle. It has the shiny look of an airport rental car. He calls to her, and it's obvious they've already met. Amy points to the pizzeria.

Pretending to be absorbed in her piece of paper, she keeps half an eye on them as Amy blinks bright-blue lids at the man.

'Very kind of you to buy me a drink and dinner. I'm starving.'

'Can't have you Hank Marvin, can we?'

Like Amy, he's a Londoner, and Agata struggles to translate the East End slang as they banter lightly. Once in the cafe, he orders a bottle of Prosecco and some pizza from the girl behind the counter. Laughter and the scraping of chairs tells her they've sat at the metal table nearest the door. They can't see her, but she can eavesdrop.

With little encouragement, Amy launches into a complaint about Carl's mother. 'I reckon we could've had a thing—him and me—you know what I mean? He tried it on. Not in a bad way. No! But his mother—oh my days! She's a nightmare.'

Amy's see-saw laugh is joined by a low, throaty laugh from the Englishman. 'You 'n me could have a thing, darling.'

Agata flinches, but Amy screeches.

'No offence, Brian—yeah—but you're old enough to be me dad—that's if I had one!' She see-saw laughs again and talks about being in care and needing money, and how she's been let down by someone who owes her, although it's very sad because he was a proper gent and now he's dead. But she's fine. She's absolutely fine, even though her finances are in a hole. She speaks in a rapid rap, too fast for Agata to catch all the details. From the tone, anyone listening would think Amy's life was a standup comedy routine instead of a small tragedy. The girl has a way of delivering a punch line, and her companion is laughing at every word.

'This guy in London was a proper gent,' she repeats. 'Never touched me or nothing. That's the mark of a gent, by the way! Just in case you didn't know!'

'I'm a right gentleman,' says the man. 'I haven't touched you, either! Just thought about it.'

A see-saw laugh. 'Yeah.' She giggles. 'Anyway, he told me I'd be well paid. Don't you just hate people who let you down?'

'I won't let you down, darling. I said I'll pay, and I will.

No strings, just the pleasure of your company. Brian Blunt, an honest man, that's me.'

'Thanks, but remember, I'm not one of those girls who turns tricks, and I've done karate.'

'Very scary!'

They both laugh. The bar girl comes over with their order. Prosecco flows and talk flows. With a drink inside her, Amy's see-saw laughter ratchets up a notch. Tipsy screeches echo into the square. Much of what is said is incomprehensible to Agata no matter how hard she concentrates.

Yolanda and Dana arrive with bulging bags of provisions and drop a double kiss onto Agata's cheeks.

'*Stronza*!' Yolanda whispers. Agata knows her sister's eyes will be on the girl's bare midriff and the bellybutton ring. 'Don't look at me like that. That's what our mother would have called her.'

'Stop!' says Dana. 'She's just a kid. She told me yesterday she was here to meet up with the Verdis.' She raises an eyebrow at Agata. 'Has she?'

Agata nods, desperate to keep listening. As her sister and partner enter the cafe, two pizza slices arrive at Amy's table.

'I'm not gonna lie, yeah.' The girl speaks with a full mouth. 'Who'd have thought? So many Londoners in a little place like this!'

'You're so right, darling. Piccadilly fucking Circus.'

'I'm grateful for the drink and food, but like I said, I'm here on business.' This is said with a lofty accent, and then the girl giggles.

Agata changes her seat to the other side of the doorway so she is sitting within sight of them.

Amy's denim jacket is slung over her chair, and she

crosses one leg over the other, wiggling her sparkly trainer. 'Anyway, thanks very much, but I ought to be going. It's been good to chat, and you're very kind, but I've gotta return Carl's van. He'll think I've done a bunk.'

'Nah, nah. Finish my pizza slice and tell me more about your—er—business.' He tips his Prosecco into her lipstick-stained glass.

'Nothing more to say. Bit weird, but all I had to do was send a package by courier and deliver a letter. They didn't trust the English post or something, and he was too busy to do it himself. He told me when I handed over the letter, I'd get the money for the cost of the Airbnb. What can I tell old Mrs. Henderson? I don't wanna do a flit, but if I have to...'

'Pr'aps I can help you, darling. Trust me. I'm Old Bill on holiday.'

The laughter changes into a cough. 'Oh-my-days!' She stuffs sunglasses on her face. 'Ignore what I've just said!'

He rises. 'I'm busting for a pee, but wait right there. I'll sort this out for you. You can pay me back when you get to London.'

'Yeah? You're very trusting.' She delays her next bite of pizza.

'Don't be like that. As I said, I'm here on my own because my girlfriend let me down, so it's nice to have a drink and a chat with someone as lovely as you.'

She giggles halfheartedly at the compliment, and he pushes his plate toward her. 'At least finish. What's the point of being in this beautiful place if you can't unwind?'

Amy demolishes his slice as he disappears down the stairs in the direction of a discreet sign.

Agata sees her opportunity. Luca has texted her about the English police officer's arrival and this must be the man —sooner than expected. She hurries over to Amy, who is fumbling in her jacket, and then hunting in her bag. The girl is using language unfamiliar to her.

'Lost something?'

The sunglasses look up. 'Oh. It's you.' She mutters expletives, tugging at the jacket pocket.

'Have you still got the letter?'

Amy's mouth screws into a tight circle, and she knocks over a chair as she sweeps the jacket into her arms. 'Fucking Babylon. Sneaky bugger. I'll bet he's not here on holiday. I thought it was too good to be true!'

'Calm yourself. What's happened?'

'I had the letter in my jacket, and at first I thought he was feeling me up when he put an arm around me, but I was hungry.' She moves to the door, and Agata tries to block her.

'This is important. I can help you. Did you know what was in the letter?'

In response, Amy puts out a hand and shoves Agata on the shoulder. 'Whoever you are, Alessandro's death had nothing to do with me. I mean, I'm sorry and all that, but I just wanna get back to London. This is getting creepy.' She points toward the stairs. 'And that man—Brian—whatsis name—he's a bloody arsehole. I'm a Black girl from South London. I hate police.' Thrusting out her chest, she calls to Yolanda at the bar. 'He said he'd pay. You ask him.'

Face flushed, she pushes Agata again before stumbling down the few steps to the road. The door of Carl's van creaks as she yanks it open and, with a crunching of gears, she drives off.

The man comes up from the toilets. 'Where's she gone?' he asks.

Agata stands opposite him, drawing herself up to full tiny height. 'Are you the English detective, here on police business? And have you just stolen something from that girl?'

His heavy brows draw together, and he looks down at Agata. He's head and shoulders taller than she is, and certainly twice her girth.

'Yes. I'm British Police, darling. Not that it's any of your business.' He reaches into a blue nylon bag and flourishes a black holder with badge, name, and number. Detective Sergeant Brian Blunt, London Metropolitan Police.

'But you're not the police here in Italy.'

'I'm meeting the local policeman.' He stuffs the badge back and zips up the bag.

'I'm his wife,' says Agata, taking satisfaction at the way he stops. 'Commissario Agnello is expecting your call.'

He moves forward. 'Well, he'll have to wait. Stuff to do.'

'You're here to interview Susan Li Verdi, aren't you? I can show you where she's staying.'

Unblinking, he stares at her with open hostility, and pulls out a piece of paper from his bag, shaking it like a lettuce. 'At the moment, I'm trying to find my accommodation. I can't get the fucking GPS to work in that hire car.'

'I help.' Yolanda places down a chit with 45 euros written in thick black. Glancing at the address, she takes a photocopied map from a pile on the counter and marks the place with an X. 'Is here. See?'

Again, Agata tries to block him from leaving. 'Do you have the letter? You should hand it over to Mrs. Verdi, or the Italian Police. You could hand it to me now, and I'll take it to Susan.'

His grin is menacing. 'Listen, darling, I don't answer to you. I report to my senior officer in London. Got it?' He slaps euro notes on the table. 'Grat-zay. Keep the change.'

For the second time, Agata is infuriated to find herself pushed to one side. She fumes.

'Well, you handled that well,' says Yolanda, who doesn't bother to hide her amusement.

They watch him get into his car and drive off in the direction of the coast.

'How dare he! He has no jurisdiction here!'

'England is still in the EU. He probably thinks he has some reciprocal rights.'

'What would you know about it, Yo-yo?' Agata feels the bruise on her ego. 'I should have kneed him in the balls.'

'And we all know you're capable of that,' says her younger sister, clearing the table. 'So what stopped you? Concern for my cafe's reputation?'

Agata pulls car keys from her bag. 'Luca is dealing with this man.'

'Not your sister's welfare, then? Typical. So, what's the fuss about?'

'Never mind,' says Agata. 'I'm going to find Amy. She's at the Hendersons' place.'

'That'll be fun! That's where the Englishman is staying. I've just marked the spot on the map.'

Agata swears. She doesn't want more humiliations today. Better Luca sends someone in an official capacity. She wonders if the letter is important. Chances are, whatever Alessandro has written is false information. Truth was never his default.

'Don't forget,' says Yolanda, 'it's the Saint's Day Festa tomorrow, and you promised to help me. I'm really short-handed this year. One hundred thousand migrants to our shores, and I can't get enough people to assist for the day. What is happening to this country!'

'I haven't forgotten,' says Agata. But she had forgotten.

Her mind is whirring: Bruno, Jett, Alessandro, Amy, and the letter, and now this English police officer, Brian Blunt. She needs to get home, write everything down, and speak to Luca.

And then, there's the matter of pumping Dr. Albina for information about a certain crime ring known as the Syndicate.

Chapter Fifteen

The ghost village of Buriano

In the car mirror, Agata adjusts her blouse to show cleavage. She smooths her hair and applies a little lipstick. She has parked the Cinquecento on the deserted path leading to the old village of Buriano. This point catches a good signal from the top of the Torre di Verdi. To her right, the vineyard slopes southward, and the sun glints on the remnants of the broken chapel windows. Buriano's buildings are lifeless and have been without residents for decades, but the ornate stonework stands as a reminder of former riches.

Agata hopes the number will connect. Two rings, and her luck is in. She recognises his voice immediately: oddly girlish, soft, and high. His video is off.

'*Ciao*, my favourite doctor,' says Agata and gives her name in case he's forgotten. 'Can we talk?'

'Eh! *Ciao bella*.' The doctor puts on the video and they stare at each other in their rectangular view. 'Long time.'

'Long time,' she agrees. 'I wanted to see how you're doing, Dr. Albina.'

'Ernesto. Please.' He props up the screen on what

appears to be a bedside table. Instead of his face, she sees a glass of wine, an open suitcase on a bed, and part of his white boxer shorts.

'You're going on holiday?' Agata makes sure only her head and shoulders are in the frame. She pretends she's still working for the agency. 'Can you spare a moment?'

'You want something.' There is no rancour to this statement. 'The lovely Agata doesn't ring me out of the blue for a social call. You want advice about transplantation?'

She watches his hands, neatly folding clothes into the suitcase.

'Did someone tell you to expect my call?'

'No, but I've accepted a job on another continent. You've only just caught me. This number will disconnect at midnight.'

She expresses surprise, and he sits on the bed, taking a sip of wine in the screen. He looks just the same. A man with an enormous nose and noticeable moles around his chin.

'I remember you with fondness,' he says. 'You didn't give me a hard time like the bastards in the police. And that American lawyer. What a bitch. Thankfully, my man chased her off. So come on. Tell me what you want. I'll give you five minutes.'

She thanks him, dispensing with her planned preamble. 'I'm working on a similar case, but one that involves heart and lungs. Again, a job with no paperwork. Are you aware of the black market in organs?'

He's taken aback by her directness and sips again. 'Well. This is a surprise. I no longer work in Italy. I'm in Croatia.'

'I see. But I was calling in case you could point me in the right direction, given your connections.'

His lips are thinly drawn. 'Oh, come on! I can only tell you about legal transplants.'

'Any information would help. The police are drawing a blank.'

He scratches the most prominent brown mole and juts out his lower lip. 'Sienna has a vast hospital. Start asking around there. You don't have to call me to do that.'

Agata has visited Sienna's hospital. There are coloured lines leading from the pavement into the large building: blue, pink, green, and white painted along the ground, with a board instructing people how to find the correct department by following the coloured walkways. In such a huge hospital, it will take time to find the right department and the right person to talk to.

'A patient died near the beach. It's also an odd case, and I remembered you worked at Cecina Hospital.'

'I never worked in Cecina Hospital.' He corrects her with a brusque laugh. 'It's tiny. I worked in a private clinic in Cecina. Only for a short time. Russian money, and if you're asking about clinics, then you are digging into the business of the über rich, and such people don't play by the rules. A wealthy person can pay for whatever medical procedure they want, but I wouldn't know about black markets.'

'Heart and lungs?' she persists. 'Any whispers in medical circles?'

He laughs. 'Heart and lung transplants are not like kidneys. It always stems from an accident. A healthy person doesn't expect to donate, and a donor could be thousands of kilometres away from the recipient.'

'How do they connect?'

He tuts. 'Such ignorance!' He sips his wine. 'I'll give

you a scenario. A boy has a crash and is left without brain stem activity.'

'As in your case.'

'Exactly. The medics discover he's a suitable tissue match and blood type. He has a donor card, so the kidney is taken to where a specialist team is standing by. The recipient could be anywhere within a couple of hours flying-time. Anyone awaiting a transplant is permanently on call for an operation.'

'Have you been involved in this kind of operation?'

He raises his eyebrows. 'I am a transplant surgeon. So yes, of course. And as you know my speciality is kidneys. But everything I do is legal, with the necessary paperwork.'

'Except for that boy.'

'We found it in the end.' He sips. She attempts to interrupt, but he shakes his head. 'Of course laws can be broken. Money talks and money heals. As long as the local men in power receive a kickback, transplants take place without paperwork. Europe is not whiter than white, but there's no suggestion of murder, you understand. People sell organs. It's the world we live in. However, the Cecina clinic you speak about is a place for Botox and breast enlargements. They sell operating spaces, and the records of the procedures are kept elsewhere.' Dr. Albina finishes his glass and stands. 'Pleasant as this exchange has been, I need to pack.'

'Thank you, Ernesto.' Agata wonders if another scandal forces him to move abroad. She lightens her tone. 'So where are you going?'

He chuckles. 'No more questions.' His face appears right up to the camera, a crease between his brows. 'I save lives. Don't forget that.'

'I know,' she says, deliberately softening her voice.

'That case was a terrible time in my life, but you were respectful. That's the only reason I've picked up your call.'

'I still respect you, Ernesto. I respect all that you do, but I'm desperate for information about someone in the Syndicate. Do you know them? Bruno has just told me that they paid your legal bills.'

The bottom lip juts again. 'So. The real reason you ring me.' The screen is pulled away. 'Be careful, Agata. Do not poke in dark corners.'

She ploughs on, hoping he won't cut the call. 'Have you heard that Alessandro Verdi was murdered? I knew him personally, and you did, too.' It's a guess, but she hopes she sounds convincing. In the screen, she sees him finger the mole.

'Alessandro Verdi.' He repeats the name slowly. 'You really don't understand, do you? I thought you were cleverer than that. The Syndicate is nothing to do with you. It is made up of a male membership for those who like their girls or boys very young.'

Her heart misses a beat, and she watches the top lip curl with satisfaction at her shock.

'You were always so flirtatious, Agata. Wasted on me, but I played along. Don't mistake me. I'm not talking about babies. I like fourteen-year-olds. The peaches—when their breasts bud. I'm no different to many men in power. And I am a good surgeon. We all have our peccadillos.'

Agata cannot find the right words. There are no right words. She says the first thing that comes into her head. 'But your file has nothing to do with underage sex. Why say this to me?'

The horse-black nostrils flare. 'You ask about the Syndicate. You deserve a little dose of reality. Didn't you realise your agency didn't save me? It was a Syndicate mix-up, and so they hushed it up and provided the fake papers. With my skills, I'm of great value to them, and so they source my pleasure.'

She slams a fist against the steering wheel. 'This is lies! My agency helped get your case dropped.'

He licks his lips in enjoyment of her rage. 'I have a new passport and a new name. Tomorrow I cease to exist as Dr. Albina, so let me enlighten you. I work for the Syndicate because I prefer fresh fruit to spoiled. That's what I see when I look at you. An old woman. But I save lives, not just with transplants but also with Off Grid Kids. That's the delightful term we use. There are many like me, with money and position. The world is full of children in need. Children of war and famine. They don't exist. They have no papers. So, we feed them and preen them.'

Her head buzzes. 'Off Grid Kids? What about illegal transplantations?'

He snaps his fingers. 'It's all to do with children who have no footprint.' He blows a kiss. '*Ciao, amore.* My advice is to stop asking questions. They will know where to find you, so be careful.' The screen wiggles, and she is looking at the hotel ceiling and a bland centre light.

'Wait! Do you know Jett Parminter?' She no longer cares what he thinks as long as she can get answers. 'Is he the head of the Syndicate?'

'Poor little Agata.' The voice is full of scorn. 'You still think you can command? You're nobody.' The call is cut; the screen goes blank. The depth of her naivety cuts her in half.

She presses fingertips against her forehead to remove the radiating pain and wipes lipstick from her mouth. The colour spreads like blood on the back of her hand, and she rubs it down her jeans. What has she learnt apart from her own stupidity?

First, there is a black market in organs, and it's virtually untraceable. Second, the Syndicate operates throughout Europe, snatching underage migrants. So, what knits them together is a paedophile ring. Off Grid Kids. She shudders.

Was Alessandro was one of them? But no! She cannot believe Alessandro was a paedophile. Twenty-five years ago, she knew his heart. It's not possible. He's not a murderer, and he was never a paedophile. And yet. She takes in a long breath. And yet, twenty-four hours ago, she thought Bruno hired her on merit, and one hour ago, she considered Dr. Albina an honourable man.

She remembers Alessandro's young wife, Mariju, and smacks the driver's wheel. The girl was eighteen when she gave birth. For the first time, Agata recognises her real failures are to spot her own prejudices. The only person whose guilt is beyond question is Jett's. Geoffrey—the boy who would punch you if you used his real name. An uncomfortable memory resurfaces. Twenty-two-year-old Jett in the drawing room with his twelve-year-old half-sister. Pushing down her memory, she gags.

Opening the car door, she pours the rest of her can of San Pellegrino into the dust. Dragonflies zap down to meet the sugary liquid, and she flails her arms, rages at them and taps their iridescent wings as they snap to bite her. Then she slams the car door. She may be a Nobody, as Dr. Albina has said, but she is determined to get justice for this murdered child.

The sun is sinking in the sky, and Luca's phone list is long. She must ring more charities before the end of the day.

Revving up her little car, she turns around, leaving the ghosts of Buriano behind. Then it occurs to her that she ought to delay going home. A more important task is to re-question the woman who was last in Alessandro's bed. Susan must surely know more than she is saying.

Chapter Sixteen

Westminster, London 2015. A year before Alessandro's death.

Karol was new to the network. The man had large, rough hands and a drunken line in enthusiastic conversation. Such garrulousness caused trouble. They shook hands, and Alessandro smoothed his palm down the thigh of his suit before ordering a drink. The meeting in the Westminster club was at Jett's insistence. A large diamond in the man's ear marked him as a nouveau riche in these surroundings. Alessandro perched next to him on a bar stool. Karol had come early. In front of him was a half-empty bottle of the best vodka in the house.

Bespoke tailoring didn't turn a Syndicate man into a gentleman, any more than Alessandro sharing a drink with him denoted friendship, but he greeted the client with a practised cordiality. The club's credentials and prices passed for respectability.

Jett said men like Karol were useful. They ran the haulage firms that imported migrants, no questions asked, and if the richer ones at the top of the network wanted glamour, so what? Jett had the English contacts to receive the merchandise, and he paid well for loyalty. Their drivers would go to prison rather than speak of the Syndicate. Money talked. Violence silenced. And power corrupted.

Years of enriching himself on supplying other people's desires had corrupted Jett absolutely. The supercilious boy was now a venal man, and the relationship between him and Alessandro was no longer the camaraderie of university days. Jett had taken possession of a certain black book, expanding his empire. While entertaining Karol would not normally have been one of Alessandro's duties, his bank account swelled on humouring Jett's increasing idiosyncrasies. It was all too easy to read Jett's mind: Set a foreigner to meet a stranger in the Lords' Club and the upper classes kept their hands clean. Jett was dismissive of certain stratas of society, and Alessandro, with his Italian heritage, would never quite count as upper class.

Karol's fat fingers withdrew five squares from his breast pocket, splaying them on the black, shiny bar. After two-thirds of a bottle, Karol liked Alessandro, convinced they were men of similar tastes. Alessandro never carried pictures of family, but he cultivated the artifice of agreement as he sipped his drink and looked through the photographs.

Finger on celluloid, Karol boasted. 'You understand,' he said, 'I never leave these images on my phone or computer. So many dishonest people. One hacker can hold your life to ransom.' He looked lovingly at the children in the photographs.

Alessandro recognised his drinking companion's predilections and prepared himself for an unpleasant hour. He knew, and he didn't know. It was his habit to look away. As the Syndicate banker, Alessandro was glad that Jett's clients were rarely forthcoming, especially in a public place. But with the barman otherwise occupied, the mood lighting low, and the Vodka bottle empty, Karol wanted to talk—and for the moment, it was Alessandro's job to listen. Information was power.

The photographs showed young, dark-skinned girls in swimming costumes. There were no smiles on their brightly painted lips. They stood, arms up, backs swayed, dark eyes brooding.

'Your daughters?' Alessandro said. It was a statement of diplomacy. Karol was from a small town in the Urals, although his forged passport said he was a Belgium national.

The man laughed at the joke and lowered his voice. 'Very good! These are my best inamorati! My little loves.' He threw some salted pistachios into his mouth. A wet crumble coated his tongue. 'Da. No one misses them. Forgotten children, so I give them a little hug.'

Alessandro knew better than to stop the upward curve of his mouth. He took another sip of his drink. Smiling. Smiling. Elbows on the bar. This was why he avoided Jett's people. Money was money, but who ate steak while looking at pictures of an abattoir?

He thought of Mariju, twenty-five years his junior—eighteen, when he'd first bedded her. But it was legal, and it was love, wasn't it? Even if her parents had insisted otherwise. At this moment, her parents didn't know Alessandro was back in Mariju's bed. Strange how the boy had changed Alessandro's world. One stroke of his son's cheek, and he was captured. God, but the child looked like him.

For the first time in his life, he had experienced the violence of love. Some of Jett's inner club liked young girls, some liked little boys, some had perversions too weird to translate. Upon touching his son's curls, a volt of fury had risen inside him. He would kill anyone who touched his child in that way. In that moment, he went from a callous banker to a revolutionary.

The celluloid eyes looked at him. He felt their reproach, and his hand tightened on the glass. Time for change. Time for Alessandro Verdi to claim his rightful place as the much-loved leader in Montecatini. Better a big fish in a small pond. This knowledge came to him late, but it was not too late. Not too late to gather his funds and raise his son as a prince in Tuscany.

After the meeting, Alessandro folded a drunk Karol into a taxi and watched it pull away. He slid into the normality of everyday London. Other people ambled about as though the world was safe. Men and women shopped without thought of the sewers. But he knew names. He held codes. Like the EU, you couldn't leave the Syndicate without negotiations. If threatened, the Syndicate would not hesitate to put a bullet to the brain. So, slowly, slowly, he began to plot his exit.

Maybe he was getting old, but the time to get out was now. A few lies, a few decoys to toss to Jett, and a few forged papers. He could do it.

Chapter Seventeen

Agata stops by the century-old drinking fountain and runs a dry tongue around her mouth. The faded fresco of Madonna and child gaze down from their stone arch. Below the paintwork, a worn lion's head and a ceramic pull-button offer water. A quick tug at the knob, and the lion spouts from an underground well. The liquid pools in the pitted stone basin below, and she splashes her face. The cold brings with it a memory of four years ago: Alessandro staying at Casa Verdi with his young pregnant wife, the blossoming Mariju. Agata had come to the stone lion, watching them in the distance. She had never experienced such jealousy. It bit deep, and she contemplated murder, gripping a knife in her hands. And then the madness receded, and she drove away like a whipped dog.

Here she is again, cupping a hand and drinking memories. He's dead now. Fate has done what she failed to do. Tears threaten to engulf her and she shakes her head. Has her former lover been caught in a criminal snare, or was he the one setting the traps? Both scenarios are possible, so she must think carefully before speaking to Susan. Curiously, it troubles her that she feels no jealousy where Susan is concerned. Agata knows instinctively that woman never captured his heart.

As she approaches Casa Verdi, the fake wife is alone, unless you count the dog, who gives a half-hearted bark. The English bull terrier isn't as fierce as she looks, and at least Susan has changed into something clean. Her eyes are topped with a black fringe of false eyelashes, and her heavy foundation gives a clownish hue in the late afternoon sun, but she appears composed. Agata doesn't attempt to give her a double kiss, commenting instead on her beautiful linen frock, the delicate precision of the golden buttons, and her sparkling rhinestone sandals. It's a little overdressed for the country, but Agata pretends otherwise. Susan offers her a small glass of red. A half-drunk glass is by her side.

'It's good.' Agata sips. 'I'm not sure my husband will ever make wine this good.'

'You too? You own a vineyard?' The eyelashes widen.

Agata is quick to cut the idea down to size, explaining their fledgling plans. Susan's thin shoulders edge downward, and Agata chats about the Torre di Verdi, mentioning its early roots as a watchtower for armies heading toward Florence. Shading her eyes, Susan is silent, but when Agata turns the subject to Amy's letter and its loss, Susan crosses her ankles tightly. She looks up from the well of her glass.

'I'm quite relieved. She wanted cash, and I've no idea how to get that amount out of a bank so quickly. Perhaps it won't be important.'

Agata cannot decipher the emotions under a face immobilised by makeup. She tells her about the British policeman arriving to question her further and sees the false eyelashes flap. 'You didn't know? I thought they might have phoned you. Have you collected the package?'

'No!' Susan speaks sharply. The dog comes over to lick her toes. She pulls her feet up onto the bench and clutches her knees.

The trill of a phone interrupts. In alarm, Susan topples off the bench, landing awkwardly on the patio, knees in opposite directions. Agata catches the phone before it drops beside her on the bricks. '*Dio mio*, you're nervous. I'll answer it.' She puts it on loudspeaker while Susan rearranges herself.

'Hello? Sue Li, is that you?'

'It's my boss,' Susan whispers. The dog plays a game of pinning her to the ground. She raises her voice. 'Hi, Elliott!'

'Don't 'Hi Elliot' me. You're holidaying in Tuscany, and I'm coping with your shit.'

Agata and Susan stare at each other. Susan pushes the dog away.

'I'm going to be brief, Sue Li. The police asked for your laptop, but we said no, because you have the codes for our system on your portal, and we have to consider our client's confidentiality. I told them to get a bloody court order.'

The lashes click open and shut, and Agata senses Susan has changed colour beneath the pancake foundation.

'Are you there?' says the voice loudly.

'Yes.'

'Do you know what's going on?'

'Do I know what? No. What's going on?' She reaches forward, but Ruby puts large paws on her shoulders and pushes her back.

'You'd better not be playing games with us.' The voice deepens. 'We wondered why the police would want your work laptop, so I decided to have our IT department check it out.'

'There's nothing on my laptop. Just work.' Pushing the dog aside, she scrambles onto the bench.

'Are you stupid or crooked, Sue Li? You've worked for us for fifteen years, and we trusted you. But you've handed over our security and banking codes to your new husband.'

'I didn't. I don't understand.'

'Like hell! He's hacked into our accounts, and it must have been with your help. Our system is state-of-the-art. Do you want to know what he did? He set up a dark web through your portal. Does that mean something to you?' The voice is not asking questions.

As Elliot's voice booms out, Agata puts a finger on the phone to stop the reverberations. 'He's been laundering money through our business. We thought he was a client, selling one painting a month. Instead, he's been using one deal to sell the same painting multiple times for huge sums with payments sent offshore and automated online invoices in your name. Are you so fucking stupid you want me to believe you knew nothing about it? If he weren't already dead, I'd murder the guy myself. This could ruin our business.'

'I don't understand.'

'Look how fast you married the bastard. You saw an opportunity to get rich and screw our company, didn't you? And now, we're going to have to pay thousands to wipe our system and reinstall security procedures. God knows if any of our clients are affected by this. We could be facing lawsuits, and if that happens, I will personally see you go to prison.'

'I'm sorry.'

'Sorry? I'm sure you're sorry, now that we know. You're also sacked.'

Susan curls into a tight foetal ball, chin on her chest,

hands tucked under her bottom. Tears start coursing down her face.

Agata speaks into the phone. 'Hello. This is Agata Agnello. I'm speaking on behalf of the Italian Police. We're here helping Mrs. Verdi, and we understand the British Police are here to re-interview her.'

An enraged shout interrupts. 'I'm not fucking co-operating with the police. We have sensitive clients. Whoever you are, tell Mrs. Verdi from us that she can avoid prison provided she keeps her bloody mouth shut. We'll send through non-disclosure forms now, and if she knows what's good for her, she'll sign. And if the fucking police want her laptop, they can kiss my lawyer's arse.'

The phone goes dead.

Tears are falling, and the black lines have reappeared. Agata sits by her side, placing an arm around the bony shoulders.

'The English and the Italians are not so dissimilar,' she says, trying to lighten the effect of his words. 'More worried about profit dividends than crime. I don't think they'll prosecute you. It would hit the news. And at least you know Alessandro's motivation. Better to know than not?' She hesitates. 'Did you know?'

Black kohl runs in grooves down Susan's cheeks, and Agata sighs. She decides to fetch a tissue and some wet wipes and returns to find the woman rocking back and forth, like a caged animal.

'So maybe you didn't know.' She hands over the tissues.

With a sudden snatch, Susan peels off the fake lashes and throws them like miniature bombs, although they float like feathers. Distraught, she wipes her face as if to remove her cheek bones.

'I'm sorry. I'm sorry. It's all such a shock. I never cry.'

'Alessandro was persuasive.'

She looks at Agata through blackened eyes. 'Did you know him well?'

'I told you. I dated him when I was in my twenties. I spent five years in London as a nanny.'

'Then you believe me when I say he was dazzling? He was lovely. He seemed so genuine. I thought he loved me. I wanted him to love me. I had no idea.'

'I believe you.' Agata remembers his face, his scent. Of course, she believes Susan. She remembers only too well how convincing Alessandro could be.

'I don't think Figaro believes me.' Susan wipes the back of her hand across a reddened nose. 'Sandro asked me to marry him. Not the other way around.' She sobs. 'It was so romantic. Sometimes, he used my computer when his was left behind at his office. He said it was to check on the status of his deals. And sometimes—' She hiccups. '—we looked at art online.'

Agata takes the scrunched wet wipe from Susan's clenched hands, gently wiping the missed blotches. It's been a day of missing what's under their noses. 'Let me get you some water, and we'll think what to do.'

Inside, she pours tap water into a large glass and makes a call to Figgi. It goes to voicemail. 'Figgi, you're hiding in your office, aren't you? Your guest has just been sacked from work. Come back now! I know you don't like emotional women, but they've found out that Alessandro was using her job as a cover for money laundering. At least the British company doesn't want the police involved. And, you ought to know there's an English policeman arrived in town who wants to interview her. Has Luca told you?'

Ruby sneaks into the kitchen and leaps, causing Agata to drop the phone. The case rolls off in the impact, and

Agata grabs both parts, smacking them back together. 'And your dog is out of control,' she shouts, but the voicemail has shut down.

Outside, she hands over the glass and more tissues. 'The important thing is to wait for the package. Hopefully, it will give us more answers. What do you think is in it?'

Susan shakes her head. 'I've never even holidayed abroad, and here I am. How can something so terrible be happening in such a beautiful place?'

Agata purses her lips a moment. 'And who hands over their work portal and codes to someone they barely know? Was that wise?' She presses another tissue into Susan's lap.

Without the false lashes, Susan's eyes are softer and easier to read. 'He was my husband. He was very keen to prove how much he loved me. I mean, he'd do stuff...'

Agata wants to hear, but a part of her doesn't want to hear. Alessandro's sex life with other women is best avoided. Stuffing another tissue in Susan's hand, she waits for the sniffling and wiping to end. Either this woman is a superb actress, or innocent of all but stupidity. After Dr. Albina's comments, Agata no longer trusts her own judgement, but on balance, she wouldn't pick Susan for a criminal capable of internet crime. She hands over another tissue.

In the past when she worked at the *Agenzia*, she felt an innate confidence in her ability to divide truth from lies. Most of her informants were women with sharp nails and hard tongues, selling knowledge of petty criminals in a never-ending game of chase the pickpocket. This weeping fake wife does not feel like an opponent, but Agata cannot rule out the possibility. The one thing she has learned today is the worst bastards bury their crimes deeply, and once the enemy enters the gates, he puts on false robes.

Chapter Eighteen

Six-fifteen the next morning and Luca and Agata are sipping espresso after a sleepless night. The sun peers across the field in its familiar purple blaze as they rehash information. Agata's constant scratching of midge bites irritates him.

He peers on the table at the large A3 sheet covered in scribbles with their pooled information. The migrant girl is next to a bubble about Golden Blood. Agata's news about Alessandro's money laundering, and possible involvement in a criminal gang, sits beside the Syndicate with *Jett?* written in red lettering. Luca has left an a voicemail message at the Hendersons' Airbnb asking to talk to the English policeman and Amy Joliffe, but no one has got back to them. When Agata asked if he had heard about this so-called British Syndicate operating in pockets outside the Mafia, Luca blew out his cheeks in disbelief. He's worked in the city. He knows a thing or two about criminal gangs, and is insistent he has never heard of them.

Agata admits that Figaro also denies such a possibility. 'Figgi told me no Mafia operates in Tuscany. He thinks

Bruno is talking about Lazio or Le Marche, districts known for foreign smuggling gangs.'

'For once, I agree with him,' says Luca in a morose tone. He is out of sorts. This morning, the country air has lost its magic, and the tractor vendor has vanished. Something to do with the farmer not wanting to sell to a policeman in case the damned machine breaks down. He looks at his empty cup. As Agata re-enters the kitchen, he scans again the A3 piece of paper. 'I want you to stop looking at migrant charities and start looking at private clinics.'

She nods. 'Dr. Albina suggested there are places where a black-market trade in organs might be operating here in Tuscany. But as for the girl's identity,'—she swears in exasperation—'I made enough calls yesterday to realise one hand doesn't know what the other hand is doing. The UN branch in Italy doesn't know what the UNICEF offices are doing. JRS Italia doesn't know what International Rescue is doing. Nobody knows what the current government is doing, because there's no cross-referencing. Migrants First exists, and it's possible they've supplied labour to the Jensen house, but I can't find anyone to speak to, which isn't unusual. Most of these tiny charities operate with nothing more than one local volunteer in an office. So, I can't get you the information you need without more time.'

'Leave it. Find the donor, and we find the illegal organ trade. Then we find who murdered the girl. My team is coming at this from the other direction.'

'So, you think the beach murder has nothing to do with Alessandro?' She pours the last of the coffee.

'I can't see it,' says Luca.

They lapse into silence. But Luca isn't as convinced as he sounds. As he turns things over, he finds his opinion changes. Why would Alessandro have the newspaper article in his mouth? Has he been here recently? He sighs. Unfortunately, such deliberations must wait. Today is all about politics. Luca hates the current political environment. A huge police presence is being co-ordinated for the upcoming protest march in Livorno. Two opposing parties are going head-to-head, and intelligence suggests there will be troublemakers in the crowd intent on violence. Many units are arriving to keep order, and he is in charge of one of them.

It's unfamiliar territory to him: Political marches usually take place in Rome, Milan, or Turin. Florence and the Tuscan region, renowned for its ability to negotiate under the auspices of Machiavelli, has had a longstanding knack for avoiding such events. He eases a finger inside his restrictive clothing. Although dressed in jeans and a hoodie, the *Polizia* bullet-proof vest rides up to his chin and makes movement cumbersome.

'Why the hell did the protestors have to choose a northern port?'

Agata answers. 'Migrants have been entering Italy through the Livorno Port for centuries.'

'I know that,' he snaps. 'I was being rhetorical.' But the question still stands. Livorno is too far north to be on today's migrant trail, even if it was a well-known destination a hundred years ago. The whisper is that organised crime is diverting police attention from something more pressing down South, and this whole spectacle is to avert their eyes while gaining press coverage. He hasn't shared this with Agata. This morning, he feels as hostile toward his wife as the protestors.

Her visit to Collodini has hit a nerve. His instincts have always been right about that man. In fact, instinct is too grand a word. The man revelled in playing a grotesque pastiche of the Latin lover. But something else has happened—he can tell she is withholding information. He says nothing, while Agata goes to pick pea pods. That's all that is growing this time of year, unless he counts anger and weeds. At the back of his mind is a worry that as fast as the vegetation grows upward, they're growing apart. The move hasn't brought paradise; it's highlighted their differences.

Without warning, a truck bounces over their field and draws up next to the house in a metallic scrunch of brakes.

Two workmen in overalls jump out with a wave and begin unloading machinery encrusted in dirt. Spitting clods of mud, they wheel them down makeshift wooden ramps and across the stone path. Luca holds up his hands in horror. On any other Saturday, they could have caught him in his pyjamas at this hour.

'Commissario Agnello,' says one, wiping his hand with his T-shirt. '*Buon giorno*. I am Renzo's son. The mayor of Montecatini offers you the loan of equipment for one week. He thinks it will help.'

'What is it?' The huge instruments intrigue Luca.

'This one,' says the older of the two men as he points, 'is very good for big brambles.' He puts large hands lovingly on the engine of the giant shearer. 'It's like a massive hedge trimmer. You hold the handles, and the long clippers snap along the ground. Brrrm. Easy. It destroys everything in its path.' He indicates the fuel tank. 'Full of petrol, Commissario. A gift from me! I live just up the road from you. See that house over there? But damn, your driveway is a bastard to find!'

Luca notes the one distant house with yellow walls largely obscured by woods. He thanks him. 'We keep meaning to put our sign on the road.'

'This other machine,' says the younger man, 'is the giant

rotary hoe. It does all the digging for you. Hold the handles, press here, and go slowly forward! Simple.' He casts an eye over the land. '*Merda*! You've got your work cut out here. Don't knock this into the electric fence, or you'll know all about it when you wake up in Heaven!' He roars with laughter.

The grumpiness seeps from Luca as he looks over the equipment, running an appreciative hand along the circular twisted blades.

'My father had this kind of machinery,' Agata says as she comes out behind him. There is little enthusiasm in her voice. 'My brother, Giuseppe, took it all to his farm near Piombino.'

'Good. In that case, you know how to use it, Commissario!' Renzo's son addresses Luca.

'An espresso?' offers Luca, but they refuse, hopping back into the lorry.

'Can we have them for two weeks instead of one?' Agata turns to Luca. 'We have so much to do this week.'

He agrees, and the older man leans out of the cab. 'Signora—for you—we try to manage without!' The younger man gives a mock salute, and they drive off.

Luca presses one of the handles. 'It looks easy enough, but they're so big. I thought we were doing permaculture gardening.' He touches the key in the ignition. 'The American article Carlo sent us speaks about making the land into lasagne peaks with newspaper and waiting for it to rot down. It's a No Dig method that doesn't release carbon into the atmosphere.' He thinks of his youngest son with warmth, longing to see him next month.

'I can't be doing with all that! This will speed things up.'

Agata's disinterest in his son's scientific endeavours reinflates his irritation. She has not even bothered to read the New Age gardening articles.

'Did you ask Figgi to arrange this?'

'No. His cousin's just died!'

'Then why now?'

'I asked for the machinery some months ago. Growing is hard work. We should have dug the soil in March. Obviously, they've only just finished with it.'

Luca wipes dirt from a brake cable before rubbing his fingers clean. 'This is a killing machine! If the Mafia were here, they'd be proud to own one.'

Grabbing the handles of the largest machine, she shoves it towards their garage. 'A bit of help, please. We can't leave them out—they'll be stolen.'

'Here, in the middle of nowhere? I thought you said no one could find us?'

'You found a dead girl on the beach, didn't you? Besides, the Montecatinese say the Albanese are everywhere and light-fingered.'

'In Rome, they blame the Neapolitans. In Florence, it's the Romans. It's always someone else,' mutters Luca, taking hold of the remaining scissor-jawed machine's handles. He pushes and grunts. 'It's heavier than I thought.' The land may redeem him, but the machinery will give him a hernia. 'Are you sure we need these? I only agreed to a tractor, because every farmer has a tractor.'

'You're a farmer?' she spits.

'We have to start somewhere,' he retorts.

Despite Agata's small stature, she is having more success moving the machine. 'Hurry, Luca. You have to go, and so do I. Today is the Montecatini Saint's Day Festa. I've promised to help Yolanda, and I need to talk to the English sergeant. Why the hell hasn't he phoned you? Both he and

Amy were out last night when I stopped by the Hendersons'.'

'Well, he hasn't.' Luca pits his weight against the recalcitrant machine, and it eases forward. 'And I told you, I rang London to speak to DI Candle, but she's not there. There's a political rally going on in Westminster. Something about their Brexit. The secretary said that half a million people are protesting in London about leaving Europe. Can you imagine? Both of us caught in protests.' He grunts. 'I can't do anything until after this event.'

She opens the worn doors of the storage barn as he experiments turning the key in the ignition. The machine roars into life and shoots forward. Agata steps up to kill the engine with a neat twist.

'You're not fit to be in charge of this,' she says.

'I'm in charge of more important things.' He clicks his fingers. 'So don't expect me at the Festa. It's just a giant party, anyway. I'll send one of the Carabiniere.' Stamping his feet to shake the dust, he leaves her to close the doors.

A rattle of exhaust, and another vehicle drives towards the house.

'What now? I'm going to be late!' Luca nips inside to snatch up his folder, emerging to see Agata greeting Renzo with a kiss on either cheek. The old man is holding a bulging supermarket bag with a Co-operativa label. Although it's Saturday, he has his work clothes on.

'*Buon giorno,* Renzo. Something else from the mayor?'

A mixture of relief and confusion washes across the wrinkled brow. 'Has he said something?'

'Your sons have just delivered the farm machines for us, compliments of the mayor.'

Renzo smiles with yellowed teeth. 'Good.' He thrusts

the bag into Luca's hands. 'I bring fagiolini seeds and some small tomato plugs.'

'That's kind,' says Agata, taking the bag from Luca. 'Aren't you helping with the Festa?'

Renzo pulls at the cuffs of his khaki shirt. 'Commissario. I need advice.'

'Can it wait? I'm heading to Livorno.' The sun emerges fully from behind the trees, and the blue sky whitens under its fierce gaze. 'Look at the time!' Luca points to the horizon, and Renzo shades his eyes.

But the old man is so agitated, he is practically dancing on the spot.

'Why don't you stay and speak to Agata? She will make you coffee.' Luckily, the stoney area in front of the house is wide enough for his car to get around Renzo's old Fiat.

'Your land is hard to find, Commissario. I wanted to come before.'

'Another time.'

Renzo wrings his hands. 'Alessandro Verdi!'

The name stops both Luca and Agata. 'Something new?' says Luca.

Renzo screws up his wrinkled face and then pops out a rehearsed speech in one giant breath, ending with, 'He was here—he came to Casa Verdi, maybe three weeks ago—he swore Natale and me to say nothing, but now he's dead!'

Luca pulls a long face. 'Have you told the Verdis?'

The old man shakes his head, looking at their path as if a way out will reveal itself. Luca and Agata look at each other. He can see she is thinking what he's thinking. Renzo has chosen to tell him—the police—before speaking to Verdi Senior.

'Does Natale know you're here?'

'No. I said I was going to get fertiliser, a little chicken

shit. She doesn't like to come with me because the bags stink. But Commissario, I had to tell someone. Otherwise we're accessories, aren't we?'

'No,' says Agata firmly.

But that isn't what worries Luca. If old man Verdi finds Renzo has spoken to the police before the family, the repercussions for Renzo will be severe. Long ago, he worked for the Verdis before entering the police, and he knows Giorgio Verdi operates like a dictator. On the other hand, Agata doesn't seem as shocked as Luca feels, which increases his irritation. He steps closer to Renzo.

'Let's make this a secret between us until we see if it's important or not. Perhaps no one needs to know. Can you stay and give all the details to Agata? We won't involve you unless a witness comes forward to claim they've seen you two together.'

The old man is effusively grateful. 'I'm sure no one saw us,' he says, shaking Luca's hand as if someone has taken a huge sack from his back rather than a plastic bag.

'I'll make espresso,' says Agata. 'Give me the details.' She goes to the kitchen without meeting Luca's eyes. She has that look that tells him she isn't giving the full story, but he's in too much of a rush.

'You need help with this land.' Renzo is reluctant to see Luca go and leans in at the car window.

'Very kind,' says Luca. 'But don't worry.' He wants to stay, but knows he must get to Livorno before Fabio. Releasing the clutch, he lets the car bounce over the stones.

At the turn in the bend where the path meets the coastal road, the frustration of the morning's events bursts from him. Luca swears and thumps the wheel as he drives. It's bad enough that the news is full of Italy breaking open with the influx of migrants, and all Europe is breaking apart in a stampede started by the English, but his little piece of paradise is also crumbling. *Coglioni* English islanders and *coglioni* Lega Nord and Italian politics—*coglioni* pick-pockets on scooters and *coglioni* murderers of children—arseholes, all of them. And the biggest arsehole was always Alessandro Verdi, though no one ever called him that. Yet Luca has never forgotten the taunting and teasing when he went to London at Verdi Senior's request. It is twenty-five years since Alessandro and his friends tripped him at every turn, making him the butt of their puerile jokes, but he hasn't forgotten.

Then he remembers meeting Agata, her kindness and her confidence. The way she took his side when the Verdi's pranks became extreme, and even a quarter of a century later, he feels the same frisson of surprise that she ditched her privileged English life to come home and marry him. He hasn't forgotten that, either.

Chapter Nineteen

They walk along the old road toward the Tower. Dressed in his best linen, Figgi is cool. Susan wears the same gold and white dress with unsuitable sandals from last night. Her attire is no match for a steep hill climb, although she looks beautiful, in a Faberge Easter egg way.

'This route is more direct than the main road. I'm sorry we have to walk, but parking is a problem on Festa days.' Despite the picturesque surroundings, he has felt the need to apologise several times. Her brooding silence makes conversation difficult.

They stop to rest in the shade of a wooded curve in the road, and he points out the old abandoned schoolhouse, ivy bursting through the roof; small stone wells that tap into underground streams; pruned olive trees, their leaf mass in the shape of a bowls; neat lines of grapevines, evidence of small-scale wine production. It is barely nine, and the folds of mist have cleared.

'Do you see the roofs on that far ridge? Agata and her husband live near there.'

She gazes out but says nothing.

By the end of the climb, he has run a monologue marathon, and welcomes the hubbub of the crowded square. Every table in Yolanda's cafe is occupied, and Sylvio's Bar Media is doing good business with early Prosecco. Market stalls line the road from the *farmacia* to the post office. Some vendors offer speciality meats and cheeses; others display colourful flowers and jewellery. As they traverse the square, children jostle them, dashing around the bronze war memorial statue in the centre. Figaro smiles, his public smile, acknowledging people as they pass. Susan attracts stares, but no one speaks directly to her.

In a special Festa outfit, Yolanda greets Mayor Figaro. The face of the medieval Montecatini Saint adorns her apron, stretching across her bosom. Behind her, the colours of the Italian flag hang next to the sign, La Pizzeria. She cuts a cheery, plump figure. 'The parking! Already, the arguments.' She brushes Figgi's cheeks with a double kiss before turning to Susan. 'You are the guest,' she says. 'Good to meet. Espresso? Free from me.'

He shakes his finger. 'I shall pay.'

She ignores him. 'So. You Susan. I speak English. You say what you want.'

Spotting Figaro, people shift upward on the cafe bench, allowing them a sliver of space to sit down.

'Agata asked us to look for Amy,' says Figgi in English for Susan's benefit. 'Has she come into the square yet?'

'Soon. She come.' Yolanda scans the road towards the post office. 'Every morning for this week, she here. She ask to do waitress yesterday. She want money.'

Figgi raises sandy eyebrows and one hand revolves in a dismissive gesture. When will tourists learn there aren't enough jobs even for the locals?

Yolanda bends to Susan. 'I speak to you English. My partner is Danish. We speak many languages. Always I say to *stranieri*, you need something, then you say to me.' She takes out a pad and pen from a pocket behind the Saint's face.

Susan's face is a Mona Lisa stare, and Figgi wonders if a full smile might crack the foundation.

'*Stranieri* means foreigners,' he says. 'In Montecatini, if you're from Rome, you're a foreigner.'

'Is true.' Yolanda's eyes sparkle. 'I tell you the *padroni* of the Tower are new to Montecatini. From Rome. They are *stranieri*.' She points her pen upward, and Susan twists around to see the imposing outline of the Tower against the sky. 'Naomi D'Angelo dress like you. Very good fashion.'

Figgi thinks Susan is blushing under her makeup. 'We have an appointment with my father in the city at noon,' he says, 'but I'll be back for the evening Festa.'

'Of course. You are the mayor.' Yolanda manages to convey both interest and disapproval at the same time. She speaks again to Susan. 'You meet the Tower's *padrone*. He is a doctor. Doctor Umberto D'Angelo. Very *simpatico*. Speaks good English.' Yolanda lowers her voice. 'He work at Lampedusa Island with migrants. Now he not work. When the girl is murder on beach, some say he cut up migrants for work. *Il Macellaio*. But eat here, and I make sure you safe.' She winks.

Figgi raps the wooden table again. 'Yolanda! None of your jokes.'

She chuckles, and some German tourists stop their conversation and stare.

'You're supplying Umberto with some of the food for the Festa, and he is paying you good money.' He catches the look in Susan's heavily kohled eyes. She reminds him of a farm animal backing away from a branding. 'Calm, Susan. The man used to work for Unicef. Now he runs the Tower as an Airbnb. There are no murderers here.' He speaks in a hearty voice for the benefit of the nearby listeners.

'But he order more food from the Trattoria than me, so perhaps he is a cornflake murderer.' She presses the menu pad against her heart in a fake dramatic gesture. 'Now, I get you coffees. Free! I insist.'

As she marches into the cafe, Figaro apologises for Yolanda's joke and lowers his voice. 'Restaurant wars! She wanted Umberto to order more from her than the Trattoria della Torre opposite. But it's true, some have nicknamed him the Butcher because of his work on Lampedusa. He used to cut the little fingers off the unnamed dead. It was the only way to keep a DNA record to help those searching for relatives. It's the common practice.' He watches her face closely for reaction, but she looks away, studying the shops.

She is as upright and brittle as a dried twig. Figgi feels a flicker of irritation. Her attitude will make things more difficult with his father, who already believes her guilty.

'The Festa brings in a great deal of money for the community. It's fun.'

'He murdered someone?' Susan whispers at length.

The Germans have gone back to their conversation and are no longer listening. 'No. She's joking.' He drums his fingers on the table. 'Some of the locals started nasty rumours, after the girl died at the beach.'

'The newspaper article. I remember. And he's from outside the town?' Her eyes fix on the Tower. 'I'm from outside the town.'

'Technically, you're a tourist. That's different. Umberto retired the year the news recorded UN personnel exploiting female migrants. It was in all the papers. Then he came here. Family money allowed him to buy the Tower. But you know what people are like; they make something of nothing.'

'What are they making of me? Why are people staring?'

He stops and looks around. Quite a few of the local families have fixed her in their sights. 'They're probably wondering why a strange Oriental lady is in town with me.'

The lashes blink. As soon as the words are out, he realises he's said the wrong thing, but he's not sure why. 'Perhaps it's your city makeup,' he adds.

Her hands wind tightly on the bag in her lap, and she looks downward.

He keeps talking. 'Dr. D'Angelo is a good man. He has two sons and an adopted Nigerian son. He did valuable work on Lampedusa.'

Yolanda returns, placing a tray in front of them. 'And here, the Devil!' The pen points again toward the Tower. A steep cobbled path joins the Tower to the lower main square. Old stone houses tightly flank the way, and in the middle, arm in arm, step a silver-haired couple. The man has a goatee beard and wears neatly pressed trousers and polished shoes. In his free hand, he holds a walking cane with a gold top. Next to him, his wife is sleekly belted into a floral dress. She has an open friendly face, and her hair is coiffed into a grey silken bun. Upon seeing Figaro, they light up.

'*Il Sindaco*! The mayor!'

'*Dottore*, please take a seat.' Figaro greets them warmly. The Germans look up and, having finished, rise and move away. Figgi motions for the couple to join them.

'This is Alessandro's widow.'

He hasn't used the term widow before, but he assumes

they don't know the full story about Mariju, and he is right. They smile and give kisses on both cheeks.

'I'm Naomi. You poor dear.' Her contralto voice vibrates with emotion as she sweeps a hand over the cafe bench to remove a speck before perching next to them. 'We're so sorry for your loss. Although we didn't actually know Alessandro.'

'But sad, nonetheless,' says Umberto. 'Please don't let that stop you coming to the Festa tonight. The Saint's Days celebrations have been a tradition here for hundreds of years. We are proud to honour the Verdi customs.'

Figaro raises a hand for more coffees, and Yolanda nods with an innocent smile.

'Where are your sons?' asks Figgi.

'Setting up the garden. We've just popped into the square to check on our menus.'

'And how is Edu?'

'Ever since the police visit, he's been nervous in company. We don't insist he's out tonight.'

'Crystal said something about that.'

They all turn to Susan in surprise at her comment.

'The American woman?' says Naomi, with a laugh. 'Ignore her. She's newer in town than we are. Terrible business with her aunt, poor lady.'

Figgi stirs sugar into his coffee. 'I must apologise for the police's handling of things. I heard about it from the Commissario's wife.'

'Edu's childhood was traumatic.' Umberto places the cane across his knees and his deep brown eyes fill with sadness. 'We thought we could give him a good life in the Italian countryside. I hope we're not mistaken.'

'We should have known about gossip and small towns, but when we had the chance to buy the Tower...' Naomi engages Susan. 'Everything was fine at first, until this murder upset the place. Of course, we have faith that Commissario Agnello will solve the crime.'

A sudden shout stops their conversation dead. An old woman in a black dress calls out to the square. She is stooped, but her cries are louder than a crow's as she shakes an empty two-litre water bottle for attention. '*Auitame, auitame*!'

In an instant, customers from Bar Media and La Pizzeria rise to her calls for help, moving as one toward her. She pushes past them and wheezes over to Figaro, gabbling details. Catching the corners of her words, the Italian cafe's customers run in the indicated direction. Curious locals outstrip everyone in their eagerness to pass the Festa stalls and the post office, jogging toward the communal water fountains. Tourists follow behind.

'Where are they going? What's happening?' Susan is at Figgi's side as Umberto and Naomi fall behind.

'Someone's injured near the communal refuse bins,' says Figgi.

The group passes the Municipal Centre, a grand, century-old civic building. People surge across the frontage, jumping the low walls to get ahead of each other. In front, a glut of young men stop abruptly by three large blue and green recycling bins. Each bell-shaped receptacle overflows with wine bottles, cardboard, and plastic cartons. Behind them, someone has dumped two dirty mattresses, and the first onlooker moans.

Figaro arrives and shoves his way through to see two sparkly trainers poking from underneath one mattress. The young men begin to lift the striped bedding, fists gripped to the ticking, but Figgi shouts for them to stop. Jostling, the crowd cranes to see what is beneath, as the boys suspend the mattress for a second. That is all it takes before they drop it like a brick and recoil. Figgi throws out both arms to prevent others from coming forward. 'Crime scene! Touch nothing.' He repeats this in several languages.

Only the nearest, like Susan, have seen the full horror: the clear incision on the girl's stomach, a moment of bare midriff flesh curled like a pork rind with a bloodied diamond in the middle, and the mass of intestines flopped in ringlets to one side, blood everywhere.

'Amy. My God, Amy,' Susan breathes with lashes wide, a black rim to the whites of her eyes.

From the corner of his eye, Figgi catches a red Cinquecento parking by the water fountains. He calls to Agata who is already running towards him. Susan reaches the kerb, doubles over, and retches in the street gutter as Agata runs past her. She takes in the sparkly trainers and splashes of blood. Their eyes meet. He whispers the detail of the incision on the girl's stomach, and she nods. Amy knew Alessandro; Amy is killed in the same manner as the girl on the beach. Here is the undeniable evidence that Alessandro's murder and the child's murder are linked. More palpable than a piece of paper in his mouth, they see at once the relevance of the girl's torso: There is no doubt the enemy is within.

Chapter Twenty

Agata grasps Susan's elbow, yanks her up from the storm drain, and propels her along to Naomi and Umberto. Susan's head is reeling, her mouth sharp with bile. The D'Angelos stand frozen by the side of the road. Umberto leans on his cane, one hand over his heart, while Naomi clutches the beads at her neck like a rosary.

'Take her back to Casa Verdi,' Agata orders. 'Go on. Go. Both of you. I'll phone Luca. Figaro and I will deal with this until the police get here.'

'Edu is up at the Tower,' says Naomi. Her voice is a gravelly whisper.

'He'll be fine,' says Agata, 'but you two need to get out of here before some idiot points a finger.'

Umberto nods. 'The Festa tonight?'

Again, Agata reassures them, addressing Susan in a half smile. 'Do you think the Notting Hill Carnival stops because of crime? Of course, the Festa will go ahead.'

Susan's rib cage heaves with shock. In contrast to the surrounding fracas, Agata is icily calm.

Coaches with tourists are attempting to park, nosing forward a centimetre at a time to fit into the marked slots by the water fountains. Agata tells Umberto that the road will soon be blocked, and they need to hurry. She pushes all three of them with a firm hand.

Stumbling behind Umberto, Susan struggles to move against the flow of pedestrians. Halfway down, Naomi prods her towards a Jeep parked outside the Municipal Centre.

'We left it here last night. The road to the Tower will be impassable today, but I think we can squeeze through the Piazza.'

Umberto manoeuvres his green beast of a Range Rover through a 180-degree turn, narrowly avoiding clumps of wide-eyed people. With a quick burst on his horn, he traverses the square before pressing the pedal to descend the hill. The Jeep skids round hairpin bends, throwing Susan against the window.

With a jerk, they pull over at the Madonna's water fountain and get out. Susan swings her legs out in confusion. Looking up, she sees a kestrel hovering in thermal drafts, head down, waiting for prey in the field. For a moment, she sees herself as the mouse. But who is the hawk? Why didn't she pay Amy? Why didn't she go to the nearest cash point, pull out some money, and negotiate for the letter? At least then, the poor kid would be back to London.

'You look green. Have a drink,' says Naomi, pulling on the ceramic knob by the side of a stone lion.

Susan takes a sip, splashing her chin. She asks why they have stopped when they are within sight of Casa Verdi, but in response Umberto and Naomi break into a heated argument in Italian. She hears Edu mentioned more than once as she swills more water and spits the remains of her vomit into the stone basin. Her phone gives a muffled ping in her bag, and for an irrational moment, she thinks it's Amy.

But the text is from an unidentified number. It is in Italian and English.

Your recorded package is ready for collection at Volterra, Cafe Priori, Piazza del Priori. Please bring identification, passport or driving licence, and this barcode.

She's never heard of the courier company. The text says they will keep the package for three days before returning it to the head office in Milan. The sun beats down on the ancient walls of Volterra, a valley's length away. It stands like a taunt on the adjacent ridge. Too far to walk.

Naomi interrupts her thoughts. 'Look, we don't know if you've heard the rumours, but I think it's best to explain.'

Umberto puts a hand on his wife's forearm. 'We don't want to alarm you, but the locals will suggest it was us,' says Umberto. 'We may be a target, especially Edu.'

'When the UN story broke.' Naomi begins, but frustrated tears follow.

'They nicknamed me the Butcher,' he says. '*Il Macelliao*.' His face is the grey of his beard. 'We'd like to bring Edu down to Casa Verdi for the next few hours. Is that all right?'

Susan can think of nothing but the package. 'I need to collect something from Volterra. It's really urgent. Can you take me there?'

Naomi is stung by her response, taking it as a refusal. 'Figaro knows we're unconnected with these murders. I promise you.' Another look passes between them.

'You don't understand,' Susan says. 'It's not about Edu. I need to go to Volterra. It's urgent. Connected to Alessandro's death.'

They look at her with blackened eyes. 'And we need to get back for Edu. That's urgent, too. Do you understand?' Umberto's voice deepens in anger.

Naomi nudges her husband. 'Wait. Why doesn't Edu drop her off. It's the perfect excuse for him to be gone.'

'Can he drive that thing?' Susan looks at the monster of a Jeep.

'He's eighteen, and I taught him,' says Umberto. It's clear he regards their troubles as sorted. Half the subsequent phone conversation is in Italian. Umberto is pleading, then smiles. 'Good. Take your usual route, and we'll meet you there.'

They usher her into the back of the Jeep and Umberto puts his foot hard on the accelerator. Turning with proficient speed, he heads back to the old road that Susan and Figgi climbed earlier. Within 200 metres, the road is too narrow for the vehicle to pass, and he edges into a secluded dead end near the abandoned school building. They wait in heavy silence. The distant sound of a police siren echoes across the valley, but in minutes, Edu arrives, panting heavily. He appears out of thin air, running through an olive grove rather than along the road. There are flakes of mud attached to his short hair. The boy's face is screwed with anger, but he gets into the driver's seat without a word. His parents wave and start walking up the hill.

'Sit in the front,' he says to Susan. 'I'm not a paid chauffeur.' His English is accented but fluent.

Scrambling in beside him, she stammers her thanks. There is no attempt at conversation as he races towards the valley floor. His control of the vehicle is astonishingly competent for his age. They pass fields of cows and tiny bridges and isolated farmhouses. Within a short space of time, they enter another set of hairpin bends as they start the ascent to Volterra.

'You drive really well, and I'm grateful for the lift.' She feels she ought to say something.

'My Babo is a good teacher,' he replies.

'Your father? Umberto?'

'Umberto is my adoptive parent. My sponsor. My Babo. My real father is dead.' The boy's eyes never waver from the road as he spins the Jeep around the steep approaching bends, following the route to the ancient city walls. Large hewn slabs of stone are dotted with white daisies, poppies, and signs for various trattorias. He turns first right, then left, then right again.

'I'm sorry for your loss,' she says. 'My father is also dead. He died last year.'

'My father was murdered five years ago by militants.'

It's impossible to respond to this. She looks up as they approach the large city gates. A thick, rusty chain keeps the portcullis raised. Underneath, a press of people come and go. He brakes.

'I'm not stopping. You understand? You get out here.'

'You're going back to Casa Verdi?'

'No.' His frown deepens.

'Umberto said—'

'I don't care what they told me. I'll park at Casa Verdi and walk to the Tower. What sort of son would leave his parents to the anger of a mob?'

Susan's fingers tighten on her bag. 'Do you really think there'll be an angry mob?' She remembers the German tourists drinking coffee and laughing next to her in the square. The crowd seemed harmless, but she also remembers the way people stared at her.

'What would you know? You've been here a minute.

We're all strangers to them. And worse—we're rich strangers with unknown money.'

Susan shrinks from the bitter words of one so young. She cannot remember ever having felt his level of anger. 'I'm sure the mayor will stop things getting out of hand.' She wants to reassure him, but maybe he's right. Relief floods through her at the distance she has put between herself and the town. In the city of Volterra, she can masquerade as just one more tourist. Then she feels a stab of guilt at her selfishness.

'If you're looking for the main Piazza, the Piazza del Priori, go up. It's at the top of that narrow cobbled road.' Edu points to huge city gates. 'Text the mayor, and he'll come and get you when all is calm.' Ignoring her thanks, Edu's hands revolve the steering wheel. The Jeep executes a rapid three-point turn and vanishes.

Chapter Twenty-One

The gates are open; two studded doors stand high enough for a giant's castle. To one side, a plaque says Porto Romano. The entrance to the city is authentically medieval, but Susan senses she is surrounded by a strange newness. Three catering vans are parked opposite the gates, serving food to a bizarre queue of medieval soldiers drinking from polystyrene containers. Others in tunics or rough jerkins sit in a partly excavated Roman amphitheatre, drinking Coke. A group of women in sacking with braided hair smoke modern cigarettes, chatting by a crumbling ancient wall. Beside them, in plastic breastplates, sandals, and leather skirts, men flip through iPhones.

Eager for social media opportunities, tourists are taking photographs. At last, Susan has her wish. She is completely invisible and unremarkable amongst this outlandish crew. Absorbed in taking pictures, a young couple walk past, chatting about the filming of their favourite American drama. She tries to catch the name, but it's not familiar.

Changing her phone from Wi-Fi to data—hang the cost—she inputs *Bar del Priori* on her app. It works. The destination is nearby and leads her under the portcullis and, just as Edu said, a cobbled street rises steeply. Ahead people jostle outside bars and gift shops. The narrow road looks pedestrianised, until a small Fiat presses through, unworried about life and limb or small dogs. She dodges to one side, flattening herself against a shop front. Weaving in and out, she walks upward toward the apex of the road, where a huge stone building creates a T-junction. She can turn left or right. The app points right.

Before her, the space opens into the large Piazza del Priori, surrounded by medieval edifices of marble and stone, more Florentine than Montecatinese. Some buildings have geometric designs of white and black marble embellished with gargoyles, but at ground level, the film crew have been busy masking the shop fronts with mock medieval surfaces. A few horses wait patiently in the shade of a cathedral, their hooves kicking in strewn straw, while film fans mix with actors and crew, chatting and looking at the camera equipment. Some costumed men have realistic knives strapped to their belts. In the sunlight, they create an aura of both fantasy and menace. Susan hesitates. Her fear is irrational, yet firmly entrenched in what she has witnessed half an hour earlier. Any of these actors could be the thugs that had targeted Alessandro or split open his messenger, Amy. Her stomach squeezes.

What if the person who took the letter is coming for the package? What if that person is now coming for her? The texts from Alessandro's phone prove someone is tracking her, and she can only hope the impromptu method of her arrival in the city keeps her one step ahead. *Il Macellaio* and his family know she is here, but no one else. She presses her bag to her chest, reassuring herself there is safety in numbers. Then she extracts her phone and texts Figaro.

I've escaped to Volterra for a coffee. Sorry.

Can you collect me at the Porto Romano when you're free? Susan.

A young man and woman hold hands and look around in awe. 'I love this place. Second year I've come. I'm so glad you could come with me.' The girl turns to give the man a kiss. 'So great you're a fan of the series, too.'

Susan asks if they know which of the fake facades hides the Bar Priori.

'Sure.' The boy looks her up and down, taking in her city apparel and full makeup. They are in casual holiday mode, but she fits in with some of the richer tourists. 'It's right there. All the bars are open.'

Thanking them, she hurries under the camouflaged doorway. Behind the chipboard fascia, a neon sign is unlit and partially covered with hessian cloth. The cafe is full of customers, both actors in full costume and visitors. Behind the till, a man in a white T-shirt takes money and gives orders to a young woman sweating in front of a coffee machine. Susan has difficulty pushing through to catch someone's eye.

'Excuse me. Packet.' She waves her phone screen.

The girl nods. '*Pacchetto*!' she calls, and the white shirted man dives into a backroom. He returns with three parcels and shouts to the entire cafe.

'Pantelli. Thomasino. Verdi.'

Two other people arrive at her side.

'*Passoporti o codici fiscale*,' he demands. The others produce an ID card and put up their phones for him to flash the barcodes. Susan waves her passport, then her mobile. The packets are duly distributed.

Thankfully, the envelope is as small as Amy suggested. It is A5 size and easily fits in her bag. Plunging it to the bottom, she pushes out into the sunshine. The light hits her eyes, sharp and relentless, just as the crew calls to the crowd. An army of soldiers hurry to take up places. As another call goes out in English and German, they leak from every stone arch and alleyway.

'All spectators, please leave the set.'

Efficiently, plastic cordons are unrolled. A man with heavy black eyeliner and thick stubble mutters curses under his breath, shoving lingerers in order to reach the inner sanctum. Moving back to let him through, a woman with gold hooped earrings steps hard on Susan's toe. Susan pulls up her leg in pain and is jostled backwards, falling into a cushion of elbows and handbags that rake her bare arms.

'Sorry.'

One hand tries to steady her, but another tries to snatch her bag. Automatically, her fingers tighten on the handles, and she grips her treasure. A second pull makes her stagger further backward, as she struggles to keep upright. The tussle jerks her shoulder, but she holds all the tighter. As she twists, she turns and falls, pitching to the ground, knocking against a tall woman, who swears at her in Italian.

'Sorry.'

A cry sounds to her left. Susan glimpses a baseball cap and a figure running. Fists are waved, but the figure darts across the Piazza, toward one of the smaller roads.

'Hey, he nearly got my bag!' A shrill voice is full of indignation and an older man makes a show of giving chase, but the crew have closed the route and refuse him access.

'Are you all right?' Someone helps Susan up before putting a protective arm on their companion. 'He tried to grab my bag as well,' she says, and they commiserate with her.

Susan presses the bag tightly to her chest as the crowd is

hushed. The film director speaks into his megaphone. 'Move on out now, please ladies and gentlemen. Actors take your positions.'

'Damn, I think he got my wallet.' A stout leather faced man is patting his pockets. 'I didn't feel a thing, but it's gone.'

Within seconds, paranoia infects everyone. There is a general clutching of possessions and fingers scrabbling to itemise jacket pockets as people peel away, dispersing down lanes. A local Carabiniere in a blue uniform and white sash arrives, asking questions in Italian.

Afraid to be caught up in police activity, Susan flees down the cobbled road towards the Porto Romano. Some indefinable instinct tells her this wasn't a random pick-pocket and that someone had targeted her bag and the A5 envelope. She holds it like a baby. A touch to her elbow makes her shriek.

Crystal steps back. 'Jeez, sorry, I didn't mean to frighten you.'

'Crystal! What are you doing here?'

'I had to collect medicines from the hospital. It's round the corner.' The American holds aloft a large white paper bag with a green cross. 'It's for my Auntie Linda. God, I can't believe my luck that the filming was here. I love 'Da Vinci's Secret'. Have you ever watched it? Fabuloso.'

Susan laughs uneasily. 'I've never seen it, sorry.'

'Huh? On your own? What are you doing here?'

'I had to get away from Montecatini. Have you heard about Amy?'

Crystal's bright hazel eyes fix on Susan who explains they've found Amy's body by the refuse bins.

'Hot damn. Poor kid. I saw a police car going up toward Montecatini. You can hear them as they cross the valley.

They put the sirens on all the way. But I thought it was some petty crime. A theft on the Festa day. I always carry pepper spray.' She takes out a small, insignificant-looking canister.

'Why didn't I think of that?' She feels better to be near Crystal, who exudes confidence. It's as if the woman has lived here all her life.

Crystal hooks elbows with Susan, jostling them through the crowds. 'Jeez. You're shaking. What happened?'

'It was terrible. She was split open.' The memory makes Susan gag, and Crystal tightens her elbow grip.

'It's okay, Sue. Don't think about it. By the sounds of it, this is the same thing as that kid on the beach. Voodoo, that's what they'll say. Or the D'Angelos. You won't be the target, so don't worry.'

Susan giggles with nerves.

'Big breaths.' She squeezes Susan's elbow.

At the Porto Romano, the film company's catering truck is without customers and the street is clearer. Susan wonders if Figgi has got her text.

'Where's your car?'

'I'm getting a lift.'

'I'm heading back now. Why don't I take you? You don't wanna hang around here on your own, do you?'

'Figaro is probably on his way.'

'Nah!' she barks a laugh. 'The mayor? Jeez, you don't know Italy. He'll be hours with the police. They'll be sitting sipping coffees and grappas while they do the paperwork. And then it's Siesta time. Anyway, there's just one road back, so if he's on the way—which he isn't—we'll easily see him and flag him down. If we get home first—which we will —then text him.'

'I don't know.'

Crystal shrugs. 'Well, you really don't know the Verdi family. They'll take any crime in Montecatini as a personal affront to their authority in town. They won't kill you, but they might even frame you. Who knows? You're new here. You're clearly not Italian. Stran-year-i. Last in, first out to prison!' She laughs and squeezes Susan's elbow again.

Her argument is uncomfortably persuasive. Susan hesitates.

'C'mon,' says Crystal gently. 'Let's go somewhere quiet and have a girly coffee. Or maybe a Prosecco or two. Take your mind off things. I'm a nurse, and I can see you're in shock. My car's here, and my ticket's running out.' She points to a battered, silver Volvo parked in one of the few slots by the old Roman Amphitheatre.

Susan mouths an okay, but as they go to cross the road, a squeal of tyres makes them both jump back. Agata pulls up. 'I've found you! I couldn't believe it when Edu said you'd come here.'

Crystal squints her electric hazel eyes. 'Who are you?'

'Agata, Yolanda's sister. The Pizzeria?'

Crystal's smooth brow barely registers surprise.

'And you must be Linda Jensen's niece,' says Agata.

'Yeah. I was going to take Sue back.'

'She has an appointment with Giorgio Verdi in Livorno, and Figaro is waiting at the police station in Ponteginori for her. I must take her.'

'Leave the poor girl alone. Can't you see she's in shock? We're going for a coffee. I can take her to Ponteginori if you want.'

'No,' says Agata in a firm voice.

Susan has never had anyone fight for her company. It is an odd sensation, and she prickles with irritation at Agata's curt insistence. A cappuccino in a cafe with Crystal sounds far preferable to a confrontation with Alessandro's uncle. She wonders how to put that politely, but Agata is unsmiling, standing with hands on hips.

Crystal lets out a puff of irritation. 'Okay. *La famiglia, la famiglia*—what did I tell you, Sue? Pa Verdi calls, and we must do his bidding.' She rattles her car keys. 'Speak later! Don't do anything I wouldn't do!'

'Sorry,' says Susan to Crystal's retreating form.

'Get in.' Agata opens the car door. 'What the hell were you thinking of? You might be in danger.'

Susan is irritated enough to speak her mind. 'Escape. I was thinking of escape. Especially as Edu said there might be a mob at the Tower.'

'What mob?' Agata tuts and releases the handbrake. 'Figgi has dealt with the crowd. Carabinieri are there, and the sad truth is Amy's death is little more than exciting gossip. No one knew her, and I'm ashamed to say that probably no one cares. They are looking forward to the Festa. Poor child. That's the way of the world.'

La Traviata is on the radio. The car flies across the valley in a blaze of colour and opera, allowing a taciturn silence between them. Agata nearly ditches the car on a corner as a beige and white camper van careens around them, but neither of them say so much as an expletive.

Along a stretch of straight road, Agata repeats her questions about Susan's movements, but Susan is disinclined to trust anyone in the Verdis' pay.

'I went to the bank,' she says. 'I should have gone before. I should have taken the money, given it to Amy, and then taken the letter. Don't you see? Then she'd still be alive.'

'We don't know why she was killed. I told you the letter was stolen yesterday.' Agata takes a left-hand road and follows a railway line.

They arrive at a bedraggled village where Agata is forced to slow. Worn cafes, functional shops, and a petrol station tell Susan this is not a tourist destination. She looks down at her feet in the car well. Dirt streaks between the painted toes.

'They've arrested Lilian Henderson, Carl's mother,' says Agata. 'That will quell the crowd. Lilian's too infirm to have done something like that, but the community is happy with an arrest.'

'What about Dr. D'Angelo?'

'After the whole mess with Edu last time, Fabio opted for a different tactic.' Agata's mouth sets in a tense line. Susan avoids further questions and hangs onto her seat belt as the car traverses a roundabout at speed. They shoot past a small wooded area and enter the next town, where the sign says Ponteginori.

'Lilian has a vicious mouth, nothing more,' Agata spits in anger as she drives the car into the police carpark. 'She's lived in Montecatini for ten years. But the locals would riot if the police arrested Umberto or Naomi today. Nothing must cancel the Festa.' She brakes and rubs her finger and thumb together in the universal language of money. 'Here you are. Now get out.'

Chapter Twenty-Two
The road to Livorno

In the last ten years, Figgi has stopped responding to his father's dictatorial demands. He is poised to take over the business from the old man. But two deaths are two too many, so he thinks it won't hurt for his father to interrogate Susan. His only concern is whether Susan will turn into a bellowing cow. He has bought some extra packets of tissues.

As they drive toward Livorno, she sits passively beside him. Her dark eyes flicker from the road to his face. They look at each other for a second before she returns to watching the fields.

'My father can be severe,' he says. 'It's just his way.'

As the wind rushes at them, she pulls a scarf from her bag and ties it around her hair to stop the strands from blotting her eyes. He catches himself thinking of a young Sophia Loren.

Speeding down thin roads, they pass small villages with nothing more than a sign for a solitary trattoria. Silently, he rehashes the hasty arrest of Lilian Henderson in his mind. It's absurd—a by-product of gossip. Some eyewitness claimed to hear Lilian shouting in the *Allumentari* about how she would kill any girl who tried to take away her son. But under such distress, rumours fly like fireflies, and the arrest—however illogical—has had the effect of calming everyone.

Agata's quick phone call confirms the release of Carl's mother. Lilian has been sent home to remain under house arrest. Figgi thanks her for completing the paperwork. On the hands-free, he checks a voicemail from Naomi, who acknowledges a last-minute demand for Festa tickets, so no harm done. Murder sells. Who knew?

A blue sign shows ten kilometres to Livorno, a green sign shows eight on the motorway. On impulse, Figgi keeps to the coastal road. This route is quieter, and he could do with the calming effect of the countryside. They pass billboards and scenic stretches of bushes, flanked by the sea. As if determined to destroy peace, his father calls. Figgi assures him they are on their way.

Susan is kneading the brocade bag on her lap, and again Figgi wonders what she was doing in Volterra. She hasn't made this clear. Why go to the bank in the city, when there is a small branch in Montecatini? Why go to the bank when Amy is now dead? Perhaps she was repaying the money into her account. That's the most logical explanation.

A row of dark-skinned girls takes their attention. Positioned at 200-metre intervals along the road, they sit on bar stools by the verges.

'How odd? What are they doing?' Susan frowns.

In suggestive poses, the girls sit like mannikins. Their arched backs and pert breasts thrust out through tight dresses, slim, bare thighs on show.

Figgi clenches the wheel. Normally he uses the motorway, and he's forgotten cruisers use this road. The Verdis have a perennial campaign to clear them away, but always they return.

Susan's eyelashes widen as she twists to look over her shoulder. They pass another four girls, each holding a mirror in a hand, some applying lipstick.

'What are they doing?' she repeats.

A man in a leather jacket, phone clamped to his ear, leans into the road, staring at oncoming traffic.

'What do you think?' Figgi overtakes a car that is slowing down and pulling off.

'Prostitution? Here?'

'Traffickers force them to repay loans.'

'Why don't they apply for asylum?'

Can she really be so naive? He frowns, aiming to put some distance between the unwanted scene and his car. 'The EU insists we process migrants in the first country of their arrival. That's either Greece or Italy. But most migrants don't want to be here. They want to get passage to England or Germany.'

'Don't they get stopped by police?'

'Of course, but the police move them on.' He sighs. 'I'm sorry, I should have taken the motorway. I rarely come this way.' He's annoyed that he feels the need to justify himself.

The kohl eyes look at him.

'Look, Susan. You have to understand how things work in Italy. The surge in far-right politics is due to the migrant situation. Minister Salvini is campaigning on a slogan: 'Prima agli Italiani'—Italians First. He says he will deport all migrants back to Africa without trial. Many are saying Italy has reverted to the way it was in World War Two, when Rome was an open city, unable to control our borders.'

'Open city?'

Of course, she knows nothing. The English only learn about Churchill. He tries to explain further. 'There have been many invasions since the fall of the Roman Empire.' Changing up a few gears, he overtakes a white goods van.

She pulls the soft bag to her lap, continuing to massage the material. 'I've lost everything. Home, family. That could be me.'

'Nonsense. You have a passport, and the Verdis will help you.'

'If they consider me innocent.'

He can't deny that. His father believes she is culpable for Alessandro's death, and the closer he comes to Livorno, the more he feels a need to reverse. Too much has happened in the last two days, and he wants more time to reflect on a course of action. 'Family is all we can rely on,' he says. 'Our country has always been this way. After the war, the communists were popular. Anything was better than Mussolini and fascism. But America hated communism and so disrupted our politics.'

'Really?'

'The American Secret Service was influential here during the Cold War. Anyway, then the Christian Democrats took over, but there was a lot of dissent. Then Berlusconi, the billionaire, was in charge. A time of great corruption. Although I know my father would say the Verdi business did well under him. Now, things are collapsing again. Many factions have sprung up. Far-left and far-right. There's even a man who campaigns in clown uniform, and he's a serious contender. Can you believe that? Also, our country is deep in debt, like Greece. Some want more EU loans, and some want to leave the EU like Britain. It's all a mess, so once more family is at the centre.'

He doesn't know why he's trying to teach her Italian

politics. It's difficult to explain politics to the average Italian. And anyway, why would she be interested?

'Crystal said something like that.'

This surprises him. She's talked politics with Crystal?

'What would that woman know? She probably watches films,' he says.

'Didn't you once go out with her?'

Figgi slows down momentarily. 'What? What makes you say that? She made a pass at me, but no.' He senses Susan doesn't believe him.

They lapse back into silence as he drives through a series of traffic lights. Signs point toward Livorno docks. The road is parallel to the dockyard with huge tankers and corrugated metal containers parked next to large industrial ships. Scurrying people dip into cafes dotted along busy roads, eager to drink cappuccinos with lorry fumes. Agata has warned him not to go to Livorno today, but upon hearing of Amy's death, his father was even more insistent for a family conference.

'We're overseeing a shipment of marble; that's why my father's in Livorno today, and not Florence. You can't trust anyone to deliver what you pay for unless you see it with your own eyes. And today, all our buyers are elsewhere.' He is about to say more when the traffic comes to an abrupt halt.

Out of nowhere, large numbers of people advance along the road.

Banner waving crowds hold aloft sheets painted with slogans. A crush of humanity is pressing down the main street, blocking the streets and pavements. The majestic city hall is a few hundred metres in front of them, its windows shuttered against the midday heat. Or possibly in anticipation of the ugly mood. Under a white bell tower, police stand at the top of the double-fronted, stone staircase guarding the main entrance where a lone EU flag flutters.

Figaro groans. 'The protests! They're earlier than expected. Sit tight; I'll make a detour.'

Carabinieri and traffic police are out in force, whistles blowing to little effect. People and placards cram the roundabout, creating gridlock. The centre plinth is barely visible, obscured by banners bearing the signs of EU nations. Flags bounce up and down above the heads of the crowd, voices rise, shouting slogans.

No all'Unione Europa, delle guerre, delle banche, dei padroni, reads a white banner daubed in black and blood-red lettering.

'Are these people against the EU? I thought that was just England.'

Figgi honks, followed by a goose-like cacophony of honks behind him. 'We have an election coming. The centre right Forza and the Five Star Movement have united to protest against Prime Minister Renzi. But it's the Lega Nord in front of us, and they'll be the biggest troublemakers, for sure.'

With distinctively different colours, more white than striped, a separate group is marching down a side street toward them.

Sinking rights. Restiamo umani is daubed in blue across more protest sheets, their shouts blending with the opposition. Everyone is yelling, anger etched on their faces.

'*Merda*!' Figgi stops honking and looks over his shoulder to find a route out, but the car is wedged between others.

'Who's this group?' she asks as Figgi swivels his head, desperately seeking an exit.

He can see no escape and throws up his hands. 'Here come the Italian Bishops' men to challenge Five Star.'

Two people with Lega Nord on their T-shirts thrust their banner upward, shaking it toward the oncoming protesters. Their voices are loud in the rebuttal of the opposition.

'Stop invasions! *Prima la nostra gente*!'

Despite being jostled, a cameraman insists on filming.

'Any minute, the riot police will arrive.' Figgi honks along with the other trapped cars.

A man with a flag reading *Prima umani* crosses their path and bangs his flagpole against the car bonnet.

'My car. *Bastardo*!' Figgi doesn't hesitate. Jumping out, he goes to push the man aside. '*Questo è un'auto d'epoca. Bastardo*! A classic car, do you understand!'

The protestor steps forward. '*Fascista*!' he cries.

There is an ungainly scuffle between the two, neither of whom are fist-fighters. Determined to protect his paintwork, Figgi lashes out with slaps and insults, while the protestor uses his banner like a matador waving a flag. Bearing down upon them, a group of police officers in bulletproof jackets intervene and begin separating the two with heavy hands and batons drawn.

'*Mia amore*! *Mia machina*!' shouts Figgi, retreating. The flag-bearer shouts back with equal invective.

A police officer bellows in their faces and then stops with a smile of recognition. 'Mayor Verdi, what are you doing here?'

Figgi recognises Fabio. They pump hands, and the flag-bearer shuffles hastily after his group, but Fabio goes after the man, pulling him from the crowd.

'What are you arresting me for?' the protestor bawls.

'Assault on an official person.' He drags him away toward a police van. Several other riot police are making arrests. 'Leave this to me, Mr. Mayor,' Fabio shouts over his shoulder and disappears.

More jacketed men arrive to meet the intersection of groups. Another altercation ensues in front of them as Figgi steps back into his car. Helpless, they watch a sea of hands waving around them. Protestors stream along the driver's side. Susan shrinks down in her seat as Figgi puts out his hands, determined to physically push away any banner-bearing activists from his beloved car. He turns on his engine and revs hard, but the sound is lost in the roar of voices.

'How did the policeman know you?' shouts Susan in his ear.

'He's Commissario Agnello's assistant, Fabio. A real Salvini man, so he was happy to arrest one of the opposition.' The action does not quell Figgi's anger.

'You support Salvini?'

'If the Bishops Party are going to put a hole in my classic car, they can fuck off.'

Figgi rarely swears in English, let alone Italian, and the tirade silences her.

The Bishops crowd are in retreat; the Lega Nord surge forward. The crowd streams around a corner toward the docks. Half the drivers caught up in the blockage have gotten out of their cars and are yelling insults at everyone. A group of Carabinieri arrive and wave at them, attempting to clear a reversing space. As an opening appears, new insults are thrown. Drivers make dangerously tight manoeuvres, intent on being the first to leave. Along with some near-misses and more honks, the congestion slowly eases.

Released from the confusion, Figgi slides the car southward. He's still in a temper; his father was stupid to put his car at risk. Muttering under his breath, he curses himself for not refusing.

A small gurgle interrupts his thoughts, and his heart plummets. Susan is crying. He shouldn't have shouted. Her entire face has changed; there are tears smudging her eyes and, once again, the kohl is striping her cheeks. Attempting to stem the black, she runs a finger under the lower lids. She reminds him of a clown from Hell, and he has to force himself to keep his eyes on the road. When the traffic lessens, he can grab the tissues, but as the congestion eases, everyone picks up speed, like water running to the sea. Again, he hears the gurgle, but without the noise of the crowd, it sounds more like a schoolgirl's giggle. He glances at her.

Her false eyelashes are brimming with tears, but she is laughing, her shoulders jerking uncontrollably.

'I'm sorry,' she says. 'I shouldn't find it funny, but... your car!'

'This is a classic Audi Quattro,' he repeats. How stupid can she be? His car is priceless. 'I had a respray a few months ago.'

'Cars first, humans second?' She can barely enunciate the words for laughter. She is rolling in her seat.

'I was protecting you as well!' But her uncontrolled hilarity is infectious, and he emits a strangled giggle of his own. 'Anyway, my father can fuck off. How does he think we could have cut through a crowd like that? With wind power?'

He has a sudden vision of his family stopping for a car crash. Years ago. And a cow farting loudly at the side of the road, and his father telling them off for laughing. He guffaws.

Susan laughs some more. 'Your father. Ha, ha, ha. I'm

innocent. I've broken no law!' More tears run down her face.

'Not even a parking ticket? Heh, heh.'

'I don't drive. Ha, ha!'

At this, they both guffaw afresh. He is in danger of crashing his beloved classic car and slows down along the smaller roads. The back of her hand smears her face; the foundation has turned a muddy grey, and she extracts her own tissue from the voluminous bag.

'Did you see that policeman's face? Ha, ha, ha.' She wipes her nose and examines the black tissue.

'I'll have to teach you to drive. Heh, heh.'

'I'll have to get a car first! Ha, ha, ha.'

'You'll have to get a job first! Heh!'

'Elliott can fuck off, too. Ha!'

'Yes! Let's tell your boss and my father to fuck off.'

It's a revelation to him—she's capable of swearing, and it's hysterically funny. 'Hey! Let's go to lunch.' He feels impetuous and light-headed. 'We haven't eaten today, and I know a place without murder and riots. Heh, heh.'

'It must be boring then! Ha, ha, ha.'

They howl. As soon as one stops, the other starts. A hiccup, a snort, a burp, a sniff, a fart, and off they go until they hit a small town. Susan is attempting to wipe her face clean. Suddenly, she picks at her false lashes, peels them off, and drops them with a dramatic wave over the side of the car.

'Do I look like a panda?' she asks.

'*Un orso*?'

'An arsehole?' she cackles.

'No, no, no. That means 'bear' in Italian.'

'Pandas are arseholes?'

They laugh again, until finally he parks and lets the

engine die. The sea lies flat, sunlight sprinkling across the glassy surface. They are at a favourite place of his, a little-known seaside village, where three cafes sprawl onto the beach, patronised by families.

She removes the headscarf and shakes her hair. He smiles for the first time that day.

'May I?' he asks. Taking her tissue, he wipes the spots she has missed, and she extracts a wet wipe, finishing the clean-up while he watches. They smile at each other, co-conspirators in running away. In wonderment, he sees that without the mask, she is far more beautiful. He wants to ask why she bothers to coat herself, but even if she answered, he wouldn't understand. He's never understood the peccadillos of women. He understands murderers, though, and he suspects she's not one of them.

Chapter Twenty-Three

As Agata leaves Ponteginori and heads back to Montecatini, a distraught Carl Henderson phones. She cuts into his tirade. 'Your mother will have to remain under house arrest until I can get hold of Luca.' Despite leaving several voicemails, she's aware her husband is busy on the streets of Livorno, and without his intervention, Fabio's hasty decision stands.

The road back has many hairpin bends. It's a law of nature that the phone always rings when she is in the most twisted part of the route, but seeing as it's Luca, she pulls over as best she can, squeezing beside a huge pile of chopped wood. 'At last!'

'What's so urgent? Eight missed calls! Don't you know there's a protest going on in Livorno? Plenty of arrests already and plenty injured. The Bishops Party followers are being squashed by Five Star. And then Beppe Grillo showed up.'

Despite her emergency, this spikes her curiosity. 'In full clown makeup?'

'Of course. And naturally, the whole crowd has

exploded with idiocy. How did our politics get so messed up that a clown can be a serious contender for Prime Minister?'

'Leave the explanations to Fabio.'

'And that's another thing. Fabio shouldn't even be here. I put him in charge of the murder in Montecatini.'

'He arrested someone.'

'I'll say! He's arresting people! Not left, right, and centre. Just Left.'

'No. I mean he's arrested Lilian Henderson!'

'Who's she?'

'The *padrone* where Amy was lodging. Carl's mother. Owner of the Airbnb near Montecatini. I've instructed the Carabinieri to release her, but the best they can do is put her under house arrest in your absence.'

'I told Fabio to go easy on the Tower people. No repetition of the way he handled the beach murder.'

'But Lilian is seventy-two with bad hips.'

'Agata! Not now! I'm in charge of fifty officers here, and there's a crowd of 30,000 converged on the Municipal Hall.'

In the background, Agata hears loud cries of *Fascisti*!

'I have no time. I'm overseeing custody while I have a pee break. Ask Figgi.'

'He's not here, either.'

'The day of the Festa? Where the hell is he? He's the mayor.'

'He took the fake widow to Livorno on orders of his Papa.'

'Today? Are they crazy?'

Before she can answer, a dirty white camper van with a beige roof careens around the hairpin bend, coming directly at her. At the last minute, it swerves, giving barely a finger's width between the two vehicles, and Agata swears, heart pounding. From the van, she hears the grind of gears and a note of acceleration. She shouts out the window, wondering if it's the same van that nearly ran her down on the road out of Volterra.

'What happened?'

'Crazy tourists. They don't know the route and travel too fast.'

'I must go.'

'Wait! Has the sergeant spoken to you? Because no one has seen him this morning. There's a dead English tourist, and he's nowhere. He hasn't even tried to interview Susan.'

'Agata! I'm in Livorno. I can't think about this now. We've got police jails full to bursting and talking about bursting, I haven't visited the toilet. I've only got ten minutes with an espresso and a shrivelled ham panini.'

'A dried ham panini! Terrible.'

'Yes. Desperate here. You sort things. I must go.'

'I'll keep an eye out at the Festa.'

But he has already cut the call.

Entering the car park at the water fountains, she is relieved to see Gianni and one other member of his team. There is no *Polizia di Stato*, and if she expected roadside weeping, she is resigned to the usual indifference of voyeuristic bystanders. It was the same in Florence; tourists congregated in clumps near police incidents, cameras in hand. The early Festa revellers are sipping take-away refreshments. A group of women wear colourful frocks, and the men are dressed in expensive polo shirts, tailored shorts, and loafers. They hover with an air of reality TV about them.

A small child wobbles, clutches Agata's leg as she passes them, and throws up with such force it splatters everywhere. She tries to muster a smile for the mother, who is frantically apologising while dragging her crying offspring away. Stamping her feet, she checks the state of her white polyester blouse and black skirt. The spatters have not reached her clothes, so she resigns herself to washing her corded sandals in the fountains. Yolanda rings.

'Where are you?'

'Have you got a spare pair of shoes?'

'Shoes? Sandals? Take what you want. You can borrow underwear if you need it, but get here fast!'

Gianni is working methodically in the tent. One flap is open showing boxes, test tubes, plastic ziplock bags, brushes, and powders set on a sturdy camping table. In a white plastic suit, his face shines with perspiration. She stops at the yellow cordon in bare feet, wet shoes in her hands.

'Signora Agata,' says Gianni. 'You want something?' As usual, his pallor and demeanour remind her of a depressed ghost.

'Luca needs some information,' she lies.

Gianni raises his eyebrows, picks up a plastic bottle of water, and drains it. 'Can you get me another one?' He waves the bottle like a metronome. 'This scene is going to take hours. Too many people trampled over everything before I was called. There's a million prints. I've called in the team.'

Agata sees the dirty mattresses placed to one side, pinned with notated cards. The body is covered in a blue plastic sheet.

Having discussed the scene with Figaro, she is armed with some rudimentary information. 'Luca needs to know if it's the same method as the beach murder. Or if it's unconnected.'

Gianni licks his lips and runs one plastic glove over the

sweat on his brow. He hesitates, and Agata pulls out her old printed official pass with *Agente of Polizia di Stato.* Gianni nods.

'So, I'm asking if they are the same or a copycat? Obviously, she's not a migrant.'

'Isn't she?' says Gianni. 'I thought she was African.'

'No. I met her yesterday, and she's definitely from London.'

'Ah.' Gianni sighs. 'This helps. Email me this information, then my preliminary report will be with the Commissario in a week or so. Or longer, if I stay chatting with you.' He throws his bottle into a plastic refuse bag that has several empty coffee containers.

'You must have something more.'

He snaps the gloves at his wrist. 'Some people think it is a game.' He lifts his nose toward the crowd on the opposite pavement.

'Meaning?'

'To guess if it is a mad voodoo murderer, or just a nasty racist attack, or something else.' He rolls his eyes slowly. 'In my experience, Agata, people believe what they want to believe. And the press want a good headline, not the truth.' His eyes remain on the crowd. 'Do you think that girl in the blue dress will go out with me if I ask?'

Impatiently, Agata casts a glance at the young girl in a tight summer frock. She is whispering to an older woman next to her. 'No, Gianni. You're dressed like a dead chicken, and she's too young.'

He turns away, but the curl of his mouth suggests he's not offended. '*Beh.*'

'Gianni,' she persists, 'is it possible it's the same killer? At least tell me that. Does she have Golden Blood?'

'I can't tell that yet, but it's possible. Her torso is open, and the incision is precise. Someone who knows where to cut and has a sharp knife. But no organs are missing. At least, none I can see. You'll have to wait for the laboratory reports.'

'Were both girls cut with a surgeon's knife?'

He stares with bleary eyes at Agata. 'There's a puncture point where an injection was administered. The knife was razor sharp. Those are the immediate similarities. But I can't say more. Now leave me to get on. Everyone always complains I work too slowly, but then they want to hold a conversation. And the later it gets, the more unbearable the sun, and the corpse cooks, not to mention we cook as well. Especially when we're shrink-wrapped. If you want to be kind, please ask your sister to bring more coffee and water. My team are going to need caffeine and hydration, and her coffee is fantastic. And ask that lovely girl who works in the cafe to bring up the coffees. I'll invite her for a date.'

Agata huffs. 'I've seen her boyfriend. He has a red Vespa. Can you compete?'

Gianni pulls at his plastic hood like a teenager. '*Beh*! A man must try. I know at the mention of my profession they walk. What can I do?'

'Try dating a female pathologist?'

He laughs with good nature and goes back to the tent. If death doesn't ruffle him, nothing will.

As she walks down to the Piazza in bare feet, Agata thinks about the tales her grandmother told her of the War. Her *nonna* would have said that there's always been a precarious balance between justice and injustice, between survival and death. But what would drive someone to kill in this fashion? And if Amy knew Alessandro, why kill her in a similar manner to the girl on the beach? Why not drop her down an old well? God knows there are enough of them lurking in the countryside. No, she surmises. This was done to draw attention to the crime. But why?

As she nears the Pizzeria, Agata checks her phone. There are no messages in response to her calls to the British Embassy or the British sergeant. No media or press have arrived to take pictures. It's as if the girl leaves no footprint. Her skin crawls. It shouldn't be this way. Someone should be shouting.

Chapter Twenty-Four

Southern Italy. Weeks before Alessandro's murder

Europe. A sea-salt ripple of relief passes along the boat as they dock. Puglia. The dead are taken off first, thrown into a narrow boat alongside their vessel. Limbs cascade at awkward angles, faces down. Wathiqa and her sister, Huda, watch in silence as their mother joins the pile. Someone is yelling as a gangplank is put into position. Behind the girls, a man pushes on the small of Wathiqa's back, eager to step on land, and another jostles at her side. She grips her sister's hand tightly.

A woman with a plastic lanyard around her neck counts as they wobble ashore. One, two... One hundred and two...

In a dehydrated blur, they walk through metal gates.

'What country?' A man in uniform is shouting as they enter. 'Eritrea? Over here. Sudan? Over here. Syria?'

They are separated like assorted ingredients in a recipe. Time has floated since her mother died. 'My sister is nine and I am twelve. Maybe thirteen.'

Two boys with full beards insist, 'We are only fifteen.'

Unaccompanied minors are instructed to sit together.

They are the first to be given plastic water bottles, while the adult boat people look at them with blackened eyes. The children gulp furtively.

Unaccompanied minors also have the advantage of sleeping inside, two to a bunk under corrugated roofs. Larger ones are put on thin mattresses on the floor. Adults sleep in separate tents, where rumours pass like cigarettes. Information is currency. Pay him, and you can get to Britain or Germany. Come here, young girl, do this and you have money. Wathiqa isn't stupid. Her mother taught her if a man puts his fingers between her legs, kick, spit, and run. She and Huda huddle.

The camp workers have dark underarm sweat patches. Everyone sweats; the spring heat is the only leveller. Wathiqa watches the constant flow of men and women with badges and red cross pouches. They speak in French and English and Italian.

A woman with crooked teeth looks at Wathiqa, examining her face and body.

'Old knife injury to your arm and face?' Wathiqa nods, and they turn away. 'No medical needs here.'

A man points to Huda, 'She's suitable for that group.' They grip Huda's arm, and her sister emits a wild scream and tries to bite the restraining hand. In disgust, they shove her back, and she cowers against Wathiqa. What happens to the chosen ones? No one says a word as five other children are taken away. One aid worker hands out paper and pencils to see who can write their details. Her little sister draws grey faces with grey tears, and Wathiqa rips up the picture.

At night, the nightmares revisit Wathiqa: her father with bullet holes for eyes, falling anew from his car. Not wanting to wake her sister, she scrambles outside shaking. Moths amass around a single bulb in the medical office, where four people exchange rolled wads. The scene is familiar. Wathiqa remembers her father: his broad shoulders leaning toward government men and the fists of money. 'Safety can be bought,' he told them. Until it couldn't.

The memory tightens her throat, but she crawls forward to listen.

The adults are arguing. 'You don't want ten noisy children,' says one. 'Take the older girl with the scars and put her in charge to keep the others quiet. She speaks some English.'

A few more fists, and Wathiqa hurries back, climbing into Huda's bunk, listening to the thumping of her heart and the whine of mosquitoes. Within minutes, two people enter the room, touching a shoulder here and there, a finger to their lips. The children rise up, eyes large. Huda swings her feet to the ground, and Wathiqa tightens her grip on her sister. Together, the chosen ones are herded into a beige and white camper van. Doors locked, it moves off in the night. Their eyes shine with fear in the yellow streetlights that leak through gaps in the blackened windows. No one speaks.

Hours later, they are released to relieve themselves on an arid patch of land. They have eaten so little that none can defecate. They squat to release urine and look around at the alien world. Everything is strange, even the smell of the air. Enormous billboards loom over an expanse of asphalt. Wathiqa tries to interpret the huge faces with beaming smiles and the strange script. The nearby road roars.

'We're charity workers. We're your friends. Here—eat, drink.' The adults toss oily bread and water bottles. They eat ravenously as the moon pales over pink mountains.

'Today we must do some tests. Don't be frightened. We're not witch doctors or anything like that. We're checking to see

if you need medicine for HIV. Soon you will be safe in lovely new homes.'

The clinic reminds Wathiqa of her uncle's pharmacy, the one the soldiers smashed. There are boxes of drugs, test tubes, pipettes, and needles in a room without windows. The children wash in cold water and change into worn Western clothes that smell of soap. Their heads are shaved. It's impossible to tell the boys from the girls.

'Don't worry. It will grow back nice and clean.'

One of the drivers chews on a biro as he daubs a little lipstick on Huda, pulling a sparkly wig over her scalp. 'Look,' he says, 'your new family will think you're a film star.'

He is the only one to laugh.

The van radio blares in a rapid babble. 'Radio Subasio, Breaking news!'

'Hey, Doc! Did you hear that?'

Biro-man shouts to the children at the back. 'Hey, kids! The politicians want to let you die in the Mediterranean. Aren't you lucky you're with us?'

What does 'lucky' mean? In the camp, the whisper was if you did something wrong, the white men put you in prison, or worse —they sent you back. She presses her legs together and sits quietly. The camper van rattles on for more hours. Wathiqa shifts beneath Huda's hot lumpen weight. Air filters through from the driver's window, yet sweat covers her sleeping sister, and the perspiration blossoms like petals across her FCUK T-shirt. The others squash to the farthest corner. Sickness is to be feared. She holds Huda's clammy hand and hums a song her mother taught her. Closing her eyes, she tries to pretend she's home.

She remembers:

Daddy arrives. Sometimes he's in Western clothes; sometimes he's in a Jalabiya. (It depends who he's been meeting.) But he always pops open a sweet fizzy drink and throws candies to them. 'Here, my princesses.' They hug him, inhaling the familiar smell of cigarettes. Mummy comes back. 'Hey, girls, finish your homework, and after, go to Auntie's to fetch the salted fish for dinner. It's Kajaik tonight!'

The memory stops as soon as she opens her eyes, and Wathiqa blinks away tears. There is normality somewhere; she just has to hold on long enough to find it.

When the adults stop for petrol, she calls to them. 'Help. My sister.'

'Fuck, she's burning up.'

'Fuck! Not her! She's the valuable one.'

How is Huda valuable? She doesn't speak languages, and she isn't good at reading or writing. It makes no sense, but no one has tried to put their fingers between Wathiqa's legs, so she has no choice but to trust them.

They whisper outside the van. The white doctor speaks urgently into a phone; Biro-man taps a tune on his teeth with his biro. Her sister tosses in pain. The children are too frightened to whisper.

The moon rises again as her courage sinks.

Finally, Doc speaks to her. 'We're going to drop your sister off in a hospital and come back later to collect her.'

Within an hour, they arrive at a half-lit building. Biro-man lifts the limp Huda, carrying her to the glazed doors. Wathiqa is restrained from following by a white-coated man who has come out to greet them.

Doc says, 'Huda will be fine. Good medicine in Italy. Be patient and look after the others.'

As the camper van is locked, the remaining children press up against Wathiqa, curling like kittens.

So she waits.

She waits.

She waits.

Chapter Twenty-Five

Marina di Cecina

The waiters greet Figaro as a friend, and he introduces Susan to the cafe owner, Izabella. The woman rises on tiptoe to give Figgi a double kiss. She nods to Susan before showing them to a table with steel legs embedded in the sand. The atmosphere is one of lazy tranquility. Susan's stomach aches with laughing, or stress; she isn't sure which. Around them, families sit finishing their meals while small children play with pebbles and shells under their feet. Livorno could be the other side of the world.

Beyond the decked area, sunbathers lie on towels draped over wooden loungers in zones of peaceful slumber. They spread across the dark golden sand. A thin, gangly man with ebony skin walks between the sun worshippers. Tickets dangle from a wooden yoke across his neck: wide-brimmed hats, multicoloured sunshades, cheap sunglasses, glass beads, inflatable beach balls. All swing in time to his footsteps. By his side, a young girl smiles—his image, his daughter speaks to everyone.

'Something for you. Quelque chose pour vous? Etwas für dich? Qualcosa per lei?'

The girl's prowess impresses the beach community; she is around eight years old, spouting all these languages. As she does her party trick, the father smiles benignly. Some, regardless of her skills, wave the hawkers away, while others are softened by the young one's approach and press Euro coins into her hand. One woman in a large striped bathing suit half-heartedly haggles for a hat to test the child's prowess.

Figaro stretches his legs beneath the table, and as his phone lights, he turns it off with a dramatic flourish. 'What is it the Americans say? This is the first day of the rest of my life!' They smile like conspirators.

In tight black trousers, a waiter comes to the table. With a professional sweep, he deposits slices of bread and grissini sticks in a thin glass, placing menus in their hands. His white shirt is so thin, she can see his pectorals.

'A drink,' says Figaro.

Despite the seaside sun and the blue of the water, her thoughts swirl. She wraps her scarf around the handles of her bag and pushes it under the table. She's had a reprieve from seeing Figaro's dreaded father, but what next?

'I'll order fresh fish, if you like. And white wine, although I rarely drink at lunchtime.'

She doesn't care what she eats or drinks. Leaning forward, she snaps a breadstick in half and points it like a sword. With the riots behind them, they are both feeling so brave. 'Thank you, Sir Knight.'

He orders a carafe of wine that arrives at speed. The young server pours for them with a flashy smile. Figgi must be famous, she decides: the Verdi effect. The wine is golden, and gentle bubbles rise to the surface. For a moment, her hand stills. When facing alcohol, there is always a frisson of hesitation. Today it is followed by the memory of Amy's burst body, and with a sudden urgency, Susan downs the drink to steady herself.

He laughs. 'If you were thirsty, we could have started with water.' An imperceptible rise of his hand, and waiters scurry. 'Or are you very British about your drink?'

She shakes her head. The wine tastes light, but on an empty stomach, its effect is fast. Tuscany has been a lesson in the art of silence, but today she must talk or drown in her thoughts. He pours her another glass, watching her intently. More in defiance than desire, she swallows it in one gulp, ending with a smack of her lips and a nervous giggle. Her body is on fire: She is six degrees from hysterical and trying to hang on to her sanity.

Figgi raises his eyebrows but makes no comment. He isn't traditionally handsome—nothing like Alessandro, she thinks, nor does he have his cousin's charismatic charm, but he has the face of a man in control. If she hadn't witnessed his rage about the car, she would have thought him incapable of anger. She thinks of the package in her bag. It must stay hidden.

Water arrives in a blue glass bottle, and Figaro pours for her. In a purposeful gesture, he takes his wineglass to his lips and attempts to copy her.

Halfway, he chokes and grins. 'I've been out of England too long, but I remember the pint glass games. You British are crazy.'

'My father was an alcoholic, but I'm not.' The comment pops out before she can check herself. 'It's been a hellish day.'

'Ahh,' he says. He looks like he understands, but she knows he doesn't.

'So, you want to pretend to be an *ubriaco*? A drunk?'

'Oo-bree-ah-ko?' Repeating the word slowly, she lifts her empty glass in a toast. 'To all the oo-bree-ah-kos everywhere. May they rest in peace.' Then her lips twist, and she feels the prickle of tears. 'Poor Amy.'

Figaro fiddles with his napkin.

'Figaro,' she begins.

'Figgi.'

'Figgi.' His name sounds like a fruit, and she remembers how Alessandro hated her shortening his name. 'You have a family. A community where you belong. I only had my father.'

'Alessandro was like a brother. A bad brother, but a brother.'

Clearly, he doesn't understand the point she's trying to make. 'You referred to me as Oriental in the square.'

'If I offended you, I'm sorry.'

'Ornaments are oriental, not people. But people see my face, and they think I'm Chinese. I've always been told I look like my mother. But I was never close to my mother. I suppose that's what got me into wearing makeup. Not that my makeup is unusual in the centre of London.' She ought to be quiet, but she drinks more wine.

He shakes his head and refills her glass.

'Alessandro never saw me without my makeup.'

'*Vero*? Really?'

'I used to get up early in the morning, wash, and reapply.' She looks out at the sea. 'And of course, he wasn't always home.'

Figgi's lips form a small *pfft*, and he drinks. 'I'm sorry.'

The wine swills in her stomach. 'You don't know what it's like to be marked as an outsider. To be told that you don't belong. Silly Soo-li. That was my name at school.

When my mother showed up to collect me from the playground, the teasing was worse. One day, I told her I wanted my father to collect me, and she was furious. She said I ought to be ashamed, and if I wanted to be like my father, I could live with him and be a drunk. And then she left.'

Aghast at how much she has said, she bites her lips. The alcohol is blunting her judgement. 'I never drink.'

'And you never cry?' Figgi's tone is gentle, but he doesn't appear to mock her.

Susan watches the father and child hawkers go to rest under one of the sun umbrellas. Another cafe owner comes out and speaks harshly to the sellers. Without argument, the two of them rise and go to the water's edge. The sun burns overhead.

She touches the paper napkin to her lips. It leaves no lipstick mark, reminding her of her nakedness. It is a strange, childlike feeling. 'My father was a sweet man. Drunk but loving. He died of liver cancer two weeks before I met Alessandro.'

Figgi looks away. She sees a red flush on his neck. 'I'm sorry for you,' he says, 'but it explains things.'

'Don't pity me. That's not why I told you.'

Why did she tell him? Restless, she wants to move and make some mad gesture. She will explode if she doesn't shake the pain from her guts. She's alive, and undeserving of life. When she looks back at her short non-marriage, she realises she's made all the wrong choices, so why is it that Amy has suffered? It should have been her.

'Amy needs a requiem.' She pushes on the table to rise unsteadily.

He stands as if to catch her.

'You don't know what it's like to be a stran-year-i.' Opening the bag, she pulls out the only Euro note she possesses. Then she rewraps the scarves around the handles, puts it on her chair, and weaves out onto the sand. If the package stays hidden, she can atone.

'How much for a hat?' she says to the little girl.

Figgi is behind her. The beach seller smiles and turns, causing the trinkets to swing back and forth. Unclipping one hat from his yoke, he looks at her. 'This?'

The child chatters. 'It is a beautiful hat, madam.'

Susan takes the suggested merchandise. It is the opposite of beautiful; it is a grotesque concoction of cheap plastic material with a red nylon bow.

'Twenty Euros,' says the child, spying the note in Susan's hand.

Susan wishes she had fifty Euros in her hand. Or a hundred. The pain weighs on her heavier than the man's yoke. They trade hat for money.

Figaro is half-smiling. 'Do you feel better now?'

'Go on,' she insists. 'Buy something!' She gives a nervous giggle. She will laugh or cry, and she mustn't cry. No more tears. Not now. Nothing is made better with tears.

Reluctantly, he pulls out his wallet. 'A client gave me a payment for his loan yesterday,' he says to explain the thick wad of notes. 'It should have been deposited into the bank.'

'Buy everything,' she orders with a dramatic fling of her arms. 'The man and his daughter should be able to go home. It's hot, and the child must be tired.'

The girl dances in delight, claps her hands, and unclips a watch, some sunglasses, and a cotton dress, handing them to Susan, speaking a price. Without arguing, Figaro parts with a few notes.

Dodging around on the sand, Susan grabs the goods he has just paid for and offers them to various people nearby. Immediately, she has everyone's attention. If one person refuses, she goes to the next until the goods find a home.

'More,' she demands, and Figgi reluctantly parts with another wad in return for a couple of sundresses in clear plastic bags and two pairs of sunglasses. She can see her energy irritates him, but she doesn't care and continues to skip among different people on the beach. A dress to a sunbathing young woman, another to an older woman with a book, sunglasses to a man and a frisbee to a young boy.

'More,' she demands, and Figgi pulls out more notes. His face is redder than before, but she ignores it. In minutes, she has distributed beach balls and phone selfie sticks, T-shirts and plastic fans to anyone who will accept them. They pass the items around. Now the whole beach is laughing at her. The crazy lady. And they laugh at Figgi, who bears a lopsided smile and a raised eyebrow. But their laughter is good-humoured, and they offer their thanks.

The beach seller and his child have only half a dozen items left.

'Come on,' says Figgi. 'We've done enough.'

'Thank you, kindest lady.' The beach seller speaks in a thick African accent.

A couple come to their side. The man wears brightly striped swimming shorts, and the woman has a bathing costume, studded with rhinestones. 'We'll buy the rest,' he says in a German accent, and Susan and the child smack their hands in joy.

The little girl twirls, saying thank you in several languages. 'Thank you. Grazie. Merci. Danke.'

'Keep the money and keep the rest of the goods. Off you go,' says the tourist to the seller, 'or we'll get no peace.' He smiles at Figgi with large white teeth. 'You must love her,' he adds before going back to his sun lounger. This embarrasses them both, and they study their feet on the sand. The seller and his daughter walk off the beach after the seller's daughter does a few more funny dances.

Izabella is standing guard at their table as they return. She has a wide grin on her face. '*Pazzi*,' she says. 'Crazy people.'

Nearly toppling over in her effort to reach her seat, Susan feels Figaro grab her elbow.

'Amy wasn't a migrant from Africa, you know,' he says. 'And this won't make much of a difference. They'll be back tomorrow trying to make money to pay traffickers to cross the Alps.'

'I know, but it's something.' She sits heavily. 'What else can we do? We have to start somewhere. And aren't we all connected? Six degrees of separation?' Her head is buzzing.

On the sand, the holidaymakers are smiling and joking and pointing. This minor act of philanthropy has spread good humour everywhere.

He stretches across the table and holds her hand for a moment. 'I wish the world was that simple.'

After such a show, they eat with inconsequential conversation. The fish is moist and falls apart in their mouths. She's starving and soaks the pieces of airy bread in the sauce on her plate, forking in great gulps with the fresh salad. When the plate is empty, her head is less giddy.

'I'm not stupid.' She wipes her mouth. 'I knew something was wrong. Why was Alessandro interested in me? In *me*? He was rich; he was good-looking. Who am I?'

'You're pretty, and you're generous,' Figgi offers.

'With your money!'

He raises his glass with a smile.

'But me?' she insists. 'A colleague told me that Alessandro had made enquiries about several staff at the

Auction House before asking me out. Apparently, he turned up at the pub after a high-end auction one day, asking questions. Who was married and who wasn't? Who had worked for the company the longest?'

'And so?'

'Alessandro was secretive. Our wedding was so sudden, so small. He proposed on the London Eye, and I couldn't say no. Whenever he was home, he borrowed my laptop, claiming he'd left his in his office. But who forgets their laptop? And he would come and go, not always answer my texts, away unexpected nights, and then return with flowers and weak excuses.' She downs a glass of water and looks Figaro in the eye. 'And do you know why I didn't ask questions?'

'Why?'

'Because I was afraid of the answers.' She swallows hard. 'He insisted I put my possessions in storage and give up my rented flat until we bought somewhere. Without him, I am homeless. When I told him of my fears, he made me open a bank account and placed some of his money into mine.' She gulps. 'And I took it.'

Izabella comes over and speaks briefly to Figaro, who nods.

'And did you know,' Susan continues, 'my phone connected to your Wi-Fi when I came into Casa Verdi? Alessandro came here without me.' She holds up her chin. 'I mislaid my phone for two days, and I think he stole it and came here without even telling me.'

'Yes,' says Figgi. 'Agata mentioned it.'

She shrugs off the obvious complicity. 'So what was he doing?' Automatically, she wipes fingers under her eyes, but there is no kohl to smudge.

Figgi holds her gaze without comment until she drops her eyes.

'I'm sorry. I should have said this earlier.' She shakes her head. 'When I saw the women on the roadside to Livorno... all my fears.'

'I think that's rather insulting to their position. You can easily get a job in London, and you have the right to live in a developed country with access to medical care. I'm not pleased about the numbers migrating to Italy, but I do understand their situation.'

She looks at her empty plate and nods. How can she explain to someone like him? Someone who belongs. She lives a life where her shoes pinch, and he wants her to say that at least she has shoes. Resting her elbows on the table, her hands support her head. 'I need to change. All I've ever done is try to fit in. If I'd helped Amy... If I'd insisted Alessandro confide in me and asked more questions... If I'd been stricter with my father over his drinking...' Fatigue and fear are causing her brain to fuzz again. She remembers the package hidden in her handbag and worries it will burn a hole in the material. Then Figaro slides his elbows forward and places his forearms against hers.

'You're not alone,' he says, taking both her hands in his. 'Alessandro used you, just as he used many people. He was my cousin, but he was a bad man. Now, I will help you. Trust me.'

His eyes are soft and loving. His words fill her heart. She is not alone. In this fragile moment, she discards the idea of ever sharing the packet. What does the package matter when they sunbathe in the afterglow of philanthropy and good food? All that matters is the warmth of their hands entwined.

Chapter Twenty-Six

The Torre di Verdi gardens

Each year in Florence, the Saint's day, *La Festa di San Giovanni,* is celebrated on 24th June with extravagant pageantry and costumes. Volterra's Festa has flag-waving and cheese-rolling in the third week in August. By comparison, Montecatini della Torre puts on a minor affair, but their local Festa is the second weekend in May, so they grab the first bite of the apple. Everyone benefits from spreading out Saints' days.

Naomi D'Angelo stands at the open gates to the Tower Gardens with a bright smile that doesn't reach her eyes. Where is the mayor? No one knows. Festivities began with a church service and hastily added prayers for *la donna inglese*, followed by ribbon-cutting and a brief history of the town. Most tourists arrive later. They are only interested in the views, the food, and the fireworks. As people press forward, Naomi snatches tickets from their outstretched hands, encouraging everyone to grab a glass and seek the platter bearers with first pickings. Roast garlic and herbs fill the air, their scent rising from smouldering half-drum barbecues. Noses are twitching, and newcomers exclaim with delight at the spectacle of colours across the valley. Volterra's pink walls are visible through the lattice of olive tree branches, and the sea is a ribbon of azure at the edge of the horizon. In the gardens, larger cypress trees offer shelter from breeze or sun, and beside them is a wooden platform where hired help dispense drinks next to the musicians' dais.

A large wrought iron archway carves through the middle of the gardens, sheltering a long line of trestle tables and benches. Grape vines twist and snake up and over the trellis, and drooping green bunches of unripe fruit intertwine with solar lights. Smaller circular tables with fat candles in balloon-shaped glasses dot the grounds, ready for later use.

Agata carries plates from the Tower kitchen to the tables beside the barbecue area. She is seeking the English sergeant, certain she saw a flash of blue sports shirt and a thick neck somewhere in the crowd. But he has inexplicably melted. How can such a solid shape disappear?

Tourists jostle to find wine waiters. Jugs in hand, Orlando and Aldo, Naomi's sons, fill up glasses as fast as they can before refilling jugs from large, boxed containers nearby. At the upper terrace, small walnut trees are festooned with oil lamps, and Agata stops nearby to search. The garden is on a gentle slope towards the valley, but even at this highest point, she cannot see the man she seeks.

Figgi and Susan arrive late, but that isn't what surprises Agata. For a moment, she doesn't recognise the fake wife without her makeup, nor Figgi, who has caught the sun on his face. They are holding hands but part when they see her. The shift is unsettling, and she wonders what has happened. Despite an earlier denial, Agata is sure Susan has collected the package, but she is reluctant to challenge her in front of so many people.

Dana thrusts a heavy silver tray into her arms. Pots of olives glisten in oil. 'Put these around on the tables and then come back to the kitchen. Yolanda's having a nervous breakdown.'

Agata advances toward Figaro with her wares, catching the tail end of their conversation.

'Must go for half an hour. I've an appointment I can't change.' says Figgi.

'Must you?'

'Figgi,' says Agata, 'I've been trying to get hold of you on your mobile all afternoon. It's turned off!' Agata knows she sounds accusatory, but she has never known him to switch off his mobile, day or night. And it is unheard of for the mayor to miss the church service.

He slaps a hand to his forehead, pulls out his phone, and turns it on. It begins to ping, and goes on pinging until he groans. 'Oh my God,' he says. 'Twenty missed calls!'

'That's your father, isn't it?' She ignores Susan's mew of surprise. 'He rang me. Me! He tried to contact Luca and then rang me. He's furious you didn't show up. I tried to explain about the protest in Livorno.'

'I can't deal with this now.'

Agata looks at him. He's ignoring his father? But she is even more surprised when he retakes Susan's hand.

'I forgot to mention this appointment. An old man, a hunter, has contacted me.'

'It's not the season for hunting,' interrupts Agata.

Figgi lowers his voice. 'He's been poaching, which is why he won't speak to the police.'

When two tourists approach, Agata hands them the

entire tray of olive bowls and waves them away. They stagger off with confused looks.

'This must be old Tomaso,' Agata says. 'He's the one who kills the porcupines.'

'Porcupines?' says Susan.

'Large African porcupines. It's illegal, but their meat fetches a good price.'

Figgi shushes her. 'He saw something last night, but he'll only talk to me.'

'If this is about Amy, I expect you to share all the information! And we must speak to the English sergeant. He's somewhere here, wearing a blue sports shirt. You met him in London? Keep an eye out for him.'

Figgi nods and slips away, but not before Agata sees him give Susan's hand a squeeze and a kiss on the cheek. As Luca has often observed, no one has seen Figgi with a woman for a number of years. He's a secretive man, so what is happening? Alessandro and then Figaro falling for the same woman? But perhaps Figgi has always coveted Alessandro's women. Agata stares at her, finding it difficult to imagine Susan as a siren for the Syndicate. But after her experience with Dr. Albina, she's prepared to believe almost anything. She grabs Susan's arm.

'Come on.' She spies Carl Henderson standing on his own. 'Carl,' she calls. 'Come keep Susan company. You're both from England.' Perhaps the girl can work magic on Carl and get more information from him about Amy.

'I'm Welsh,' the man says with resignation. 'There is a difference, you know.' He smiles at Susan, in a lost-boy hopeful fashion. Agata thinks that where Carl is concerned, maybe magic isn't necessary.

As with all medieval constructions, the Tower kitchen is in a pit at ground level, reached through two large wooden doors. The living area begins on the drier, higher, first floor. In the cavernous basement, there are no windows, and the space is lit by fluorescent strips attached to the buttress points. The paraphernalia of modernity is in contrast to the damp mustiness that oozes from the walls. Modern white melamine cupboards line one wall, doors ajar, showing rows of pickled and oiled produce; olives and artichokes in greenish oil sit side by side with cherries and peaches in thick reddish liquor. On the right, cakes, cheese rounds, unlabelled bottles of wine, and clean plates are stacked for later in the evening.

'I'm taking a break,' says Agata to Yolanda, who is slicing meat with an electric circular knife. She stops and throws up her hands.

'What! Right now? No! We've only just begun.'

'I must find someone. Give me ten minutes.'

'You promised!' Yolanda calls as Agata walks out.

Having checked the sergeant is not in the gardens, she chooses to leap up the metal staircase to the Tower's front door. She wouldn't put it past him to go snooping. The man hasn't even shown up to register Amy's death, yet she's learned he came back to quiz Dana and Yolanda about the story of the Butcher. She knows his sort and is determined to make him reveal the contents of the letter. Now, with this fresh death, the link between the Italian and English investigations needs to be strengthened.

A hard push to the heavy studded main door reveals a room with polished medieval stone walls and stylish furniture. Ornate lights are positioned on low marbled tables next to deep leather sofas, and a wide screened television burbles on low volume into the emptiness.

In the corner, stone stairs lead upward, and she ascends to find herself in the Tower guest kitchen. Toasters and microwaves shine next to a sink filled with dirty coffee cups.

Upstairs, she hears laughter and climbs a circular stone staircase carved into one corner. The stairs become progressively narrower and steeper. On the next floor, a room divider separates the bedroom from the stairwell. It is high enough to obscure the apartment, but low enough to allow appreciation of the medieval vaulted ceilings with mosaic brickwork and baroque chandeliers.

A brief knock, and she enters. No one is there. Low lights cast a halo around modern cubist artwork on the walls. The windows are in the form of arched and recessed casements, flared with the sinking sun. On the far side of the valley, Volterra's windows blink a Morse code back to the Tower. Below, the party sounds dampen. Agata tiptoes past the double bed and looks down at the gardens, searching again for a glimpse of blue aertex shirt, but it's impossible to distinguish the guests at such a height. She tries a side door that reveals a sliver of an empty shower room.

More laughter, and again she ascends. The next floor is identical in design, the views extending further. The party is now no more than a muted suggestion, but the laughter is closer. She opens a door to find the American woman and the older of Naomi's boys on the bed. Mercifully, they are not yet in *flagrante delicto*, but there's no doubt what they have in mind. Crystal's bright pink T-shirt is rucked up to show a racy bra, and Aldo's trouser belt is undone. Upon seeing Agata, Crystal bursts into laughter. Aldo jumps up, a flush coming to his handsome cheeks. He sees to his trousers.

'Hey, spoil sport,' says Crystal. 'It was just getting interesting.' Her bright hazel eyes challenge Agata.

'Please don't say a word to Mama,' says Aldo, and he scoots to the door. 'She's sex mad, that one!' He blows Crystal a kiss and speeds down the stairs.

'It's not true,' the woman protests with a grin as she adjusts her clothing. 'He's the one who suggested this room. He's not Mama's innocent boy, by any means. I was just snooping, and he caught me. Isn't it fabulous?'

Despite the difference in age, Agata can see how Crystal might be an attractive proposition for sex, and vice versa. It's a moot point, who suggested what. 'I'm sorry to intrude. I was looking for the British policeman. He's wearing a blue aertex shirt. Have you seen him?'

Crystal's brow doesn't move, but her eyes suggest a frown. 'I think I saw the guy you mean taking a piddle in the olive grove earlier.' She tucks in her shirt. 'Aldo caught me sneaking up to the roof. I've heard it's got incredible views, but he said we can't go up because of the firework guys. Health and safety.' She laughs. 'Shame! A roof top setting would be real romantic!'

Together they descend, and Crystal walks off, just as Yolanda accosts Agata. There is no getting away from her sister now.

Chapter Twenty-Seven

With reluctant steps, Susan follows Carl around the Torre di Verdi gardens. They join a queue, and a burst of laughter at their side refutes any notion that the town is shocked by the morning's gruesome discovery. When Amy spoke of Carl, Susan hadn't expected this balding, middle-aged man in a faded black T-shirt. He smiles, and she finds herself reminded of a dormouse with whiskery stubble and cheese-white teeth.

'I heard about your arrival and wanted to introduce myself. My mother and I live over the hill and look after the mayor's dog when he's away. Mad creature. Someone dumped the dog on him, but he's rather fond of her.'

Susan looks at her feet. To her dismay, they are coated in small black insects the size of speckled dirt. She wiggles her toes.

Carl doesn't notice. 'I suppose they're talking about Ma and her house arrest.' He gives her a pleading look. 'I liked Amy, but she'd only been with us for ten days. The whole thing is ridiculous. You don't think Ma did it, do you?'

As Mrs. Henderson is an unknown quantity, Susan grimaces. 'Did Amy tell you why she came here?'

'She said she'd been paid to deliver something. Not drugs. She was very insistent about that.' He wrinkles his nose and twitches the whiskers around his mouth before slurping some wine. 'Obviously, mother didn't like her. She doesn't like any of our younger female guests, especially if I like them. But we're *stranieri*, you see, even though we've been here for ten years.' He sniffs, then returns to gazing at her with his wide blue eyes and begins the story of his life.

Trapped, Susan nudges up the queue and hitches her bag further on her shoulder. Although she and Figgi stopped at Casa Verdi for a quick wash, their dash up to the Tower has made her perspire. The package weighs less than a small apple and is still in the bag. There was no time to hide it in the house, and she wants to check it out by herself. Her ill-ease is further spiked when she catches sight of a man in a blue aertex shirt. He is half the garden's width away, waving at someone, but then disappears towards the thin cypress trees. Carl's voice has lowered an octave, and he bends to whisper in her ear.

'If it weren't for the Montecatini Festa, they'd be abusing the Butcher, but then where would they go to have their fun!' His fingers make contact with her bare arm, and she flinches as if touched by a mosquito. In that second, she loses sight of the man.

'Don't worry, you're safe with me,' says Carl and continues his assessment of the locals. Agata is running through the crowd with a tray in hand and disappears in the direction of the blue aertex shirt. If Agata catches him, will they share the letter? What will it say? Susan feels sick.

Carl continues to talk about his mother's attitudes towards his girlfriends. If he is to be believed, there are many, but none that can be said to be Miss Right. He pulls Susan toward a drum of sizzling meat. Smoke dances into their faces, and before she can refuse, he slaps on squares of beef and portions of chicken, then pushes her forward.

'I'm not really hungry,' she says. 'I had a big lunch.'

'Don't be like that. Amy would have wanted you to eat.' He is focused on getting them a seat and manoeuvres her next to him at the trestle table. Reaching across, his stomach protrudes over the table edge as he picks up a bowl of salad just within reach.

There is no one to use as an excuse to leave, so she sits awkwardly. Servers are trundling along the table length, offering cuts of salami and prosciutto from an outstretched platter. The sight reminds her of Amy's split sternum. Her stomach flips.

'Actually, I'm really grateful to you for sitting with me. Normally I would sit with Ma.' Carl stretches out again for oil and balsamic vinegar vessels. 'I'm lucky I can work anywhere with a good internet connection—and yes, before you ask, I'm much too old to live with my mother, but she hasn't got anyone else and, as I said, her arthritis is awful.' He dollops salad onto Susan's plate before piling his own. Chunks of bread are passed around in a basket as Carl outlines the predicament of finding a girlfriend while living with a parent.

'I know my mother is difficult. When I met Amy, I wondered about her. She was tough, she could cope with my Ma.' He drinks and then burps gently. 'Y'know, I wanna live like a normal guy. But no, it wasn't to happen.' He drinks some more.

'When did you last see Amy?' If she must sit with him, she might as well glean some information.

'Dunno.' Carl burps. 'She came back last night, but we

were booking in a couple of new guests. She must have gone out again. We told the police we didn't notice. Poor Ma.' He shovels in a large mouthful of salad.

Someone lights the candles, and citronella plumes rise into the dusk. Solar lights come to life and blink in the trees and the vines. A man with long, stringy hair is filling the wooden platform with equipment and musical instruments.

'The thing is,' continues Carl, waving a knife, 'Ma is chronically insecure about being left old and alone. I can see what she's doing to me. I'm not stupid, y'know, but I thought Amy and Mother. Maybe? I was going to ask her out.' He accepts another refill of wine from Aldo (or it could be Orlando as Susan can't tell the difference between Naomi's sons), and drains the glass, mopping up oil with bread and pushing it into his mouth, 'Yeah of cour', ev'one is sayin' we did it.' He swallows. 'But I tell you, everyone's, like, talking up their arse.' He waves for a wine bottle to be passed down the table. 'You'd get on with Ma. Would you like to come to lunsh?' he slurs.

This is too much. She has no difficulty imagining him as a murderer of lone women, and fears she will make another emotional outburst, only this time, it will be violent. She excuses herself and flees to the perimeter fence, where she spies Crystal talking to one of the D'Angelo boys. Crystal leans against him with a coquettish air and doesn't move when Agata joins them with a plate full of bruschetta.

'Well! Hi!' The intense hazel eyes are lidded. She is either slightly drunk or slightly high. Her gaze takes in both Susan and Agata with a sardonic smile. 'God, I just love this lifestyle. I'm making a night of it. My brother's here, and he said he'd do Auntie Linda's medicines.' She giggles. 'Have you met Aldo?'

He smells of burnt barbecue and musk, and his handsome face is flushed with heat.

'Where is he? You said he was in the garden.' Agata glares at Crystal.

'Who?'

'The English sergeant.'

'How should I know?' Crystal shrugs.

'I thought I just saw him,' says Susan.

'Really? Where did he go?'

'Toward the Tower or maybe toward the olive trees behind the fir hedge there?'

Agata shakes her head and leaves, distributing food left and right without attention.

Crystal entwines her fingers into Aldo's glossy black hair as she speaks to Susan. 'No Figaro? They say he's very Roman with time.'

Aldo objects to the inference with good humour, and Crystal laughs.

A broad man with a full beard appears from the woods. His thick, reddish hair protrudes from under a baseball cap, and he's wearing a blue aertex shirt. It's definitely not the policeman who interviewed her in London. A case of right shirt, wrong man.

'Have you met my half-brother, Robert?' Crystal says, and the man nods a hello in an indefinable accent. 'We don't look alike! Same dad, different mom.'

'Ja.' He nods. *Does Dutch sound like German*? wonders Susan. She hasn't travelled enough to distinguish.

'And I'm free to stay at the party!' Crystal strokes Aldo's cheek, 'Fancy a rematch?'

The man called Robert whispers in Crystal's ear, and she frowns but waves him away. Further conversation is interrupted by an irritable Naomi. In the solar light, her nose has a sheen of perspiration. She insists on Aldo's help.

'*Subito, subito,* I'm coming,' he says, not moving.

The stringy guitarist begins a lament, and Crystal's brother leaves, walking toward the Tower gates. Susan wants to attach herself to Naomi, but the older woman is pulling at her son's sleeve, insisting he helps.

'Mamma!' Aldo rolls his eyes in a display of comedy for Crystal's benefit, but he does as he's told, and Crystal goes in search of another drink.

'Fireworks at midnight. You'll love it.' Naomi treads warily to avoid the snaking wires that run from the musician's dais all the way to the electricity supply at the Tower. Although it has been professionally marked with yellow tape, it is like crossing a river. There are tired creases around Naomi's eyes, and her voice has sunk an octave into a nicotine and caffeine brogue. 'Thankfully no speeches. God knows what would be appropriate to say after this morning.'

'How is Edu?'

She points. A second man has joined the guitarist, and Edu is by his side fingering a computer console. 'I thought he'd hide away, but he's doing well. Whatever you said to him on the drive to Volterra must have been helpful.'

Susan stares at Edu plugging in various leads and sorting the metal spaghetti with ease. What did she say? He knows more than she does.

Chapter Twenty-Eight

Montecatini della Torre. One month before Alessandro's murder

The enemy was inside the gate, and such a revelation was painful to Alessandro. He had always prided himself on being the guardian of Montecatini, even if his family saw otherwise. This was his territory. His right. His to inherit.

His fifth cigarette of the night glowed in the purple predawn as he smoked and tossed around solutions. The Torre di Verdi blazed against the paling nighttime sky. A cuboid of stars. Knowing he was at the end of his twenty-four-hour visit, he stretched with fatigue. He had signed documents with a local notary, delivered fake passports, and looked people in the eye before completing large transactions. This deal was outside the Syndicate's remit, so he needed to be careful.

But in Montecatini, he felt safe. Renzo and Natale would never give him away. When Renzo had handed him the local paper, Il Gazzetino, the old man had spoken about the strangers in their midst, and Alessandro read the information with concern. Such a secret could never stay hidden. Not in this community.

A quick glance at the relevant paragraphs, and the newspaper article meant more to him than it did to Renzo. Is that what they did with the child? He hadn't asked. Best not to ask. That had always been his motto. As long as the payout was good. He understood that children would be handed over to the Syndicate. He understood some of the adult migrants would be sold. That was the traffickers' price. He understood those hired to run the Italian leg of the operation were currently operating a side racket: a kidney here, a liver there. So he had thought nothing when they said they were making an overnight stop near a hospital, and on his patch, he knew the perfect hiding place for a night. But according to Renzo, one night had become a month. A month! No one could hide for a month. You couldn't keep a secret for a week in Montecatini, let alone a month. Locals saw everything.

Predictably, the traffickers had blamed Karol. The Russian man oversaw this stretch from Puglia to Belgium, and the fat man was well known for his brutality with anyone seeking to skim profits. Many of the drivers disappeared on Karol's orders, so the couple were afraid. They asked to remain hidden and begged Alessandro to allow the deal to go ahead. All they needed was time to collect the funds, so they could pay Alessandro his million-dollar payout, and then they would disappear to South America. He had agreed. But not for a month. And not for a murder on his territory. The child was not meant to die, let alone be buried on a beach. And what idiot had allowed the Cecina beach location to be connected to Montecatini della Torre?

Finishing his Marlboro, he ground it into the ashtray. It was never wise to wait. Like a smouldering cigarette, deals had a finite window of opportunity. Everything was in place, and the updating of border regulations, inevitable with England leaving the European market, meant the Syndi-

cate's system was about to undergo a major change. His negotiations to purchase Buriano were nearly complete, and Jett had given him his black book to check up on clients. It was more than a gift; it was a sign. Now was the time for him to extricate himself. For the final fanfare, Susan was in position. She would draw the flak. If he was to extract himself from the Syndicate's tentacles and grab the untraceable money, he had to keep going.

The list of his last few errands, a breadcrumb trail, formed in his mind. Glancing at the Torre di Verdi, he imagined medieval guards watching for invaders. At the first sign of trouble, they dispatched riders to Volterra to alert the city. The horsemen would gallop to the city walls, shouting: The enemy is at the gate! Cesare Borgia comes with his murderous Spanish soldiers. Put down the portcullis! Pull up the drawbridge! Make ready the vats of boiling oil!

But no one watched anymore. The hillside community had grown flaccid on peace and tourist money. Marauders and Mafia passed right under their noses.

He made a fist. 'I am Alessandro Verdi. And I will win.'

With a flash of inspiration, he sat at his childhood desk, uncapped a pen, and drew out the old notepaper with the Verdi crest. Then he began to write a letter. Not so much a breadcrumb, more a whole slice.

Chapter Twenty-Nine

Agata sneaks past the kitchens to avoid her sister. Once more, she runs up the Tower stairs. If she wants a fitness workout, this is it. Second time around, she ascends further to the fifth and final floor. For a moment, she senses someone behind her. A shoe's scuff, a breath? Or is it the echo of her own feet against the stone and the pumping of her heart? She isn't sure, but more raucous laughter pushes her to climb the narrowest part of the staircase. Above her, a rounded lid opens onto the flat roof of the Tower.

Poking her head up, she sees crenelations, invisible from the ground. An artificial light illuminates a bright circle in the centre of the platform, and around it the land unfolds in a 360-degree silhouette. What a watchtower this is! From country to sea, all is visible. To one side, Volterra's walls are lit like a battleship at sea. In front of her, three people squat, inspecting a large, paper diagram on the floor.

'*Ciao bella*! You can't come here,' calls one of the men. In front of them, cones and boxes sit with numbers and tags surrounded by cables crisscrossing in complex formation over the ground.

As they stand, she notes the parapet is no higher than their waists. When she explains that she's looking for a man, they shout with laughter and wave hands in the direction of a large shape in a darkened corner. There is the English policeman, slumped over a wrought-iron table, head on his arms. It looks too uncomfortable for sleep, and yet his eyes are closed. A heavy sunshade folded like a bat's wing stands on one side of him, a round computer mast the other. Sentries on guard.

'He's drunk,' the firework men say. 'We came up here and found him finishing a bottle on his own. We told him to leave, but maybe the stairs are too much for him. He'll pitch and fall.' They make some further caustic comments about drunken Englishmen.

'He's a British policeman,' she says.

They laugh all the harder. 'Look, we're taking a break for a smoke and food before the event.' A man with a goatee beard scratches his crotch. 'Can we leave him with you? He needs to go before we start the explosions.'

Agata asks for help, but they turn her down flat. 'Our insurance only covers us for certain things. S'pose he falls and cracks his head? We'd be in dead trouble.'

'He'd be the dead one if he falls down those stairs!'

With a mock apology, they leave, and she hears their continued laughter echoing on the stairs.

In a temper, she shakes the sergeant by the shoulder and shouts. His eyes are red-rimmed as they open. He slurs, 'Hey darling. You promised you'd service me.' She thumps him on the back and swears at him. He groans and repositions his head to face away from her. Agata pinches his fleshy upper arm. He releases a rumbling snore. His position makes a body search difficult, but she digs determinedly in his trouser pockets and his shirt. Where her fingers are going, she'll soon find out if he's faking. But he doesn't stir, and there is neither a letter nor money.

'Where is it?' she shouts in his ear.

For a second, his bloodshot eyes re-open, and he manages a leer. 'No deal, darling. I'm no fool.' He tries to tap his nose with a finger. Misses. His arm swings down by his side, and his face hits the iron table. He resettles to sleep.

The best course of action is to ask Naomi's sons, Orlando and Aldo, to assist in moving him down to one of the bedrooms. He's too heavy for her on her own, and it will be pointless to speak to him until he sobers up. Descending the stairs rapidly, she thinks there is a tapping noise behind her. She stops, unsure. Anyone could be in these rooms. There's no security. But she doesn't want another episode of walking in on half-naked bodies.

'Is anyone there?' she calls out. 'Can you help me move this guy from the top?' A millisecond of echo chases her voice and then silence. She is running out of time and continues, thighs protesting, as she winds down the steep staircase. At the base, she bumps into an angry Yolanda.

'They're clamouring for more.' Two large platters are thrust into either hand. It's fastest not to argue, and Agata re-enters the gardens, struggling to balance the trays. Fruits and cheeses and marzipan cakes are spread out for the third course. People will eat until they burst to get the price of their ticket.

Fireflies blink across the field, and solar lights give a hazy glow to trees' branches. Someone has lit the oil lamps, but it is too dark for Agata to see for any distance. People are tramping backward and forward to use the ground floor toilets in the Tower area. Naomi's boys are nowhere to be seen. She finds Susan hovering in a dark recess, clutching her bag.

'Where's Figgi?'

'Here,' he says.

They both jump as he appears, breathless, out of the gloom. 'I've run back.'

In relief, Agata outlines her dilemma and asks for his help. Figgi suggests they need at least two large people to move him, and they look for possible volunteers.

'And the letter?' asks Figgi.

Agata sucks her teeth in irritation. 'No letter. I checked. Which reminds me, what was collected at Volterra?'

Figgi looks at them. In the solar lights, his skin is a pewter mask. 'The Englishman collected the parcel from the courier?'

The guitarist stops, and there is scraping and movement as another band pulls instruments onto the decked area.

Agata is hissing with impatience. 'Not him—you, Susan. You've had all day, and I know you picked up something in Volterra. Haven't you discussed this with Figgi?'

Her face crumples. 'I'm sorry. I forgot.'

'It'll be worse if you hide it,' Agata insists.

'Hide what?'

'You're as bad as each other,' she says. 'You didn't tell me Alessandro was still in touch with Mariju. I had to hear it from Yolanda. And she doesn't tell you about the package. Do you want his murder solved or not?'

Figgi puts up a hand as if to stop the traffic, claiming ignorance. Susan insists the package has been safe in her bag.

This is not a time for diplomacy, and Agata does not hold back on her anger. 'You're idiots. Anyone could pick-pocket you. You both need to go. Don't you see? There's no police here at the Festa because of the Livorno protests. Just one Carabiniere guarding the murder site.'

'It's worse than that,' says Figgi calmly. 'Old Tomaso claims he saw two men with Amy. They were parked near the closed copper mines in the woods. He couldn't see their faces, but one was tall and thick-set. Does that fit your sergeant?'

Agata chews a lip. 'When was this?'

'About two in the morning.'

Her mind races to find connections, but the dots refuse to join. 'We'll have to wait for the policeman to sober. Let's hope there's a copy of the letter in that package.'

'But what if it's something to make me look guilty?' Susan is twisting the buttons on her dress.

Figgi puts an arm around her. 'We'll tackle it together,' he says.

Sun, sea, sand, and sex? Ignoring his father's calls? Maybe this girl isn't so stupid after all, thinks Agata as Figgi leads Susan away. She calls after them to hurry.

They nod, and Figgi says, 'In any case, I brought my car up the hill, and it is blocking someone in the overflow parking.' A look passes between them before they run down the path out of the gardens.

For a second, Agata forces herself to breathe and calm down: inhale, exhale. She examines her emotions. A part of her is desperate to clear Alessandro's name. A part of her is riddled with good, old-fashioned, ugly jealousy. Susan was the last woman in his bed. Sheepish Susan! She is twisted up like a fox in a snare.

Turning back to the garden, she goes to find assistance in the form of Naomi's boys.

Chapter Thirty

Agata spies Umberto near the musician's platform. He is crouching, speaking softly. Edu's legs are tightly folded to his chest, one arm gripping his knees, while the other pounds the grass in a fist. The boy stares blankly ahead and mumbles.

Orlando comes from behind her, sinking at Edu's side.

Edu's brow is deeply furrowed, mouth drawn back in a grimace. 'He called me names, bad names. I only tried to help. Why would he threaten me?' A sob breaks from his throat.

'Who?' says Agata.

Umberto speaks to her quietly. 'I asked Edu to go and check to make sure the firework organisers had everything they wanted.' He fingers his wedding ring nervously. 'Perhaps I shouldn't have. Now, Edu tells me a foreign man became abusive to him on the stairs, but I don't know who.'

'The English sergeant? The one sleeping on the roof?' Agata shakes her head. 'But he was almost unconscious when I left him.'

'Or pretending!' says Orlando, anger rising on his step-brother's behalf. 'See how the police do this to him!'

As he rocks back and forth, incoherent words tumble from Edu's mouth. Then he throws back his head and growls at the sky. Orlando sits shoulder to shoulder with him, urging calm.

'He's been on edge all day because of that girl's murder,' moans Umberto.

'When I find that policeman...' But Orlando is cut short by a look from his father, and in the next second, Edu rises in one volant movement, toppling his brother.

With flailing arms, the boy punches the sky, and one fist lands on Umberto's chest, making him stagger backward. Then he runs, over the fence and down the hill. The loudness of the music prevents anyone from noticing this exchange, and within a second, the silhouette of trees swallows him.

Orlando helps his father to rise. 'Papa. Leave him. You know what the therapist said. He'll go to his special place and talk to himself until he's calm again. In the morning, he'll be embarrassed.'

'What was said to him?' Agata peers into the shades of grey beyond.

'Anything. Nothing,' says Umberto.

'Or something,' says Orlando. His whole body is screwed in anger.

'I blame myself for not insisting he stay inside.' Umberto wipes his eyes.

She cannot fathom how the sergeant woke up sufficiently to threaten anyone, but she feels the pain of the family and touches Orlando's arm. 'Come on. We'll find him and question him.'

As they climb the five stories of the Tower faster than

she had thought herself capable, Orlando leads the way, throwing open doors and shouting, but no one is in the building or at the top. Agata's breath comes in short gasps. The table and chairs are awry, and Sergeant Brian Blunt has gone.

'Where is he?' says Orlando, sidestepping the firework cones. 'He deserves a hard slap. I'm going to find him.' He turns and runs down the stone steps.

Agata looks around. Nothing else is disturbed. Even the smallest of firework fuses remain in place. She thinks of his fogged eyes and the slurred speech and moves to the nearest crenelations, peering over. The drop makes her feel queasy: it's so far down. Below, the crowd dance in a coloured tableau. One side is closely wooded and dark, but she cannot see anything in the shrubbery, and imagines if someone fell, at the very least, there would have been a shout.

Carefully, she retraces her steps, checking in every bedroom in case, by a miracle, he has stumbled down to a guest bed. But as before, each floor is empty. Crystal and Orlando's illicit adventure shows on the crumpled sheets, but the rest are smooth, awaiting residents. Each duvet is plumped, and the satin sheets are glistening in low lighting. Not a drunk man nor a clutch of lovers, nor even mischievous children in sight. She glances out the windows of the first floor, trying to see if the sergeant has staggered to the garden party to continue drinking, but the solar lights create a diaspora of guests, and it's hard to identify anyone.

Outside the kitchen, Yolanda pushes a wine box into her hand.

'Come on, Agata, what are you doing? We're working flat out here.' She wipes her perspiring forehead.

Reluctantly, Agata goes out, refills wine glasses, and

collects dirty plates. But she is becoming increasingly anxious. Has the Englishman woken like an enraged bear and caused harm? And if he's threatened Edu, who's next?

'Have you seen the English sergeant?' she asks Naomi, who is balancing two trays of espressos.

'No. Have you seen my husband?'

'He may have gone looking for Edu. There was an incident.'

Naomi blinks in displeasure. 'I'm not surprised. I told Edu to stay home. We're all upset, but Umberto should be helping. And Edu needs space and peace.' She doesn't ask what has happened, instead casting a reproving glance at the musicians. Dancing and decibels are increasing. 'I'll crack Umberto's head when I find him. Last I saw him, he was with the guitarist, chatting. And we have to clear the tables before the fireworks. When people look up, they trip and break plates and glasses.' She hurries off.

At the garden entrance, Agata looks down over the low stone wall toward the main piazza. She strains to see what's happening in the square. Perhaps the sergeant is making his way back to the Airbnb, though goodness knows how safe he would be in charge of a vehicle. A few men carry boxes of supplies, and the area is lit in the ghostly phosphorescence of two streetlights. All the cafe lights are out, and the metal tables and chairs are in vertical clumps. She studies a four-door Fiat as it drives off toward the windmill hills, but she cannot remember the make of the sergeant's rental car. Behind the Fiat, a foreign car with stickers pulls out and disappears up the road past the refuse dump. Someone hops into a camper van. She's not sure if it was the mad driver who nearly caused her accident earlier or another tourist. It looks creamy, but the light distorts colours, and anyway, she'll deal with that another time. The van goes slowly between lingering pedestrians before driving down the hill. Nothing looks unusual. The fireworks can be seen for miles around, and each year some prefer to watch in the calm of their own homes or from the higher viewpoint of the Miniera carpark.

With the knowledge her sister will be incandescent in the morning, she descends into the square. Jogging up the road to check on the forensic tent, she finds one lone Carabiniere slumbering in a deckchair, a bottle of wine at his side. His jacket is open and his sash askew. A smattering of flowers have been left around the tent with mixed messages. Some wish the English safe haven in Heaven; others insist that the Montecatinese would never do such a thing. Young revellers are fooling around at the water fountains—boys splashing giggling girls.

'Wake up,' she says, and the policeman gives a guttural snore, readjusting himself on the chair.

'Oh! Signora Agnello! *Buona notte*!' He smiles, running a hand over his face. 'Please don't tell anyone. I couldn't help but have a little snooze.'

She looks at the bottle by his side.

'It's Renzo's last year's vintage.' He puts fingers to his mouth and kisses them. 'The best he's ever made. The Verdis will miss him.'

'He's retiring?' Renzo is full of secrets, she thinks.

'So he said. A better offer elsewhere.'

Hard to believe such gossip, but it's a conversation for another time. 'Have you seen a large man walking or driving slowly past here?'

'Signora! You must be more specific.'

'A large Englishman?'

He laughs with good nature. 'I know exactly who you mean. No.' The Carabiniere stands up and stretches. 'But to be honest, I'm just guarding the body. And a lot of cars have passed going to the Miniera for a good view. So I can't be sure.'

'Hasn't the poor girl been taken yet?'

He gives a rueful grin. 'With the trouble at Livorno, there's been no one to move her. Not one ambulance or paramedic. And we can't release her body to the undertakers—it must go direct to Pathology. Poor little one. At least we bagged her, and she sleeps peacefully on the ground. I heard she was pretty.'

Unexpected sadness catches in Agata's throat, but a noise from across the road distracts them both. The teenage romps have escalated, and the air is split with laughter and lewd comments. She holds back from yelling at them. Have they no respect?

The Carabiniere gives a gentle shrug. 'Life goes on.'

This is no time for sentimentality. Hurrying back to the Tower Gardens, she suspects her sister will commit murder if she realises her absence, but when she enters the field, all eyes are upward as the fireworks begin. A roar followed by a screaming sound opens the display. Everyone tilts their heads to catch the whirls of colour exploding against the black canvas of sky and hills. Screeching pinwheels and a volley of booms are followed by gold and silver in a fanfare across the olive groves. These are overtaken by blue and pink blossoms that coat the Tower before collapsing to the horizon. More bangs and popping sounds, and guests shouting appreciation. Agata imagines Edu hiding terrified amongst the trees.

For ten minutes, she hovers, checking and re-checking each square metre of the party as the fireworks light up the gardens. Nothing. She is angry at herself for leaving the policeman. What is happening to her instincts? She was once so proud of her street smarts. Why has she become unable to spot when someone is play-acting? It's the move to the country that's to blame. That and Luca. This is all his fault. A phone vibrating in her waitress' apron yanks her from her mental tirade.

'Agata, come and see this immediately. It's serious.'

She doesn't need a second invitation. Throwing down her apron into a pile of dishcloths by the kitchen's doorway, she speaks abruptly to Dana, who is loading crockery into the industrial dishwasher. 'I can't stay. Police business.'

The owner of the Trattoria della Torre smiles and nods, smoking in a corner. He offers to help in her place, and Dana waves her away. Running, she dashes to retrieve her car. Thank God, it is a Cinquecento and she can just manage to get out. In her eagerness, she bumps a wing mirror but keeps going. She avoids the crowded route past the municipal building and takes the alternative short cut that goes along the hillside road of Via Giuseppe with its overspill parking. As she negotiates the steep road down, a scrape on her chassis makes her curse. The steepness of the turn catches everyone in a hurry, but not even an injury to her beloved car will halt her. She forges down the hill.

Chapter Thirty-One

Ruby dances in the kitchen, and Figgi holds her back. 'You're too late to deter intruders,' he says to the dog as he opens the door.

Agata stops on the threshold. Drawers are open, cupboards hang ajar, and tea towels lie like rag dolls on the floor. Susan runs down the circular stairs and beckons her up.

'I don't know how they got past Ruby. An English bull terrier with big teeth!' Susan's eyes are pools of fear.

'We forgot to lock the door,' says Figgi.

Agata watches Figgi drag Ruby upstairs, as if she is responsible for this unexpected turn of events. The dog whines and scuttles down the corridor to the living room, heading straight for her dog bed. A firework illuminates the sky with pink rain.

'Susan's bedroom is also a disaster,' he says. 'But I think we frightened the intruders when my car turned up. I saw a black shadow running up the hill. If they've run to the woods, I hope wild boar skewer them!'

'Figgi has sharp eyes. I saw no one.'

So, thinks Agata, she's calling him Figgi now?

In the *salotto*, all is well; the oils are on the walls, and the alabaster eggs are in their stone nests. Antique silver candlesticks shine in the low lights near a mahogany table.

'Do you think they wanted the letter?' says Figgi. 'We don't know how many people Amy told. Or if the British policeman said something.'

For a minute, they discuss the disappearance of Sergeant Blunt, the package, and the letter. Susan stares at her feet while simultaneously twisting the buttons on her dress. She reminds Agata of a child being summoned to the Headteacher. Figgi puts on reading glasses, pushing them up his nose, and beckons Agata to the centre of the room where a tiled coffee table has been set on a cotton twist rug. A desk lamp trails a cord to throw bright light onto the contents. As Agata kneels, she sees their images in the panes of the darkened French doors. The last bursts of fireworks blot the reflection for a moment, then the landscape returns to black with only the lights of Volterra for a compass. A side window is open, and the crickets fill the void left by the last of the Festa celebrations.

The table bears its gifts. She examines them with Susan by her side; a small black leather-bound book with clasp and keyhole; a tiny silver key, tarnished and worn; a thin silver plaque barely attached to the leather, worked loose by time, but still bearing Sir John's monogram; and three pieces of A4 paper with quarter creases, smoothed out side by side. As an inventory, she wants to say, this should not have caused loss of life.

The book is recognisable, yet when last viewed on her employer's desk it held no hint of menace. She was younger then, and wonders if naivety played a part. The silver edges are more scuffed than she remembers, but the contents are probably the same: names and numbers in a pre-mobile phone era. She can still see Sir John's face when told of Jett's games with his daughter in the drawing room. A hard mouth, but a curious absence of shock. Is it possible that Jett found like-minded clients within the pages? The people seeking Off Grid Kids? The thought makes her both angry and despairing. How civilised is the 21st century? She bends to study three pieces of paper. Figgi leans over her shoulder and hands her white gloves.

'I use them to look at old architectural plans. We thought it best to avoid putting our fingerprints on them.'

She is impressed by his forethought and slips them on. They have the consistency of butter, although they are too large. Fumbling, she picks up the first page while Figgi paces the room. As his reflection follows him in the glass, Susan twists her dress buttons fiercely.

The page in Agata's hand is nothing more than a printed internet search of private clinics in Tuscany. It includes the Cecina Clinic, but nothing has been starred or underlined. The other side is blank. On the second sheet, there is another printout with the heading of Golden Blood. 'So he knew.' She sucks her teeth. This is a bitter blow, but without a date, she can't be sure whether he printed it before or after the child was killed. She turns it over, but there is no clue as to whether he was complicit in the girl's death.

Figgi stops and faces himself in the large glass doors. It is as if he hears her thoughts. 'I cannot see my cousin as a murderer, but he was involved in some way. I am sure.'

Agata wants to agree. There are many crimes they could lay against Alessandro, but not one of violence. Greed, perhaps? She hesitates. Susan would be best placed to know, but she remains silent as Agata examines the final sheet. A photograph has been enlarged and printed. The date at the bottom shows it was taken days before his death. Despite the granular texture, the head and shoulders are clear enough, although she finds it difficult to distinguish if it is male or female. Someone has folded the edge of a white hospital body bag to reveal the upper portion of a corpse. The zip is visible in the diagonal line, and the pallid complexion and dark lips are covered in a frosted coating that spikes the lashes. The skin colour is also difficult to decipher in the shot. Either it is dark, whitened by extreme cold, or pale, darkened with freezer burn. The angle of the shot has captured part of a chest freezer door and a manufacturer's marks, but it is indistinct.

'Is that the Tower kitchens?' Susan leans forward, and Agata catches her drift.

'They have a big freezer in the Tower kitchen, but tonight it has been full of meat and vegetables. No body parts there now. Perhaps the letter would've told us.' She wriggles her legs to one side. Her eyes and feet hurt with all the running around she's done since five this morning, and she is struggling to formulate the correct questions. 'Does any of this mean something to you?'

'Susan hasn't done this.' Figgi stops his pacing to squat opposite them at the table. 'I found out that Alessandro was here briefly, shortly before he died.'

'How?' asks Agata, acutely conscious that he has not imparted this information before tonight.

'I have cameras in the house. I installed them when we banned Alessandro from coming here.'

By the expression on Susan's face, it is clear she knew nothing, but she recovers and points. 'Look over the page,' Susan instructs. On the other side are scrawled the words: *What have you done?*

It's not clear who the note is for, or whether the question is written in condemnation or query, but the handwriting is definitely Alessandro's. She has his letters from years ago that remain seared into Agata's memory.

Figgi stands again, paces to a sideboard and takes out a blue glass bottle of water. He pours three glasses while insisting she look inside the black book. The gloves make turning the pages awkward, but she presses against the covers and allows the leaves to rustle open, landing on indiscriminate pages. With a strange reverence, she reads a past history. Many of the surnames hark back to her days in the Knightsbridge house. No addresses, just ex-directory phone numbers. Here are the direct links to people who held power a quarter of a century ago. Some have died, others may be in retirement in country mansions, but who still holds the reins? Her thickened fingers turn to the back of the book and the ink changes. Names have been added recently. And in biro. Sir John never used a ball-point pen, insisting on using his Montblanc fountain pen. Again, she recognises Alessandro's script. Five names are in blue, and three are underlined in a red biro with two sets of codes beneath. She chokes in surprise and sips the water before pressing open that final page. Susan's name is in the middle. *Susan Li Verdi.*

'In my job at the auction house, I had to check payments for sales and purchases.' Susan speaks in a whisper as if admitting to a crime. 'The top numbers are offshore accounts, Cayman Islands in the main. I recognise the codes. Quite a few of our customers used these bank accounts when large amounts were involved in a sale. And the numbers and words underneath are passwords. Some have email accounts. With this information, anyone could gain access.'

This doesn't answer the question. Susan edges away from Agata. There are five names on the last page. Karol Berzins, followed by a joint account in the name of David and Christine Boeker. Next to each is the figure of three million dollars. Susan's name is underneath. Her account is listed as having received two million dollars, two weeks before Alessandro's death.

'People have killed for less money,' says Agata as she rechecks the zeros.

'He insisted,' Susan whispers. 'Alessandro made me open an account and take two million of his funds. He said it was to prove he loved me. So I wouldn't worry about money. He didn't want us to have a joint account.'

'Is that the price of love today? I must tell Luca.' Agata is immune to Susan's embarrassed button-squeezing. 'Why didn't you tell us before?'

Figgi puts out a hand, and they clasp for a second. 'It proves her innocence. She could have run off with it. Instead, she's come here at his request.'

'So why make that request?' But Agata has a theory. 'It's possible, by placing you here, you become central to the crimes, and a suspect of both the Verdi family and the police.' She cannot fathom why Figgi isn't treating Susan with more hostility. It must be love. As they look at each other, shaking heads, one inescapable fact surfaces in Agata's tired brain. 'Let us not forget, Sandro expected to live. Who knows how he would have followed this up? Might he have asked for the money back?'

'He was using Susan. Isn't that obvious?' Figgi bears the same expression Agata remembers from his dealings with his cousin from many years ago. Each time they sent him to sort Alessandro's transgressions, Figgi's chin would jut and his lips tighten. He is still the boy wanting his cousin to be publicly harangued instead of privately reprimanded. Is this the reason he is keen to take over his cousin's latest paramour? Some ghastly desire to trounce Alessandro?

Her eyes squint over the inked markings. Then she points with a clumsy, white-gloved finger. 'I don't know Karol Berzins, or the Boekers, but the last name on the list is Jett Stillttiger. It's Jett. The Jett we knew from that summer.' She explains to Susan. 'Twenty-five years ago, I introduced Alessandro to Jett. He's what the English would call a bad apple. Recently, I found out that he took his stepfather's black book when Sir John died. Look at the account in his name. Just 500,000 dollars, probably the cash you need to open an offshore like this, no questions asked.' She tuts. 'Of course, it's an anagram, and bound to be a false account set up by Alessandro. It's his way of giving a warning. Don't hurt me, and I won't hurt you.'

Susan swallows and looks confused. For a moment, the buttons get a reprieve. 'An anagram? I only know Karol. I've met Mr. Berzins.' She looks at Agata. 'Alessandro took me to some business party where there were underage girls in bikinis. I was told it was a pool party, advertising swimwear for children, but I didn't see any photographers. Or other women of my age. Just men and young girls. Afterwards Alessandro told me they were art collectors, not friends, and I wouldn't see them again.'

Agata curls her gloved hands around the book. 'Underage girls? That sounds like Jett's idea of fun. It seems even more likely that your marriage was designed to make you visible.'

Without makeup, it is easy to see the fear spread across Susan's features. But there is also a tinge of anger in the unadorned eyes. 'I didn't want to do it. Any of it. He insisted I create the account and take his money.'

Figgi squeezes her hand, and Agata tucks the photocopies back into the black book and places it in the envelope. Peeling off the gloves, she holds the parcel to her chest.

They stand and move to the corridor. 'We need to hand this over to Luca and find the location of the freezer,' she says as a yawn surfaces.'You agree it's too important to be kept in the Verdi family?'

Figgi nods. 'I've got hunting rifles in the cabinet room downstairs. When you go, I'll get one out.'

At Susan's ill-suppressed shiver, Agata snaps her fingers. 'Wake up. This is the countryside. Everyone has rifles, Susan. Rifles and mosquitoes. Not just wine and olives.' She notices Figgi place his little finger to Susan's wrist. 'Meet me at La Pizzeria tomorrow at ten, and I'll drag Luca along.'

But she doubts any of them will sleep.

Chapter Thirty-Two

Tired as she is, she makes a two-minute detour to the old mines. Perhaps she will find the sergeant slumbering in his car. The Miniera Hotel shut down a year ago, a faded last-century glamorous establishment needing expensive restoration. Typically, the local *comune* could not agree on future use, so a camping site has sprung up as a short-term measure. Tourists park and pay for hook-up at the Mining Museum in order to have electricity and Miniera Wi-Fi. But it's an inefficient spot. Anyone can come late and leave early if they don't mind the lack of facilities.

Inside the open gates, she drives past the scuffed sign of *Il Museo della Miniera*, with its arrow pointing toward a rough sign of *Campeggio*. Five camper vans stand in a row, their pitches lit by a single neon light.

The silence suggests sleep. Either that or the occupants continue their revelries at the Tower Gardens. Agata looks at each vehicle. There are Dutch and German plates, but no Italian rental car, and if one of the Casa Verdi thieves has gone to ground, she lacks the proof to invade. Even so, if she sees the beige and white camper van, she will happily bang on the door, wake the occupants, and give them a piece of her mind. But it's not there. Disappointed, she sniffs the sulfurous post-firework air.

Gruelling willpower keeps her eyes open. She gulps air from the open window, driving past the boundary of the ghost town, Buriano. A speck of light shines deep into the territory. Car lights? Rough campers? As she slows, it extinguishes, and all is dark. There are too many acres to search, and anyway, Agata suspects poaching. That's not her fight. Not tonight.

Mouth open, Luca is asleep, naked in the bed. His body smells of the crowd, and she's tempted to wake him out of spite. Then she decides she needs sleep more than an argument and climbs into bed. He turns towards her. 'We win. Yes, Italia!' His limbs tense then relax, and he snores.

Her mind cannot rest. It flips through new and old information. Is Susan really the innocent? Agata remembers her being sick into the gutter and decides no one could fake that level of shock. But the woman admits to knowing Karol Berzins and taking two million into an offshore account in her name. Why hasn't she mentioned this before?

And what about Amy? Is her murder a copy-cat? Or is it the same killer who was disturbed before removing the organs? Carl's mother is not the killer—that's Fabio being stupid. You may as well accuse Crystal of being a slut and cart her off to jail. *Pffft*, she murmurs into her pillow, and Luca mumbles in response. The sergeant hasn't tried to speak to Luca or Susan, so what's the English game? Perhaps the British have blindsided the Italian police. But where did he go, and why upset Edu? If you want to be invisible, you don't target the locals when you're the outsider. Perhaps he didn't see Edu as a local. *Bastardo*!

Turning in discomfort, her thoughts rest on the Tower freezer. Is it a case of *where there's smoke*? Has the Butcher helped dispose of bodies? But if Alessandro was the man organising Syndicate offshore accounts, why expose his source of income? And what was Figaro doing liaising with poachers? Surely the Verdi family do not stoop so low? In the darkness, her wildest thoughts fly like phantasms. Alessandro was friends with Jett. And Jett was... her sleep-addled brain can only form shapeless monsters. As Luca snores, she elbows him impatiently, too tired to sleep.

And then she slides into an uneasy slumber of dreams and nightmares.

A few hours later, she wakes to see the clock showing five-thirty. Semi-conscious, she is in another world where Jett is fastening a hand around her neck. She can hear his voice telling her she's never to repeat what she saw. Her body jerks as she tries to bring up a knee into his groin, but her leg refuses to do what she wants, trapped against Luca. Then her eyes open, and she slides next to her husband's warm back. As her eyes close, it is Alessandro who turns to face her. He kisses her, and her whole body responds, until he says, 'It's all about revenge.'

She is wide awake.

Sweating, she sits up in panic. The sky lightens and the harsh cry of pheasants punctuate the dawn. Despite the heaviness of her limbs, anxiety crawls in her brain. Her bare feet welcome the cool of the tiles, and she pads downstairs to throw open the kitchen doors. The sun emerges with its customary purple stripe between the dip of hills. Agata must murder something or go mad. She checks to make sure that the notebook is still in her handbag. Jett's name haunts her. Stillttiger? The anagram isn't difficult, but it means Alessandro knew. He knew and did nothing. Is there a special circle in Hell for people who turn a blind eye to paedophilia?

Children were forbidden to enter the ornate drawing room, with its gold leaf coffee tables and leather buttoned chesterfields that smelt of privilege. This was the domain of Sir John and his wife, where old portraits with flint-black eyes watched everyone's step. Agata had just come on shift and was using the back nursery stairs when she heard the child's voice. Padding down the corridor, she pushed at the door with the stealth of a burglar. For a moment, the afternoon sun dazzled, then she saw the profile of her eldest charge. The girl was ten years old, capricious but affectionate.

'No, Jett.' There was both defiance and uncertainty in her voice. 'No more.'

Jett stood, flicking up her skirt with a fireside poker and laughing. 'You're not a baby—show me again!'

As Agata stepped into the room, the child looked at her with a mixture of alarm and embarrassment. In one hand, she clutched her knickers; in the other, she held a small Monsoon bag, her favourite label.

Jett's pale face flushed but he remained where he was, leaning against the mantlepiece. 'Don't worry,' he said as the girl stepped back. 'It's only the foreign help. Not your proper nanny. Your English nanny smacks your bottom, and you enjoy it.'

'That's enough, Jett.' Agata spoke with the precision of a knife.

The girl offered back the bag, but Jett laughed, encouraging her to keep it. Agata instructed the child to return to her siblings, and for once, the girl didn't say she was too old for the nursery. Scampering past Agata, she bolted down the corridor.

There was a silence as each wondered what to say. Jett was an ex-Eton boy, knocking around London without a place at Oxford. He turned, poker in hand, and faced her with his usual bitter sneer. But Agata's outrage was stronger.

'Don't you dare behave that way with your half-sister.'

In two strides, he was in front of her. A sudden thrust, and he pushed the poker against her throat. Her hands went to the metal, but he was taller and heavier, making her gasp.

'Who do you think you are?' His weight pinned her to the panelled wall. 'If you say a word to my stepfather, I'll have my mother sack you.'

She lashed out, landing a hard punch full on his eye-socket, and he recoiled, swearing, as she ran.

Agata was twenty-three. It was the last summer of her contract. With little time to lose, she went to see Sir John. No point in seeing the mother; she knew who held the power in the house.

The study smelt of polish and old paper in leather bound books. He sat behind the imposing desk. For five years, she had seen the children's father move and speak in slow, hushed tones, reassuring ministers, removing agitation from men in suits. A whisky here, a tea there, cut glass or fine china. His involvement with the children was limited, but his involvement with the country was as secretive as it was frequent. According to the nannies, he was the man who restored order in the volatile British Parliament, regardless of which political party was in power. What would he make of this?

A momentary frown, and then he gazed at her with his deep blue eyes. She saw neither anger nor sadness. The gaze of a gambler. 'What should we do about it, Agata? Hmmm?'

'It's your call, Sir. I'm sorry I hit him, and I'll leave early if you want me to, but it was the only way to make him release me.' She took a breath. 'I've said nothing to Jett's mother about the row, and I don't think your daughter would want the nature of the game made public.'

His frown was terrifying, but when it cleared, his smile was sincere.

'You've an old head on young shoulders, so you'll understand the family deals with this in its own way. Behind closed doors. You've signed...'

'Of course, Sir.'

'I like you, Agata. You've proven yourself unflappable. The children adore you, and I feel I can trust you.' He patted the black notebook beside him. 'I'm wondering if you'd like to work for me when your contract finishes this summer? Here, in my offices? Usually, I ask members of the family or Oxford graduates, but I could do with someone who possesses natural common sense and understands European ways. We British can be too insular, don't you think?'

She turned down the offer.

That summer, she argued with Alessandro about Jett and broke off their relationship. That summer, she flew back to Tuscany and suggested Luca might want to take her out. A shy boy, he'd needed a prod. That summer, she told her parents she was homesick and no longer wanted to live amongst people where money and privilege superseded decency. But she never gave details. And she did not return to her parents' home in the countryside. Her actions were prompted by one unassailable fact: Jett never forgave. He bore grudges and settled scores. Best to leave.

In Florence, she and Luca promised to focus their lives on small justices and simple family values. And loyalty.

It is a promise she has failed to deliver.

Her morning routine sees her walk past the electrified fence, but she doesn't detach it. She has no desire to uncoil the hose and bring plants to life. This morning, she wants to kill. Kill her past, kill her demons. The old overalls hang in the garage, and she pulls them on, grabbing the handles of the menacing ground trimmer. Luca thinks he can make compost lasagnes (some stupid American notion about permaculture), but brute force is what's needed to tame this Italian life. Vegetables won't appear out of the ground by a look and a wink. Country is about sweat and brutality.

With a roar, the scissored trimmer kicks into life, and the four sharp blades snap, snap, snap. Immediately, the undergrowth parts. With stems as thick as thumbs, brambles split open to reveal their flesh, and curling vines fold. The engine's fierce vibrations shake her to the pit of her stomach, travelling up wrists into arms and shoulders. Mosquitoes rise from their dark slumber and fly in the morning mist, attacking any suspicion of bare flesh. Spitting them from her mouth, she continues metre after metre, pushing the machine, hacking to the right and to the left, leaving a crushed battlefield behind her. She will win this war.

Suddenly, she's aware of shouting and kills the motor. Her limbs continue to vibrate. In boxer shorts and bare feet, on the edge of the field, Luca stretches out his arms with a look of utter astonishment. 'What the hell are you doing? *Amore*! It's six in the morning. It's Sunday!'

'We must find the English sergeant. Bad things will happen today. I feel certain of it.' The words come tumbling out, and Luca attempts to cross the smashed land. He steps on something sharp, winces, stumbles, and puts out a hand, touching the electrified fence. A vicious shock zaps him, and he recoils, holding his arm as if shot.

Agata sprints over broken weeds to arrive at his side. 'Are you okay? You fool!'

In response, he encircles her in his arms and plucks an insect from her hair.

'*Amore*,' he says tenderly, 'I will take any injury for you, but do we have time for an espresso before you electrocute me and kill more plants? My dangerous lady.'

She puts her head against his shoulder, sharing the weight that is in her heart. 'I love you,' she says. And suddenly, she feels this is the truth, and she's been hiding it from herself for many years, always insisting she loved another man. The man of her youth.

'I'm glad,' he replies, 'because I love you, too, even if you wake me after four hours sleep.'

They kiss. It's the kind of kiss they haven't shared in a long time, and it kindles a fire in both their bellies. *He's a good man*, she reminds herself. *He's a good man, and I've not always given him enough credit*. He's a good man, and she's taken it for granted whilst yearning for another.

'I prefer to try permaculture, but you want tradition, okay! If we can tolerate each other's differences, we're halfway to Heaven.'

Heaven, she thinks. 'Let's go to bed!' she says, and his eyes light up.

He smells of sweat and she smells of mud, but he kisses her again with a young man's passion.

After twenty-five years, she realises the man who deserves her love has always been at her side. And it is her secrecy that has divided them. They wrap arms around each other and ascend the stairs. When this case is over, she makes a silent promise to herself, she will suggest a second honeymoon. Before their sons come home—before Dino gets back from Thailand—before Carlo comes back from University—before they grow any older and more forgetful and stupid. A real honeymoon. Without Alessandro haunting her dreams.

Chapter Thirty-Three

Coffee hisses through the *machinetta*, and he pours, insisting on serving Agata at the table. His fingers stroke the back of her neck, combing through her wet hair.

'Permaculture, the no-dig method, will be easier, but if you want tradition.'

'Whatever you want.' Her body purrs.

'The good news is I've just checked my voicemails, and the English sergeant left a message yesterday afternoon. I was so busy I didn't see.' Agata yips and turns as his fingers smooth her neck muscles. 'Calm. All is well. He's waiting for his superior to contact him before speaking with us. The English had their own problems over the weekend. Half a million people through London protesting about this Brexit thing. I think Vanessa Candle was also busy.'

She recalls her vain quest yesterday evening, but the Tower Gardens recede to a cloudy memory as Luca continues to work magic on her shoulders.

'He will probably ring later today to plead a hangover. Figaro once told me that was the British way.'

She is too happy to be bothered about other countries and rises to give him a kiss.

The phone rings with a loud rendition of *Nessun Dorma*. 'See?' he says, 'I changed my ringtone to the English football theme for the World Cup. The English are terrible at football, but they love Italy. That is also the British way.' He answers without checking the number as Agata nibbles his ear, but they both pull back when a hysterical voice bleeds from the phone. Luca grimaces, puts the phone on the table, and presses for audio. It is Naomi.

'Commissario, Commissario. *Aiutami*! You have to come at once. Help. We need help. Help! Orlando found him round the back in the bushes. He was smoking. He's not breathing. He's dead.'

Agata interrupts the frenzied stream. 'Orlando's not breathing?'

'No! I mean yes. But they will blame us. They will lynch Umberto. His neck is at a strange angle, his eyes are open, and he's all scratched up from the thorns.'

'Umberto's scratched?'

'No, no, no. He fell deep into the undergrowth. You wouldn't see him unless you were looking on the north side. One of our prize chickens got lost. His head is smashed in.'

'The chicken? Who fell? One of the firework team?'

'No! But, you know what they're like! Anyone who is *stranieri*! We're not from Montecatini! *Mah-donna, Mah-donna. Jesu Cristu, Dominum nostrum.* Why is this happening to us? We didn't do anything. He fell, but how? One of the firework men said...'

'Naomi!' Luca raises his voice. 'Are you saying that one of the men from the firework company fell off the tower?'

'No! But they must have done it. It was them. Not us. That man had shifty eyes, and he was drinking too many

Peronis. We give the party. We smile. We pay cash to the helpers. They drink our beer, but they will say it is Umberto. He's innocent! You believe me. Do you believe me?'

'Naomi! Stop! Who's dead?' Agata shouts at the phone.

A wailing ensues, and another voice enters the conversation.

'Commissario Agnello, this is Orlando. I found the English policeman dead in the bushes. I didn't touch anything, but it looks like he fell from the top of the Tower. The sharp rocks next to the old perimeter wall caved in his head. It's not as easy to fall as you'd think. You'd have to climb over the metal security poles.'

'I thought the sergeant went downstairs.' Agata rings her hands.

'Commissario,' says Orlando. His mother can be heard sobbing in the background. 'We need police. Do you want me to ring the local Carabinieri?'

Luca swears. 'Orlando,' he says. 'Get a sheet. Cover the body. Don't let anyone go near. I will ring my team, but we may be some time. Most of us worked a twenty-hour shift in Livorno yesterday. It'll be like raising the dead.' He stops, acknowledging his choice of phrase.

As calm as his mother is hysterical, Orlando assures him of his co-operation.

'Is Edu back?' asks Agata.

'He came back after the fireworks and has just woken. We haven't even told the early morning helpers. When Mamma screamed, I said it was a rat. You can't see the north face of the Tower from the gardens, so none of them have been there. I was searching for the chicken.' He speaks quietly. 'We're eager to protect my father and Edu for as long as possible. Yesterday's murder of that English girl reignited some ugly rumours. Mamma is right; they will find Papa guilty even though he was with guests all night. And if anyone saw Edu in the olive gardens...'

'Enough. We're coming!' Luca finishes the call and grabs paper and pencil, forming an impromptu list of people to contact. He underscores some names. 'First a wash. You smell lovely, but I smell like a pig's bladder.'

'We'll both go to the Tower,' says Agata, examining the list. 'But first, we have to speak to Vanessa Candle. Together. She speaks no Italian.'

They hunch over the phone.

From somewhere in England, a switchboard operator answers on the number they've been given. A woman explains that DI Candle is out on operations and cannot not be contacted until Monday. Agata speaks slowly and firmly, giving details of the death of a serving British police officer, and the voice changes tone, agreeing to pass on the call.

Then Luca phones Fabio. It goes straight to voicemail. 'He's probably drunk in some fascista bar with his mates. He made so many arrests yesterday, and none of them Lega Nord.' Irritably, he speed dials another colleague, subordinate to Fabio. A young woman answers instantly and agrees to be on site in half an hour.

While Luca showers, Agata dresses. Together they brush hair, clean teeth, and make more calls. Gianni the Forensic answers with unaccustomed speed. He is the only one who has had a quiet evening. Many arrests, some in hospital, but no deaths.

'It's a funny thing,' he says. 'You'd think going to a violent protest would be more dangerous than a firework display, but you see some odd things in my line of work.' He agrees to be there in an hour.

'That's two,' says Luca as he buttons his shirt. *Nessun Dorma* warbles from the bedside table, and he dives for it.

'Commissario Ag-nello? This is Detective Inspector Candle. Tell me the phone message is wrong. Where's my sergeant?'

In a three-way conversation, they detail what has happened. Vanessa Candle swears liberally, needing no translation.

'Unbelievable.' Even in a foreign language, her lack of sympathy is clear. 'He didn't contact me as instructed. He said he'd interviewed Susan Li Verdi, and it was all *No Comment*. I told him to come back. Then I received a voice-mail yesterday at lunchtime saying an English girl had been killed, but it was nothing to do with our case.'

'That's not good,' says Agata. 'This is all lies, Vanessa. He stole a letter written by Alessandro Verdi meant for Susan Li. But he refused to share it with Luca, saying it was a matter for the British Police.' They give a brief explanation, and there is another bout of swearing. They are both learning swear words in each other's language.

'I'm taking the first plane over,' she says. 'If need be, I'll pay for the ticket myself. Can someone collect me at Pisa?'

'We'll ask the mayor. You've met him, Figaro Verdi?'

'We did try to contact you,' says Agata, 'but Luca was out at protest marches in Livorno and I understand you had the same problem in London. It was a busy day.'

Vanessa growls. 'Bloody politics! It gets in the way of policing, but Sergeant Blunt came over in a covert operation. That's why we didn't make a fuss about it. Officially, the death of Alessandro Verdi is now under the jurisdiction of another unit.'

'Officially,' says Agata, 'we are meant to have stopped

investigating the child's death. But I am convinced they are linked.'

'Organised Crime Squad said the deceased was involved in smuggling. That's all I know. Maybe people smuggling? Have you got hold of Mrs. Verdi's phone?'

Agata has resorted to doing Luca's tie as his fingers are fumbling. 'We will discuss all when you get here. We'll work with you if you work with us.' She finishes the knot, and he pulls on his jacket.

'You have my word. Our country is split about whether we remain in Europe or not, but in my book, co-operation is the way forward. Let's teach the bloody governments a thing or two.'

Chapter Thirty-Four

The parking bays around the square are jammed. This is no sleepy Sunday; police cars fill every spare corner, forcing Figgi to inch up the steep, cobbled road of Via Giuseppe to the overflow parking. He scrapes his exhaust on the stones and curses. There is one bay free at the far end near a grassy slope. Figaro has told the *comune* that the road is only fit for horses, and still the men with tractors find excuses to veto the cost of repaving the area. But Susan is untroubled by roadworks and would have been happy to run barefoot to the square. Why does the nightmare keep going? She touches her bare face, wishing she had put on full makeup.

'Why did Inspector Candle demand I return with her to London? Am I now considered a suspect?' She has asked the same question on and off since receiving the phone call from London.

Figgi pats her arm. 'Calm. You were with me last night.'

Strictly speaking, she's aware they weren't always in each other's company, but she's ready to say anything to clear her name, especially as the truth seems determined to damn her. She may not have married Alessandro for his money, but she can't deny how it looks, and she wonders for the hundredth time why no one accused Cinderella of being a gold digger.

Figgi parks, and they squeeze out by the trees. She looks at him as he brushes pine needles from the shoulder of his jacket. It troubles her that it's been barely a week and already she can't conjure Alessandro's face. In the whole eight months of their marriage, how many hours did they spend together? From this distance, the valley is a timeless scene. But she isn't timeless; she's forty, and what does she have to show for it? Her life with Alessandro was meant to be the beginning of something better, and yet, here she is in Tuscany, a step away from prison.

'Come on,' says Figgi. Judging by the line of his mouth, his thoughts are running along different lines. He strides eagerly into battle.

A hungover gaggle of holiday makers sit on chairs and benches in the piazza, staring at the police vehicles with curiosity. Some sip coffee. Bar Media is shut, but the pizzeria is open and serving. All look at the road to the Tower, which is closed with police tape. Agata is tapping her foot by the bus stop as they arrive. They move to the pizzeria cafe.

Offering three steaming cups on a tin tray, Dana's eyes are half-closed. 'Don't tell me they've found someone dead from exhaustion in the Tower kitchens, because it wouldn't surprise me. Why did you wake us, Agata?'

'I'm not saying anything until one of the Carabinieri makes an announcement.' Agata is neat and fresh in comparison, dressed in a clean, white blouse and her customary tight Levis. The only change is in her hair, which falls loose in strands over her shoulders. She sips the coffee, standing up while Susan sits awkwardly by her side.

'Don't worry,' murmurs Figgi next to her.

As they gulp espressos, Agata explains she is waiting for Gianni. He is an hour overdue.

'I don't understand,' says Susan. 'He could have interviewed me anytime, but he didn't.'

Agata checks her watch. 'Figgi, you agreed to go to the airport? Vanessa Candle's flight lands in fifty minutes. Sure she'll recognise you?'

Figgi nods. 'She took me to identify Alessandro's body.'

'I was too cowardly.' Susan looks into her cup. 'I couldn't bear to go to the morgue.' She looks as if she wants to shrink from Agata's unspoken criticism.

Figgi gives a swift squeeze to her hand. 'Stay here. Natale and Renzo don't work Sundays, and I don't want you at the house alone. Not after the intrusion last night.'

A camper van makes a daring effort to manoeuvre through the slim space and eases across the square. Belching oil, the vehicle manages to reach the other side and gathers speed down the hill toward Volterra.

'That damn camper van!' Agata spits. 'He nearly ran me off the road yesterday. How come these tourists are bigger maniacs than the drivers in Sicily? I've been trying to catch the owner to give him a piece of my mind.'

Dana comes out with some pastries. 'The Miniera,' she says. 'I'll bet that's where the camper van was parked last night. But don't worry. Murders come in three, so perhaps the driver of the camper van will be next.' She tries a feeble laugh.

Figgi pulls out his car keys. 'We've already had three murders. The child on the beach, my cousin, Alessandro, and the young English girl, Amy. The British policeman makes four.'

Agata refrains from mentioning the person in the photograph.

'I'm talking about here in the town of Montecatini.' Dana puts a hand on her hip. 'Maybe we should put up a plaque to this English Amy. Photograph yourself here by the refuse bins.' She stops. 'Wait, did you say that big guy is dead? The one who was in La Pizzeria two days ago?'

Agata slams down the coffee cup and leaves the piazza, pushing through four locals holding an animated conversation. Figaro moves away without comment as Dana stares after him, pale eyes widening. She turns to Susan. 'Stay here. Eat now. Eat *dolci*! Don't move!' She goes inside, shouting for Yolanda.

Alone on the bench, Susan is transfixed by the sugar dusted pastries. Her mouth feels like cloth. Once again, she is acutely aware of her stranger-status. If only she could curl under a duvet, blot out the world, and be safe. But where is home? And where is a place of safety? She remembers the little girl and her father on the beach, all smiles and twirls. How do they cope? How can the child be happy when she doesn't know where her next bed or meal is? At least Susan has two million in her offshore account, but will this money see her charged with murder?

Her phone trills, and the name Alessandro flashes on the screen. A surge of adrenalin bites into her. The mobile trills and trills. She presses delete. It trills again. Again, she presses to decline. A message flashes up. With shaking hands, she reads:

I'm here. I'm alive. Need your help. Don't tell the police. Come at once.

Crystal is helping us. xx

The words are bright, and then they fade. She pokes and stares at it again. Her heart bounces as she looks around the square. Where is he? How is he alive? An English group has just arrived at La Pizzeria, and everyone is laughing and joking about an encounter with the film crew in Volterra. Three small children play hide and seek around the war memorial. A couple of old women with goat-like legs are hauling huge string bags away from the *Panificcio*. The bright sun strengthens and deepens the Tower's shadow across one side of the square. She can hear Yolanda chatting with customers in her peculiar English. In a parallel universe, Alessandro is alive and well.

With effort, she stands, although her legs will barely hold her. She takes a few steps forward. She has no choice. No matter what he's done, she's done things too; they can only solve this together. She starts to walk away from the Piazza toward Casa Verdi.

At the kerbside, a car stops abruptly, and she recognises the driver. 'Hey. Sue! Get in.' Crystal beckons to her. 'Come on.'

The bright hazel eyes are darker, flatter, and Crystal's expression lacks its usual jocularity. She leans over and pushes the car door open. 'Get in. He's been trying to get hold of you. Are you on your own?'

Susan climbs into the car. 'I don't understand. Alessandro is dead.'

'Did you identify the body?'

She swallows hard. 'Not me. Figgi.'

Crystal grimaces and turns the car around, which considering the parking and the police vehicles is an act of sheer willpower. 'I thought so.' Hitting the kerb with her tyre, she curses before setting down the hill. 'I told you the Verdis weren't to be trusted. Figgi was in Casa Verdi last night, tearing up the kitchen, probably searching for your packet. I know I told some fibs, but Alessandro wasn't sure if we could trust you. I've never had a fling with Figgi. At first Alessandro thought Figgi would help him, now he realises he's the one behind the murders. And he'll kill Alessandro if he knows he's still alive.'

'But why?' Susan clamps one hand on her trembling knee. 'Who was in the morgue?'

'Christ knows. Some unlucky Joe. The Syndicate organised it. You know about the Syndicate, right? You're one of them. So you know the Syndicate and the Verdi Mafia are at war.'

She fishes in her memory. Who said what to whom? But with everything that's happened, the water is too murky, and she denies all knowledge.

Crystal's brief glance suggests she is surprised. 'But you're Syndicate,' she repeats and shoots a curious look in her direction. They slide around a hairpin bend.

To Susan the conversation may as well be in Italian. None of it makes senses. 'Am I? Is that who killed Amy? I didn't kill Amy.'

'That was Figgi. We think she'd read the letter and tried to blackmail Figgi. Poor girl didn't know what she was getting into.'

Fragments of time enter Susan's thoughts: Figgi coming back to Casa Verdi the night Amy was killed, the way he controlled the crowd when the corpse was found, his disappearance at the Festa yesterday. She only has his word that he met with the poacher, Tomaso.

'And the British policeman?'

'You have to understand the Verdi family will stop at nothing to protect their reputation. Old man Verdi would have locked you up if you'd arrived in Livorno. You're damned lucky that protest was going on.'

'Figaro has been so supportive.'

'He can't kill you here in Montecatini, can he? Not while you're under his protection. Too many awkward questions.'

'But Alessandro was the one money laundering.'

'Weren't you in on it?'

'Me?' Her bag slides off her knees as they jerk around the tightest bend. 'Are you Alessandro's first wife?'

Crystal barks her coarse laugh. 'Christ no! What makes you say that? I found out about the Syndicate when I worked at the detention camps. I'm an anaesthetist, not a plain nurse.' Crystal's large hands grip the wheel as she takes the final turn, and Susan's shoulder presses to the car door and jerks back. Then the car brakes.

Paper flutters on the gate, taped to the top bar. Someone has put up a sign on the Jensens' property. *Migrants No! No alle migranti!* It is scrawled in large, black continental lettering. 'Yeah, yeah. We'll be gone soon enough.' Crystal shrugs and crosses the boundary. The downward path has more holes than a billiard table, and they rattle over stones, stopping at the cement stippled walls of the house. 'Alessandro bought this property a month ago, only he didn't want Figgi to know. He's used it as a base.'

Something clicks in her brain—her phone recognising the Wi-Fi, his insistence she take the money and come to Montecatini, the package, his question: *What have you done?* It's not what she has done in the past, it is Alessandro who wants her to do something in the future. But what? She is afraid to show how little she understands.

A dirty cream and white camper van is parked to one side. As they arrive, Crystal jerks up her thumb to a driver inside the van. Eyes hidden by mirrored dark glasses, the driver returns the gesture and sets off. Crystal parks in his space. Gangly limbs run from behind one straggly fir tree to the next, and then a head pokes out and stares at them. Crystal waves to another man, who appears at the top of an external staircase. He isn't Alessandro, but someone with a wrinkled brow and straggly red hair, receding at the front. A white fuzz of sunlight blinds her momentarily, and she puts up a hand. What will she say when she sees Alessandro?

Chapter Thirty-Five

With half-closed eyes, Fabio stands near Luca. Two further plain-suited detectives are leaning their backsides on cafe tables. A smell of exhaustion and last night's booze hangs around their heads like flies on old meat. The police presence has grown in the square, and Luca clears his throat to silence the chatterers. He has positioned himself on the decking outside Bar Media in order to address the crowd.

'The Tower is off limits. It is now the site of a criminal investigation.'

People surge together, blocking the road to discuss this curious turn of affairs. The word *Il Macelliao*, the Butcher, is whispered with thin lips and black looks. Some glance over their shoulders as if a knife-wielding maniac will burst in amongst them.

Luca holds up his hand for a second time. 'We will need witness statements from everyone attending the Festa in the two hours before the firework display. My assistants are here ready to speak to you.' Next to him, Agata repeats the request in English, and mouths fall open.

A camper van with beige trim is nudging into the piazza. It is having little success as people refuse to move, so it turns up Via Giuseppe as an alternative route out of town. In a second, their haste is halted by the harsh scrape of axle on stone. The vehicle wedges, and the engine revs loudly. The van rocks but cannot free itself, and the tyres squall. Locals are used to such accidents; deep striations scar the stone year after year.

'You can't take that turn so fast,' says one old man, grinning at the catastrophe.

A burst of engine power or even a hefty push usually releases them, and others call out 'Foot on the accelerator!' as they gather behind to give a shove.

But the camper van's axle and exhaust pipe are so deeply embedded, the vehicle cannot be released. The groan of a handbrake and swearing in a foreign language are audible in the momentary hush. The driver revs the engine again, determined to break forward or backward. The vehicle lurches but then subsides, unable to make a centimetre in either direction. Local teenagers bang on the doors. 'Give it up. We'll get someone to tow you.' In response, high-pitched screams come from inside the cabin with returning thuds.

Instinctively, the helpers retreat as a couple of Carabinieri come forward. In the wing mirrors, the driver sees the men in uniform. Both doors fling open, and two men jump out, running at full pelt up the hill. Swerving, they run past the overspill car parking, dive off the road, and head into the woods in the direction of the windmills. With a shout, Luca orders his team to take chase.

Fabio hangs back, and motions to his subordinates to run. Along with the two Carabinieri, they sprint upward and are soon lost to sight.

'They won't catch them,' says Fabio with a smirk. 'You can tell they're illegals.'

'You've disobeyed my order,' says Luca.

Fabio raises his eyebrows. 'You meant me?'

Agata crosses the square. She puts a hand to the back of the camper van, but it's locked. Two people try to wrench it open with no success. With an exasperated shout, she grabs the keys from the front, throwing them to the nearest man.

As the doors fall wide, the whole square fixes on the interior. Six small children cower, dark-skinned and skinny with partially shaved heads. The crowd is silent; not even an exclamation passes their lips. It's hard to tell if this strange cargo is boys or girls, but they are all tearful and dressed in old cotton tops and worn shorts. Some are barefoot, while others wear flip flops. On the dirty floor of the camper van, a plastic bag has spilt its cache of wigs: blonde, black, brunette, and sparkly pink in the exaggerated styles of performers. On a rail, hanging against an inner window, separating the driver's cab from the cabin, are a series of small sequined outfits.

Agata hesitates. Seeing their terror, no one knows what to say. Then Fabio strides towards them. 'Who are you? What are you doing here? Speak!'

Dana launches herself forward and shoves his shoulder, causing him to slip. He raises his hand, but her fists are screwed into a knot, ready for a fight. 'They're kids,' she shouts.

Brushing his shirt, as if she has despoiled his outfit, he snarls. 'Crazy woman! I'm a police detective. And you're nothing but a foreigner. You dare speak to me like that?'

Dana points a finger at him. 'Shame on you,' she says, and then turns to Luca. 'Shame! Commissario. If these are the migrants everyone fears, they're children! Not criminals.'

From behind, Yolanda places a hand on Dana. 'Calm down. They must be part of the Migrants First scheme.'

Dana faces the crowd. 'They told us the charity was using teenage boys. Hooligans.'

Under the scrutiny of so many eyes, the children cower further to the back of the van.

'Nobody said anything about hooligans,' says Luca, but he's drowned out by disconcerted chatter around him. Everyone wants to blame someone else for the misinformation. The crowd erupts into gesticulations and hot-headed accusations.

'They're little and hungry,' observes a woman in black with wrinkled cheeks. She stands by the camper van door and raises her voice into a shrill cry. 'They need feeding. A good *minestra* will help. Come on, little ones, come out.'

Of course, a broth will save the day. A muttering arises in support.

'Let them have something to drink,' says Luca. 'Questions can wait.'

'And if they escape?' says Fabio.

'Escape!' says Agata, who finds her voice. 'Who's the crazy one!' She takes a child's hand, but it is like trying to get wild animals to leave their lair; they all pull back. Yolanda, Dana, and Agata urge them forward and slowly, slowly they are brought to sit at the cafe tables, eyes wide with the horror of so much attention. The curious jostle for a closer look. A few local children climb the one tree in the centre of the square and stare down. Bar staff offer San Pellegrino cans, and the crowd's attention splits as some observe the police's efforts to free the camper van. The dead

Englishman is forgotten as the van rocks forward and backward to cries of encouragement. Agata gets in the front cab, switches on the engine, and works with them to disentangle the machine from the stone.

With a grinding squawk, the vehicle breaks away and slides backward to block the road. A huge cheer breaks out, but now, nobody knows what to do with it. It's too big to park in the remaining centimetres of space.

Agata examines the paintwork. It's definitely the same van that has nearly run her off the road on two occasions: beige and white, a broken metal logo, small wheels low to the ground, and blacked-out windows at the back.

'Does anyone have some newer outfits we could give these children?' one mother suggests, and energised with a helpful task, a number of people run off, leaving others to conglomerate near the shops. Dana brings out several plates of biscuits.

'Come on. All the children can have one. Make them feel at home. Share.'

A few Montecatini mothers push their little ones to the table to take the free food on offer, but the skinny children won't raise a hand or a smile. They sit still as wax.

'Why didn't someone say it was children in the Jensens' house?' Yolanda speaks accusingly to Agata. 'I'm sure we were told it was teenagers. We would have reacted differently if we'd known.' Those around her nod in agreement.

'How do we know they've been at the Jensens'?' says one. 'Are there others?'

'Look at the Dutch plates on the camper van,' says another.

This is all the evidence they need, and Agata opts not to challenge them. More than anyone, she knows the wording on the website of Migrants First. It refers to teenagers of sixteen and above. These children are too young to fit the description.

A boy of nineteen walks slowly down the cobbled tower road, hugging the houses.

'Edu!' calls Yolanda. 'Come here and speak to them. Tell them they're safe.'

Like the children, he turns stiff and mute, staring at the crowd who stare back. A sweep of his eyes takes in the scene, the six small children with shaved drooping heads, the camper van with open doors in the middle of the road. Without a word, Edu heads back to the Tower.

Agata growls at the crowd. 'That's all your fault. Look at yourselves. Look how you treated that boy. You should be ashamed. He came here for safety, and you've painted him the enemy.'

'Who are you to accuse us?' says a large local man, making a fist.

Her eyes gun him down. 'Use your common sense,' says Agata. 'People like Fabio and his media make the noise that fills your brains. Look at the children.'

Fabio straightens up, makes a rude gesture behind Luca's back, and slings his suit jacket defiantly over one shoulder. There is a mutinous silence, broken by the return of the chasers, who walk down Via Giuseppe with a small, sallow-skinned man in their custody. The crowd cluster toward the captive. The man's arms are pinned behind his back, and he struggles ineffectually in the officers' grip. A plain clothed detective walks in front, telling everyone to clear a path.

'We only got the one. The other is gone, Commissario.'

Fabio moves forward like a king bestowing an honour.

The man is cuffed and put in the police car. 'I'll take him in for questioning,' Fabio says to the crowd. Luca tells him to phone first and see if any of the cells are vacant. After yesterday's cache, who knows? Attention shifts again when a honk heralds the arrival of Figgi's sports car. Access in and out of the Piazza is completely blocked, and Figgi stops at the edge and gets out. Beside him is a smartly dressed woman in a grey suit and flat black shoes. Her dark hair is pulled into a slicked bun, and she looks around, taking in the chaos. Being the centre of attention doesn't appear to phase her, and Agata is more relieved than she wants to admit. There aren't enough police to deal with this emergency. Any extra is useful.

'Inspector Candle,' she says, going to shake her hand. 'Agata Agnello.'

Vanessa returns the shake with a firm grip. 'The English speaking half.' She looks at the migrant children who stare back. 'What's going on? The mayor said he'd take me straight to identify my sergeant.'

'Luca is phoning head office. We've arrested someone who is suspected of trafficking minors, but the sergeant's body is still in the Tower Gardens.'

Vanessa's gaze queries the link, and Agata turns up the palms of her hands. Phone clamped to Luca's ear, he shakes the English policewoman's hand and points upward. Vanessa looks at the Tower that looms behind the Trattoria. 'Wow,' she says, then moves to business. 'You think my officer's death has something to do with child trafficking? But maybe these kids are locals?'

Agata clicks her tongue. 'This isn't London. It's a small town. How much did the mayor tell you on the drive from the airport?'

'Enough. I'm still convinced Susan Li Verdi is involved.

It's too much of a coincidence that my man dies and she's here.'

Figgi's eyes scan the crowd. 'I told Susan to stay at La Pizzeria. Where is she?'

They look around until Dana speaks. 'If you want Susan, she's with Linda Jensen's niece. I told her to stay here, but I heard her phone ring. Next thing I know, the American collected her in a car. I don't know where they went.'

'The Jensens aren't here,' says Silvio from Bar Media. 'I had a text from Stefan Jensen yesterday wishing us a good time with the Festa. They're in Holland, and they've sold the house.'

In a flash, Agata remembers looking over the Tower gate last night. Her hand hits her head. How stupid! The camper van was going down toward Casa Verdi, not up toward the Miniera. Not a tourist, but a regular visitor. She has allowed stereotype to overcome logic.

'You read the news and they tell you what to believe and then you see what you expect to see.' She stamps her foot.

'What does that mean?' asks Figgi.

'We see what we expect to see.' Agata clutches at his sleeve. 'The locals thought the migrants were hooligan teenagers, even though no one actually saw them. They thought the Jensens were here, although no one had spoken to them. Edu is accused of a crime, not because there's any evidence, but because he was once a migrant. And I assumed the sergeant was drunk at the top of the Tower, because he's British.' She waves her hands across the crowd. 'And all the tourists are the good guys because they spend money in bars.'

'What?' says Yolanda.

'When was the last time anyone actually saw the Jensens?'

'It's sold,' repeats Silvio. 'I'm telling you, they're not here.'

'Susan is in danger,' says Agata.

'If you're going to find Susan Li Verdi, I'm going with you.' Vanessa is stern. 'The dead don't move. Right?'

'From down there, anyone can see a car approaching from the piazza,' says Agata. 'We need to take one plain car down first.'

It's an academic issue as the square is gridlocked, and Luca motions to Fabio to oversee the removal of certain vehicles in order to follow them. 'Mr. Mayor, your car is the only one available to move. So we four can go immediately.'

Figgi nods without speaking. They squeeze into the Audi sport, and Figgi manages a three-point turn. As he does this, one of the Carabiniere restarts the camper van. The engine coughs and dies. Clearing a way through will not be a short procedure.

Vanessa sits in the main passenger seat next to Figgi. Luca and Agata squash behind. '*Merda*. You'd better be right about this,' he murmurs to Agata. 'At least I've got my gun. I didn't have time to check it in after the riots.'

Agata looks at him fondly. 'Don't be silly,' she says. 'Hypodermic needles and drugs are the link. Alessandro died from an allergic reaction to an injected drug. Gianni found needle marks on Amy, and I think the sergeant was drugged. The migrant child was anaesthetised and died in an operation. As for whoever is in the freezer...'

The car swerves and skids across the hairpin bend. He feels for the gun in the holster. 'But then, aren't we going in the wrong direction? Dr. D'Angelo—'

'Doctors, nurses, vets. Many people know how to administer an injection or get hold of drugs.'

A deer bounds across their road. Jumping out of the woodland, it traverses to the field on the other side. Figgi brakes, swears, and instantly puts his foot back down on the accelerator.

Chapter Thirty-Six

Someone is crouching behind the low-slung branches of a fig tree. It could be a girl or a boy wearing T-shirt and shorts. Whoever it is, their face is hidden in overgrown vegetation. Then a flash of dark skin, and they run a short distance to duck behind a thick-stemmed rosemary hedge. Bees rise like steam from purple blooms.

'Wathiqa,' Crystal shouts.

Silence. Susan sees the head bob up and retreat.

'She won't go anywhere.' Crystal nods toward Casa Verdi. 'She's terrified of Ruby. We told her the dog will eat her if she leaves our land.'

'And she's waiting for us to take her to her sister.' The redheaded man comes to her side.

With a jolt, she recognises him as Crystal's brother from last night. Minus the baseball cap, his semi-bald pate makes him look older. His brow is creased like crepe. They flank her, and together they move toward the external staircase.

At the top, Susan realises the view from the Verdis' mansion is misleading. From there, the straggling firs bordering the road hide the majority of the building, leaving a glimpse of roof and upper door. She had assumed the house was similar to Casa Verdi but smaller. Up close, she sees her error. Although half the size, this property is a worn shell. A few metres of land have been cleared for cars, but the rest grows wild, captured in a net of weeds. Neglected olive trees thrust out overgrown branches, their trunks partly obscured by scrub grasses. And the walls are not polished stone but dirty stippled concrete with blown render.

'I thought you had people working on the land.' She notes the thick-bladed weeds that burst from dry cracks in the outer staircase. Small green lizards, unchecked by a dog, run in ripples between broken slabs. Even the shutters are ready to drop and fall, leaning on loose hinges.

'The Jensens had no money to maintain their property,' says Crystal. 'There are years of decay here. Letters from the Municipal Council show a mountain of debt on *comune* taxes. That's why they sold it to Alessandro.'

Delaying her entry, Susan spies the edge of an empty pool, khaki mottled in mould and masked from the road, but she's too shocked to query the subterfuge. The man pulls on her upper arm. 'Come on.' She tugs at her memory to remember his name.

'Where's Alessandro?'

'Inside.' Crystal ushers her into a high-ceilinged corridor, and the brother partially shuts the door, allowing the light to elongate across a worn, tiled floor.

The hall is half the length of Casa Verdi's. Through half-open doors, Susan glimpses several bedrooms containing bare mattresses.

They jostle her toward a galleried landing with a thin metal railing. In the centre of the high ceiling, a large-bladed fan circulates dust motes. Down below, the shabby living area has picture windows on two sides. Nobody is there. Her legs shake like dry leaves. Does she want to see Alessandro? He's not who she thought he was. But then, neither is she. They were both acting a part.

Sunlight stripes across an old sofa, cracked with heat. Rusty fly screens block the open windows that look out over the sloping hill visible from the Verdis' property. From this angle, sheep can be seen grazing in the lower fields, protected by three dogs. If the girl behind the rosemary bush is frightened of Ruby, she must be terrified of that free-roaming pack. They are the size of lions.

The man pushes Susan to sit. Her bare legs burn on contact with the leather, and she searches the room, willing Alessandro to be in a corner, but there's no hiding spot. A huge, stone fireplace is empty save for a medical cool bag in the middle of the hearth. Two enormous brass candlesticks with spiked collars stand like sentries on either side. They are darkly tarnished with disuse, and more reminiscent of instruments of torture than light-bearers. Beside the chimney breast a sturdy wooden door is closed, and a large key dangles above with a severed iron blade. The exit looks blocked.

Her knees touch a pitted, wooden coffee table. 'What's this?' Laid out in neat formation is a mobile phone, two pads of A5 paper, three plastic biros, and a large syringe containing a clear liquid. Her attention fixes on the hypodermic.

From behind, the man presses on her shoulder as Crystal sits next to her. 'Supplies,' she says.

Susan looks from one to the other in confusion. 'Where's Alessandro? Where's your aunt?'

'This is Dave Baker, my partner, not my brother,' says Crystal. 'Sorry about the chicanery. Alessandro said you were working for him, and we believed him, but then we got the letter.' One of the phones illuminates with a message visible to Susan.

Twenty minutes eta

'Twenty minutes, Dave.'

He nods, licking his lips nervously and extracts a piece of paper from the pocket of his shorts.

'You don't know who we are, do you?' says Crystal. 'I thought you would realise, but unless you identified us, we weren't going to trust you. Here. Read.' She smooths the paper on the table.

Dave's face is creased with stubble and anger. Any trace of yesterday evening's accent has disappeared. 'And we're owed an explanation,' he adds.

Dear Susan,

I'm writing this before jumping on a plane. I'll text you shortly with more details. I've been hacked and fear for my life. And this is your doing.

I checked our offshore accounts. You transferred two million from the Boekers' account into yours. These are the people you were helping to launder money. I told you they were dangerous. Now you've put us both in danger.

The Boekers don't know you by sight, but they know me. So I've sent the book to Montecatini. If you take it to Figaro, he will accompany you to the police. Don't trust him with our information, but you must give yourself up. It's the only way. Speak to the police. If the Boekers are arrested, maybe we can be safe.

Please don't betray me again.

Alessandro x

. . .

They launch questions at her.

'What's in the book?'

'What money? Our money hasn't been touched.'

'Of course, we paid him. We had a deal.'

Her head reels. She answers what she can and tries to assure them that their names are not mentioned in the leather notebook, but they scoff.

Dave sits on the stairs. 'What I don't understand is why did he think *we* were after him? The only people we had to fear were those in the Syndicate. Why give us up to the Syndicate? It must have been you.'

Susan has trouble tearing her eyes from the table. Inside the syringe, the clear liquid shines in the sunlight. And then the penny drops. She clasps her knees to steady herself. 'You're the Boekers, aren't you?'

The look between them tells Susan that Alessandro will not save her from his grave. For a moment, she is relieved this exonerates Figgi. He hasn't falsely identified Alessandro's body. Then, silently, she rages at herself for being so naive. Alessandro has set her up. It's what Figgi has been saying all along.

'Why is there a man in a freezer?'

Crystal picks up the hypodermic needle as if to stab her. 'So he took a photo of that, as well? Dave, you've got his phone. Didn't you notice?'

He pulls out a small mobile from another pocket. 'He must have had two phones. I didn't have time to check his Clerkenwell office. It was all I could do to gather up loose ends in London and come straight here. You spoke with him last when he was in Italy. What did you tell him?'

The hypodermic points at Dave. Crystal hisses. 'We had police crawling all over the town, and then one of my drivers wanted a bigger payoff to keep his mouth shut.' Her voice rises in fury. 'I had to tell Alessandro something. He told me to leave, but we needed to stay. I said it was important no one found the driver's body before the second half of the deal went through.' She jabs a finger at Susan. 'You were supposed to be our partner in this. Alessandro was the banker, and you were laundering the money through your auction company.'

'Me?' Susan bleats, and her legs begin to shake.

Dave picks up a wooden chair from under the window and throws it against the galleried wall. It bounces and breaks into pieces. 'We should have gone while we could,' he shouts at Crystal. 'I'm sick of people trying to chip away at our deal. First the driver, then Brian Blunt, and that stupid London bargirl. If we'd paid them all, there'd be nothing left.'

They face each other, ignoring Susan, whose mind sharpens.

'I have a photographic memory. Give me a computer, and I'll hand over my money to you. Two million. Then you can go. I won't tell the police anything.'

She is lying. With fear flooding through her, she can scarcely remember her date of birth, but she will say anything to buy time. 'His family won't support me. They think I married him for his money.'

Dave laughs. 'Who cares about the Verdis? It's Karol you have to worry about. Karol and the Syndicate.' He comes close again, spitting on her in his frenzy. 'If you're not Syndicate, who are you? We nabbed some of their children, their merchandise, for our own profit, and they don't take kindly to people cutting in on their action. But as for your two million, it's not enough to keep us safe. We're waiting for the final payout. Seven million.'

Crystal pushes him back. 'Leave it to me, Dave. Check on Wathiqa. They'll be here any minute.'

'She won't go anywhere without her sister. She thinks she's still alive.'

Susan's hand twitches and drops the pen. She bends to pick it up again. 'The murder on the beach?'

'Jeez. You know nothing, but you wanna talk? Just write a confession. Say you're the one who thought of all this. Then we can all go our own ways!'

The sun blurs Crystal's face as Susan swallows. 'The migrant children don't know they're used for body parts?'

Dave's feet are wearing a dust trail on the floor. 'What do you think?' he snarls and kicks the pieces of wood, making the splinters dance. 'Anyway, not all of them are a tissue match. Most go to be Off Grid Kids, for fuck's sake. Undocumented. Destined for private brothels.'

Juggling phone and hypodermic, Crystal explains. 'The Syndicate paid me to screen them for disease. So, if one of them had a valuable blood group, I took advantage. Golden Blood, man! Worth a fortune. Alessandro knew about our sideline, and he was cool. He said you knew. But then we had a phone call warning us that someone was squealing to the Syndicate. It had to be you.'

'No,' says Susan. 'I would have gone to the police.'

Picking up a large spindle, Dave throws it at a bleached print on the wall, and it drops, shattering glass. 'I'm the police! Did you imagine there's justice for unaccompanied minors?' he spits. 'Is that it? Don't you know they're caught between governments who don't want them and a public who despise them? The papers are full of anti-migrant stuff. If Salvini gets elected in Italy, they'll let them all drown in the Mediterranean: man, woman, child, and beast. And you,' he says as he points, 'living in a luxury flat in Canary

Wharf with your fat bank account! You took the money like everyone else, and you closed your eyes. You didn't ask how Alessandro made his pile, did you?'

Her fingers shake with adrenalin. She is guilty. Of course she is guilty. Who isn't? All of England is guilty. The whole world is guilty. But at that moment, contrition is not on her mind: A primeval need to survive consumes her. Her nerves are bleeding as she clings between a rock and a hard place. It's true, she wanted to help herself to a better life. Alessandro offered her a rich marriage, and she accepted: a Faustian pact. All she had to do was be subservient to the man with the large bank account. But now, as the end approaches, she is desperate to break the treaty. A whip of bitterness strikes her as she recalls the many days when her father was alive, and she used to wake and wish to die from misery. Now, all she wants is to live. Surrounded by dust, splinters, and decay, she makes a promise to a god she scarcely believes in: If she gets out of this house alive, she will be a different person. She will make the rest of her days count—she will give every penny to charity, work for the greater good. Anything. Anything at all.

Crystal snaps her fingers. 'I've got it. Confess to killing Alessandro. He was their banker. That'll do it. Write it down. We don't need to kill you. If we're caught, we'll show the letters to the Syndicate, but if we get away, you're free.'

All their lies are painfully thin. They won't let her live because the dead can't give their version, and Crystal has killed people for lesser reasons. Susan fumbles and loses the pen between clammy fingers. It clatters on the tiled floor. She picks it up and writes an uneven black scrawl, a jumble of meaningless apologies and confused confessions.

The phone illuminates, and Crystal pokes it, letting out

a whoop. 'First half-payment in the bank. Second when we hand her over. Get Wathiqa ready. They'll be here in five.'

Dave makes a fist of relief.

Outside the window is a Tuscan scene fit for a tourist. Susan absorbs the shades of green, the depth and length of the valley under a powder-blue sky, and signs her death warrant. Snatching her note, they momentarily read it together and in the lull, she slithers Alessandro's letter into her bra.

'Wait.' She scrambles for another lifeline. Any minute now, she will rise and run. Run as she has never run before. Run, even if she dies trying to evade capture. 'Yolanda will say I got in the car with you.'

Dave laughs. 'Like we said, the only thing anyone has to fear is the Syndicate. The Carabinieri are clowns.'

The rumble of an engine outside precedes a crackle of tyres on pebbles.

'The buyer.' Crystal goes to the window and presses her nose against the mosquito screen. 'What the fuck?'

Light footsteps in the corridor reveal the thin spectre of the gangly child. In better light, Susan can see it's a girl, leaning over the galleried landing, fingers twisted on the banister like bird claws. One arm is a mass of purple and grey welts from an old injury. Susan can't tell if she's crying or angry. 'Police got the van. Mikhel, he run away, but he take your car.'

Crystal swears and points toward the girl. 'Never mind. You're about to be collected to see your sister. You'd like that, wouldn't you? She's better, so we don't need to take any more blood transfusions from you.'

'Hurry up,' says Dave. 'Deal with Susan. I'll hand over Wathiqa. We'll head over the fields and take a farm car.' He climbs the stairs towards the galleried landing. 'C'mon, Wathiqa.'

Susan prepares to scream and tell the girl to flee. This may be the only thing she can do to redeem herself. But the teenager pounds her fists on the railing. 'No!' she shouts and throws back her head with a howl. 'You told me Huda was alive, but Mikhel says you kill my sister. He said the other driver help hide her body and ran away.'

As if to catch a stray cat, Dave approaches, arms out with guarded steps. Head down, the girl charges him. Butts him hard in the stomach, forcing him down the stairs. Then flying past him, she runs toward Crystal, arms flailing. There is an odd smile on Crystal's face as she stands, needle in hand.

Chapter Thirty-Seven

Figgi's car stops at the top of the Jensens' drive, and they all look to the lowest point of the valley, where a solitary vehicle is travelling at speed.

'I don't see any car at the property,' says Vanessa. 'Have they left?'

'Luca.' Agata puts a finger to her mouth. 'Someone's still here.'

Thin voices bleed into the air with the insect life, and everyone scrambles out to listen. Agata steps forward.

'Get behind me, Agata.' Luca draws his gun from the chest holster. 'I'm going first.'

As they get closer, they can hear indistinct, angry conversation between several people. Vanessa stretches an arm toward Luca. 'You need to call for backup, man. You can't go in alone.'

They strain to hear the muffled conversation, and then someone shouts in distress.

In an instant, they split into twos. Vanessa and Luca move up the crumbling outer stairs to push gently on the front door. Figgi joins Agata to skirt around the side of the house, creeping under windows and avoiding dry vegetation.

Inside, the shouting becomes clearer.

'Wathiqa, we've organised a better life for you,' a man's voice speaks in English.

'You killed her!' The child's accusation is shrill, strangled with emotion. 'Let me go!'

'Calm down. We're going. Do you want to be sent back? If the police catch you...'

'Wathiqa. It's not what you think.' Crystal's American voice is easy to recognise. 'Your sister was sick. Peritonitis. She was going to die, anyway. We didn't tell you because we didn't want to upset you.'

There is a sob and a shriek. 'You lie.'

Crystal's words turn from butter to brick. 'Let's not forget you're an unwanted migrant in Italy. And we all know what happens when you're an illegal, don't we? We've told you often enough.'

A slap, a howl of pain, a scuffle. Agata is unsure whether to intervene or whether to leave it to Luca and Vanessa. She and Figgi are now under an open window, blocked by a fixed metal fly screen.

'Don't mark her, Dave. The client won't like it.'

'She's already scarred. It doesn't matter. He wants her for her blood.'

'You sent me texts saying you were Huda.' The young voice sobs. 'You made me give blood for her.'

'I sent the texts to calm you,' says the man. 'Crystal, this conversation is pointless. Finish that one off.'

Another scraping sound, and Crystal shouts. 'Susan, put down the hypodermic. You don't know how to use it.'

'Release her.' Susan's voice is deep and barely recognisable.

Unable to stay still, Figgi rises. Agata pulls at his arm.

'*Polizia*. Stop.' Luca enters, and Agata rises in relief. Everyone in the room is facing the galleried landing, where Luca stands at the top with a drawn gun. His entrance creates a second of silence, in which Crystal leans across and grabs the needle, shoving Susan hard on the chest. Susan topples backward with a shout, knees against the sofa, so that the furniture upends and her head smacks on the floor.

Simultaneously, the girl wrenches free from the man, aiming a vicious kick into his crotch. He folds in pain, and she runs toward the closed wooden door. A scuffle and a grunt, and Vanessa pins the man's arms behind his back. Luca follows Wathiqa, but Crystal grabs her first, putting the needle to the child's neck.

'*Lasciala*!' he says, gun in hand advancing. The child reaches out to him but is held fast by Crystal.

The hypodermic flashes as Crystal lunges with one arm, sinking it below Luca's chin, while continuing to grip Wathiqa. Luca drops the gun to clutch at his neck. The firearm skitters along the floor into the prone body of Susan. His knees buckle. Agata shouts. Wathiqa twists, and Crystal struggles to hang on to the girl's bony wrist.

Figgi and Agata shout, pushing and pulling on the fly screen. The old wooden frame splits under their pressure, toppling forwards. Agata is the first to hoist herself onto the windowsill and jump down.

In a flash of movement, the young girl grabs the large brass candlestick and swings the instrument like a discus. It vibrates in the air for a second before the brass spikes connect with Crystal's head. Blood spurts across the child's T-shirt and lands on Agata's legs. Crystal's eyes stare. Her mouth opens. The child drops the implement with a clang of metal on tile. The pumping blood makes everyone recoil as the American slumps to the floor beside Luca. Her lips move wordlessly, and her eyes blink.

In a frenzy, Agata trips over the mesh, skins her knees, stands, then dives towards her husband, whose entire body judders with a seizure. 'Luca, Luca,' she shrieks, pulling out the needle and throwing it across the floor.

Figgi follows with a smack of wood as he half-lands on the coffee table. Everyone is shouting. The girl dashes for freedom, and in one gazelle-like leap jumps onto the broken fly screen, springboards onto the windowsill and then out. She drops out of sight, momentarily reappears, then vanishes towards the pine boundary. No one thinks to follow her.

'What was in the injection? Tell me!' Agata shrieks at the man held by Vanessa.

'Give me Luca's cuffs,' Vanessa shouts. 'This guy isn't getting away.'

'What was in the injection?' Agata is cradling Luca's head. His face is pale, and he's struggling to breathe.

Figgi pulls the cuffs from Luca's jacket and hands them to Vanessa. 'We have to get him to hospital. An ambulance will take too long.' He kneels by Susan.

Vanessa cuffs the man at one wrist, attaching it to the metal stair banister. She kicks him hard, and he howls. 'Answer her.'

Agata yells again. 'Tell me, or I'll break your arms!'

The man twists against the cuffs. 'Horse anaesthetic. From a vet. Enough to kill.'

'Hospital.' Figgi pulls Susan up from behind the sofa. Dazed, she touches the blood that matts on the back of her head. 'Hospital,' Figgi repeats and goes to assist in lifting Luca, but he is fast becoming a dead weight. His eyes roll to the back of his head, and Susan joins them to take one arm.

'That door.'

'The downstairs door won't open,' says the cuffed man. 'I think Alessandro broke the key deliberately.' He rattles the cuffs on the metal balustrade as the three of them struggle to drag Luca up the stairs.

'Let me go. I'm police,' he shouts, legs sprawling across a step.

Vanessa pulls back one arm and punches him neatly between the eyes. Blood squirts from his nose. 'Stop whining. I know who you are, DCI Baker. If Agata doesn't break your legs, I will.'

The man wipes his streaming nose with the back of his hand, curls on the step, and lets them pass. Vanessa joins them, assisting with the remaining limb, and the four of them struggle across the landing, down the external stairs, and up the path to Figgi's car. Luca's unconscious body folds awkwardly as they place him in the back seat.

Agata climbs in beside him, slapping his cheeks. 'Luca, stay awake. Stay with me. We'll have you to the hospital in twenty minutes.'

'Get in,' says Figgi to Susan. 'They'll check you out, too.' He looks at Vanessa. 'Sorry, no room, but the Carabinieri will be here shortly.' He sets off at speed. Suicidal speed. But no one will argue. And thank God, he knows these roads well.

Vanessa wipes her forehead and adjusts her shirt that has come loose in the struggle. She looks up towards Montecatini. She can see the slow crawl of cars on the edge of the Piazza.

A shining black sedan car with blacked-out windows approaches from the bottom of the hill. She turns and watches it execute a neat half-circle, swivelling to face in the direction from which it has just come, before stopping by Vanessa. The driver's smoked window slides down just enough to show a man of indeterminate age wearing dark glasses. His hair is short, his jaw square and lightly bristled.

'You American lady? We come for child.' The heavy vowels stamp the man as Eastern European or Russian. Vanessa isn't sure.

She stares at him, unflinching. 'Who are you?'

'We come for Wathiqa. We have an agreement and papers for adoption.'

'I doubt that,' says Vanessa. 'Not real papers, anyway. You want to give me your names?'

'Are you American lady?'

'Clearly not.' Vanessa couldn't fake an American accent even if she wanted to. 'The American lady is dead, and the child is gone.'

'Says who?' The man frowns. 'We contact her just now.' He steps out of the car, placing his broad frame next to Vanessa.

A lesser person would be afraid, but Vanessa has squared up to worse. She doesn't move an inch. Years of training make her a difficult person to intimidate. 'You want to go in and check? You'll put your prints all over a murder scene. Be my guest.' She pulls her badge from her pocket. Behind the dark glasses, he studies the writing, one hand on the outline of a gun beneath his jacket.

'Okay. So I'm British Police, but the Italian Police are coming in minutes. This is a crime scene. Understand?'

His hand drops. 'My boss has legal papers to adopt.

Nothing illegal here.' He steps back into the car. 'We go back to court, and we find child.'

The window slides up, and they depart, scraping the verge and shooting down the hill. Vanessa notes the Italian car registration. Probably rented or borrowed. 'Not if I find you first,' she says. She sighs. Of the many insults she has collected over the years, it's the first time she's been mistaken for a pimp mother. She wipes a bead of sweat from her forehead. 'Hell will freeze over before I hand any child to you scum,' she says out loud.

Her eyes trace the black sedan as it appears back on the main road heading toward Pisa. It is hard to believe such ugliness exists in the midst of this beauteous landscape, but Vanessa is not overly sentimental. Her thoughts are with the task in hand. Now seems a good moment to capitalise on her unique situation: a British detective in Italy, who has taken a senior British police officer prisoner. There's no protocol for this situation that she knows, so what deals might be struck? She turns and heads back into the house.

Chapter Thirty-Eight

Retracing the corridor, Vanessa notes the abandoned bedrooms and a dozen sweat-stained mattresses. If the living room is only accessible from the landing, what is behind the locked door below? The place reeks of disuse. Baker is rattling the handcuffs against the iron balustrade, using his free hand and the sports shirt to mop the blood still seeping from his nose.

Retracing her steps, she reaches under the sofa and loops the gun handle with a spindle from the floor. Then she goes over to Crystal's still form. The smell of blood and the stationary ribcage tell their tale. Vanessa makes a cursory check for a pulse, but no one could survive such a deep spike to the temple. She stands up, knees cracking, and gives a quick dog-like shake. It's not the first time she's witnessed a violent death, and it probably won't be the last. Baker will have a shiner, but the nose doesn't look broken.

'Is there anyone else in the house?'

Baker mumbles a reply, and having satisfied herself that immediate medical care will be of little use, Vanessa drags one of the remaining chairs to the base of the staircase and stretches out her legs. He's pale but defiant, and for a moment, they eyeball one another. What is her position in this fiasco? She can tell he's thinking what she's thinking. Technically, he outranks her.

'Okay. Let's talk.' She doesn't afford him title or privilege.

He yanks on the cuff, speaking in a voice thickened by injury. 'I'm undercover.'

'Cut the crap. We're already on to your unit. Why do you think my sergeant was sent here?'

Baker lets the bloodied T-shirt drop back onto his chest. He spits red phlegm on the stair. 'They'll put a target on my back. I need witness protection and a new identity.'

Vanessa leans forward. 'That's a lot of demands from someone chained and facing a thirty-year jail term.'

He hocks again to clear his throat. 'You want to play it by the book? Even if I say nothing, I'll be dead in two days in an English prison. Probably less in an Italian prison. The Syndicate will take me out.'

She assesses this statement. She hasn't got to her current rank by playing everything by the rules. Her climb has included a mountain of insults and copious sliding-the-line moments. Once she put a fork deep into a colleague's wandering hand. It did her reputation wonders. Sometimes you need luck, and sometimes you need leverage. Maybe she has both in Baker.

'I can't do you deals. Above my pay grade. Let us begin with an off-the-record chat. If I hear something convincing, I'll phone and plead your case. If not, we'll leave it to the Italians.'

Baker wipes his nose with a hand and looks at the gun. He hesitates. 'Water.'

She keeps a hip flask. Few of her team know that. 'Have

some whisky. A bit of anaesthetic for your nose. Then you can tell me why my sergeant went awol. He was only three months off collecting a fat pension.'

Baker tips back his head and drains the flask. The clock is ticking, she thinks. She will lose advantage when cars come from the square. 'C'mon. Save your miserable skin.'

So he talks. The confession of a man who has little to lose.

Baker admits he's a gambler who wound up in the Syndicate's pay around the time he met Crystal in a big Florida poker game. When the US authorities put out a warrant for Crystal's arrest, she fled and sought him out, seeking money and a job. Her medical training made her useful to the Syndicate. One flash of a lanyard, and authorities hand her children from the migrant camps. Everyone trusts a blonde medic with a ready smile.

It's a life of looking over their shoulders, and what they both crave is plenty of money in a country without extradition, somewhere beyond the Syndicate's control. Crystal comes up with a plan. Black market organ donation pays well. She knows this from her illicit work in Florida. Instead of illegals from South America, she can use illegals from Africa. She has the black-market contacts, and the Syndicate are paying for her to do the blood tests. It's a great sideline. He's appalled, but she persuades him the money would buy their dream escape. All goes well. Their riches multiply until Crystal tests two girls who are sheer gold. Golden Blood. And even better, a rich oligarch is seeking organs for his sick son. Baker contacts Alessandro, the Syndicate banker, requesting offshore accounts and fake passports. In his role as a go-between, Baker has met with Alessandro quite a few times.

Alessandro asks few questions for an agreed share of twelve million dollars. The banker doesn't know that's the price of two healthy girls with the correct blood and tissue match.

The larger girl will donate her organs, and the younger will be used as a blood bank. But the younger one falls sick, so they swap their plan, bringing the surgery forward by several weeks. This involves the Italian stretch of their journey instead of the Belgian leg. The oligarch insists he will only take the second girl if his child survives. So they wait. The sick child can't be moved, but seven million makes the waiting worthwhile. When they ask Alessandro for a safe house in Italy to complete the transaction, he offers them his newly acquired property in Montecatini. He warns them to stay clear of his cousin, Figaro, and all will be well. But days turn into weeks.

Baker's nerves shred. Waiting is fatal in this game, and he can predict how the dominoes will fall. First domino: The hospital refuses to take the girl's body. No paperwork, no legal burial. Second domino: The driver who helps Crystal get rid of the body demands a higher cut. Crystal tells Baker she's sorted it. Third domino: Alessandro reads a newspaper article about the girl with no lungs and no heart. He develops a sense of morality. Or so it seems.

The third domino surprises them the most. Alessandro is the man who takes payments from the rich for Off Grid Kids. But he turns up and tells them to clear out immediately. They promise, but when Alessandro and Baker get back to England, Baker gets a call saying Alessandro is going to inform the Syndicate of their activities. He panics. Alessandro has given them fake passports, and in return, they've given part payment. Baker thinks he can talk to him, persuade him to delay any such rash thoughts. Crystal explains how he can administer a drug to make Alessandro more suggestible. They're not monsters. They're not into inflicting pain. But right in front of Baker's eyes, Alessandro shouts and begins to fit, yelling about the news article in his pocket. The hired goons stuff the paper in Alessandro's mouth in temper, and then vanish, leaving Baker with a dead banker. Seeking to tie up loose ends, Baker takes the dead man's phone. There's a message on it to someone called Susan Li, the wife.

Now he's really panicked. He calls Crystal, who suggests their exit plan.

First, he pulls rank to get the investigation brought into his department. Then he buries the files. Flies out to Italy. They must leave immediately, but Crystal refuses. She persuades him to wait. There's seven million coming their way, and they are going to need it to live freely in South America. And besides, there's one less cut to make with Alessandro dead. Besides, she says, they can find out what's in the package. Incriminating evidence must be buried.

Some questions were answered by Brian Blunt. He's no fool and recognises Baker straight away. Nor does he believe the story that Baker is working undercover. But he's happy to have Alessandro's cut. A rich retirement beckons, Blunt says, except the English bar girl has steamed open the letter. It means nothing to her, and she doesn't know them. Susan Li is the problem. But in the middle of the night, Crystal sorts Amy in her own special way. Let the police chase their tail for a voodoo murderer.

Now both Baker and Blunt are uneasy. This is too much, they say, Crystal's ruse to point blame on a voodoo murderer won't work. But Crystal insists it was better to cauterise loose ends. They've come this far.

Alone with Baker, she persuades him it is safer to drug Brian's drink and tip him over the edge of the Tower. Damn

Italians keep interrupting her plan, so she calls Dave. It needs two—one to drug and one to tip—but when it's done, the last domino is in sight. They don't have to give Alessandro's share to anyone. All that is left is to grab the wife and check the parcel. It's possible Susan has been directing the traffic toward the Syndicate. So, a quick injection and leave her in the house with a confession pinned to her chest. Then the Syndicate won't look their way. Job done. No witnesses, no problems.

Hand over Wathiqa. Take all their money and run.

Baker's legs twitch against the stair's lip. 'I'm a gambler and a petty criminal. Not a murderer. Not a paedophile. Crystal was different. For her, taking a life was easy. Migrants were numbers on a balance sheet to be sold or dumped. She's been doing this game a long time. Anyone who got in her way was cut out. That's why the American authorities froze her assets and put out an APB. This past week, I wondered if I was the next cut when we reached South America.'

'My heart bleeds for you, Baker,' says Vanessa, picking a fingernail. 'As for Crystal, she sounds like a psychopath. There's many back home in England who would vote her to be Home Secretary.' She sniffs. 'But I need names.'

'I was paid to let lorries with hidden migrants pass through at port. Turn a blind eye. The Syndicate took over on British soil with their own gang, and any unaccompanied children were taken out and put separately into a black limo at an agreed meeting point. Sometimes Alessandro handed me pre-ordered forged papers to pass on to those who had contacts in England, but beyond that I don't know what happened to the people in each shipment.'

'A name.' Vanessa struggles to keep her expression

neutral. A part of her wants to punch him again. 'A name, Baker. Who's the top man?'

Baker rattles his chain. 'Someone in the aristocracy, but I don't know. Honestly, I don't have specific names.'

'No names, no deals.'

Baker wipes a thin trail of blood on his upper lip. 'Every time the press says police have broken a trafficking ring, what they really mean is they've caught the bottom feeders.'

'You're not telling me anything new.' Vanessa puts the hip flask back in her pocket. 'This won't get you off the hook. We've got two guys in custody with Hickock, ready to swear to aggravated burglary on the Verdi death. One nod from the Syndicate, and they'll place you at the crime scene.' She stands and stamps her feet. A police siren has started up in the distance. 'So, you killed my sergeant?' Despite her dislike for Blunt, Vanessa almost feels sorry for her nose-thumbing colleague. If he had done as he was told, he'd be alive today. His sense of superiority and his prejudice against women in rank has been his death warrant.

'Most of my unit is working for the Syndicate,' says Baker.

'We thought as much. Now they'll let you take the fall. C'mon. The Italians are arriving, and it will be out of my hands. Save yourself.'

'Karol Berzins.'

'A woman? Carol who?'

'No. A big, fat Russian guy who's swimming in money from people trafficking and drugs. He keeps a mansion somewhere north of London. He'll be your big collar. And also, my Superintendent, Hutchins. He'll try to drown me, but I made sure I kept a little evidence. When I get back, I'll give it to you. But I need a new identity, because I'll always be at risk.'

Vanessa compresses her lips. 'This Carol guy. And your commanding officer? Anyone else? The Verdi family?'

'Alessandro Verdi, but I don't know about his family. Crystal tried to get in with Figaro, but he's a closed book to outsiders. And I don't think Susan is part of the Syndicate. We talked to her, and she's dumb as hell. Alessandro said she was in on it, but after today I think that was one of his ploys.'

'Anybody else?'

'Crystal told me the names of the immigration workers who hand over the children in camps. You need to take my information seriously. Ripping out a girl's heart under anaesthetic is mild compared to what the Syndicate will do to me to ensure my silence. It's big business.'

A breeze blows up from the valley and through the broken window frame. Mosquitoes toss in the ceiling fan, and horns honk outside.

'Help me,' he pleads. 'I won't press charges for my broken nose.'

'Fuck off,' she says, speed dialling. 'Mr. Verdi? How's Luca?' She frowns. 'I'm sorry to hear that, but it sounds like it's out of your hands now. How much influence do you have here?' A small smile curls at her lips. 'In that case, come back immediately. It will be worth your while. And mine.'

A shout, and Vanessa fishes out her Metropolitan Police wallet for the second time with a sigh. She's experienced enough to know that many rookie police aim for a civilian suit, especially if they're standing next to a man with a bloody nose. Police crawl along the galleried landing, checking for the non-existent gunmen. 'It's your lucky day, Baker,' she says, as she holds out her badge to the law officers.

Chapter Thirty-Nine

Reaching the centre of the olive grove, Wathiqa can go no further. The soles of her feet scream. She's lost one flip-flop and thrown the other, and she sits to inspect her injuries. The balls of her feet are lacerated and bleeding. Blinking against the sun, she checks there are no people chasing her, but the horizon is empty, save for small birds of prey who hover expectantly. Head in hands, she slumps, lacking energy to flick away the insect life that settles on her cuts and creases.

'*Hai bisogna da qualcosa*?'

In a flash, she jumps up, ready to fight, kick and spit.

A thin, young man is so still in the shadows, he could be part of the landscape. He sits cross-legged, leaning against a tree, pad and pencil in hand. Next to him lies a clear glass bottle of water.

Seeing her gaze, he says: '*Qualcosa da bere*?'

She says nothing, but thirst makes it hard to look away. Perhaps she can grab the bottle without him grabbing her.

His tongue pokes out as he observes the browning blood on her T-shirt. He speaks in English. 'You running away?

When I run away, I come here.' His head tilts up to the clear blue sky. 'This is a good place to hide.'

Her focus is still on the bottle.

'Go on. You must be thirsty. I've watched you come across that field like a deer on two legs.'

She understands but she doesn't want him to know that. Not yet. He repeats this sentence in a different language, then shrugs, bends, and continues to sketch. His face is ebony, darker than hers, but who is he? And why is he here?

Her mother trusted the boatmen to get her to Europe, men in agbadas, men in khaki, white men with rifles. But Mother died, and no one helped. She trusted the American, Dr. Crystal, to get her and Huda to safety, but her trust was misplaced. She trusted the Italian hospitals to make her sister better. But they let her die.

Who does she trust now?

He takes a drink from the bottle and offers it to her.

'Finish it. My Babo gave it to me. He told me to stay away from home. The police are there, and I don't like the police.'

The boy has decided on the English language, and perhaps her expression shows her understanding. But her mother warned her about well-dressed men: They are not all they seem. Yet he is young, and his expression is friendly. She hesitates.

'My Babo was my sponsor. He says when I feel bad, I must draw the things in my head. That way, they are on the paper, not in my brain. So, I draw the soldiers and the dead.' For a second, he lifts his pad of paper for her to see, then snatches it back.

Wathiqa inches forward, plucks the bottle from his side, and moves back, draining it in one. The crickets play a tune between them. 'You know the American doctor?' she asks.

Confusion wrinkles his brow. The pencil stills. 'Do you mean that nurse with the Dutch family? I've heard about them, but never met them. We're new here. We used to live on Lampedusa Island.' He puts his head on one side to look at her. 'My real father is dead. And you?'

The bullets in her father's head flash before her eyes, and without warning, her limbs collapse under her. She sits, pulls her blood-soaked T-shirt to her eyes, and weeps. Nobody disturbs her, not even the dragonflies. For a few minutes, fat tears fall, then she calms herself. The boy is drawing again.

'You trust your Babo?'

He nods, not looking up from his sketch.

'Can he find my sister?'

'Is she lost?' he says.'My Babo wrote to the Red Cross to find my cousins.' He examines her feet. 'My Babo can give you bandages. He is a doctor.'

The boy's eyes are gentle, without aggression. She stares down at her feet and presses fingers around the most painful parts.

'I know a secret passage,' he continues. 'They go from these fields to my home. I use it whenever I need to run away and hide. It comes up in the Torre di Verdi gardens. Want to come? I can get you plasters and some flip-flops. No one will see us.'

With unhurried movements, he packs away his pad and pencil into a blue rucksack and pulls out a phone and a large key. Then he walks a few metres, scrabbles underneath a spiny, low-lying shrub, and puts the key into a half-hidden metal plate on the ground. It springs open. Below is a gaping dark hole with earthen steps heading downward.

'Our tunnel!' He speaks with pride. 'Orlando and I cleaned it when we first came. My Babo said the Tower watchmen made it in the time of Cesare Borgia in case murdering soldiers surrounded them. Come. I will put on my phone torch, and you can follow me.'

Wathiqa sees the black hole and the boy gesturing for her to follow.

In a burst of longing, she wants nothing more than to follow his light to safety—somewhere she can sleep without fear, somewhere there is food and water, given without threats or coercion. But where is such a place?

Her mother would tell her to run. Who goes down a hole with a stranger expecting light at the end of a tunnel? But how can she keep running on her cut and bleeding feet? She is exhausted and listens to the police sirens wailing nearby. They will find the doctor with a spike in her head, and the police will come for her. Or she goes with this strange boy, maybe to be imprisoned by other forces.

Which way to go?

Chapter Forty

Figaro arrives back and parks his car nose to nose with the police. With a quick command, he tells the Carabinieri to wait outside before turning to Vanessa.

'Do you mind? There's something I need to ask him about Alessandro.'

'You're not going to kill him, are you?' Vanessa is only half joking. 'I could fill you in on our chat, rather than you becoming a murderer.'

Figaro smiles, although his eyes are tired. 'I'll never be a murderer,' he says. 'I am a man in a suit. I am the mayor.' He makes it clear he has questions that are irrelevant to the police. Questions about his family. Vanessa knows she has no jurisdiction here, and the Carabinieri wave him on as if this is a regular occurrence with local crime scenes.

Figgi pushes back the sleeves of his white shirt, ignoring the blood splatters on his cuffs, and enters the house.

Baker looks at him fearfully. 'What do you want? I've told Vanessa all I'm going to say. I'm doing a deal.'

Figgi sees the trembling in the prone man's legs but says nothing.

'So, you going to kill me? With everyone outside? Revenge for your cousin's death. It was an accident. I swear.'

'You're an amateur, aren't you?' says Figgi without sympathy. 'My mistake. I thought you were a professional. I thought you were going to put a neat little bullet in his brain like any decent hit man. Why drug him and stuff newspaper in his mouth? And even stupider, an Italian newspaper! You brought the trail right back here. *Coglione.* What an idiot.' He looks over the railings at Crystal's body below and shakes his head. 'You'll be found guilty of Alessandro's murder. Crystal was here in Italy the whole time.'

Baker's mouth falls slightly open. 'It was you. You made the phone call telling us Alessandro was going to betray us to the Syndicate?'

'We have some very good friends in London, and one of them was having Alessandro followed. A little problem with their daughter. From them, I was able to find out about you and your corrupt games. I don't involve myself with the English Syndicate and they wisely keep out of our way, but we all realised you were part of them. So, I gave the instructions for someone to phone you. Naturally, I assumed you'd deal with Alessandro to protect your business interests. And then, Alessandro's wife would never have to know the extent of his dealings.'

Baker's mouth is working, as if his brain cannot catch his tongue. He swallows. 'But Alessandro Verdi is your family. *Cosa Nostra* and all that. Why would you do that?'

Figgi's eyes narrow. 'The trouble with Alessandro was he didn't want to be part of the family. He wanted to be bigger than the family. He wanted to take charge.' He scoffs. 'That was never going to happen. As long as he stayed in England, I didn't mind, but he wanted to come back to Italy.' Figgi advances down the stairs 'He came here, dragging the dirt of the English Syndicate into Montecatini. I'll admit, I didn't immediately recognise Crystal was involved. She was clever. I thought the Jensens were here. As did everyone. And then I realised. But how to get you out of town without panicking the people, without destroying the tourist trade and our good reputation? The Verdis protect this district.'

Baker writhes in panic. 'Why didn't you ask us to leave? Christ, man, Crystal went to see you.'

'Crystal made a clumsy pass at me. She should have just got down to business.'

'I don't understand. Why didn't you kill Alessandro when he came to Casa Verdi?'

Figgi grimaced. 'I was elsewhere. But in any case, family don't kill family. But if one of ours get killed while swindling someone else...'

The handcuffs rattle as Baker pulls ineffectually against his chains. 'You're going to kill me, aren't you? An eye for an eye. Mafia retribution.'

Figgi stands next to him looking down at his sprawling helplessness. 'Am I holding a gun? No. Do I want to get my hands dirty on little people like you? No. This is what I'm going to do.' He leans down and lowers his voice. 'I'm going to get you out of here, provided you do exactly what I tell you to do. Firstly, the young African girl goes free. We erase her from the crime. There are no illegal migrants on my territory.'

Baker shrinks against the railings as Figgi walks passes

him to Crystal's body. His fingers pluck a white handkerchief from his pocket, and he picks up the candlestick, wiping it carefully before pressing the implement into Crystal's dead hand.

'The letter?'

I don't know. It was there. Someone took it. Probably that stupid Susan girl. Alessandro accused her of being involved.'

Figgi nods and completes the artificial scene. 'Alessandro died on British soil. He was involved with British Mafia, or the Syndicate, as you call them. When we find the other body in this house, the one in the photograph, we will blame it on the American woman. We will say Susan was here asking questions about Alessandro. I wasn't sure about her at first, but she's an innocent caught up in a dirty world. You will be a witness who saw Crystal inject Luca and then try to kill Susan, accidentally killing herself. Understand?'

'Your police won't believe that. The forensics won't bear it out.'

'Luca Agnello is in hospital, unlikely to survive. Agata will like this version of the story. She has a soft heart for children and an understanding of true justice. As for the Carabinieri! They will believe what I tell them to believe.' He straightens up, folds the bloody handkerchief into four, and re-tucks it in his trouser pocket. With a litheness befitting an athlete, he nips up the stairs, ignoring Baker's trembling body. 'The Private Investigator's report commissioned by Alessandro's father-in-law will be sent to the British Police. Do as I say and I will ensure your safety here, but what happens when you are back in your own country is up to Vanessa Candle.'

'Please. My police force will bury me. Take me into

your family business. Let me work for you. I know the smuggling gangs here. I can be useful,' pleads Baker. 'Don't sell me out to the English Syndicate.'

Figgi curls his lips in derision. 'Play nicely with the Italian authorities, and I'll think about it.'

Chapter Forty-One

Montecatini della Torre. Four months later.

A dry summer has sweetened the grapes for *vendemmia*, the picking of fruit. Soon the olive harvest will begin and the *fratoias* will whir in the industrial olive presses. All the flesh and stones will be pulped into a smooth oil, like the summer events that are being pulped into smooth stories. Apart from all the police and the paperwork, there has been an earthquake in the south, with the tremblings felt all the way up to Florence. A few cracks in the Piazza and surrounding buildings have kept local builders busy, but now the roads are sorted.

September is a good time to be in Montecatini. Locals and dignitaries climb to the upper piazza, built long before the modern road. Odd that the most ancient structures survived unscathed. The church takes up one side of the small, cramped square, with space only for a horse and cart. But no hearse needs to risk its paintwork through the ancient stone arches. Today is a memorial service, not a burial. Alessandro's body remains in limbo in England, snared in bureaucracy. In any case, the Verdi family graveyard is in Florence, so the Montecatinese are content with this ceremony of smells and bells and a golden plaque.

Families press into the cool of the medieval pews. Today, Alessandro Verdi is to be remembered with reverence and fondness. Their prince, the bringer of parties and joy and cash. The stained-glass windows are blocked from the sun by the Tower, but strains of gold, crimson, and blue coat the pews. Noble colours for a noble son.

The elderly Signor Giorgio, the most senior of Verdis, has made a rare appearance to give a homily of tempered words. The feud between Alessandro and his family is no secret, but Giorgio is suitably reverential, speaking of Alessandro's life with love, while abstractedly fingering the lapel of his bespoke silk suit. His face is so lined, it is impossible to tell if he is happy or sad. Hands are kissed, cheeks are kissed, and Giorgio Verdi leaves without a word of past discord. Legends must be allowed to grow, and every family has its share of arguments. Alessandro was the man they hoped would one day return to be mayor, and for months, in every bar, they have been reciting their memories of the boy who would never be king.

Slowly, everyone moves from the Tower's shadow down the hill to Casa Verdi. Few decline the offer of good food and wine. Yolanda and Dana have been cooking for weeks. On one side of the terrace, Natale stands, a wisp in the heat, wrung dry by grief. The gift of the old Jensen house to her family cannot stem her tears. Red-rimmed elders support her. She is no longer in the kitchen at Casa Verdi but comes as a guest. It is the passing of an era.

As the old community adjusts history, there is an awkward first meeting between Susan Li and the real wife, Maria Giuliana. The beautiful Mariju is the principal guest of honour. Agata does the introductions and finds that Mariju knew of Susan all along.

'You were a friend of my parents many years ago in London?' The young woman addresses Agata. Her mouth is full of small, white, pearly teeth, and she curls a finger around long black locks that tumble like a Botticelli painting at her breast. Her youthfulness makes the crowd feel protective, and there are many comparisons to a Madonna and child.

'I knew your parents, Alfredo and Priya. They were at University together with Alessandro,' says Agata. She omits to explain the nature of her relationship with Alessandro. She is a fifty-year-old woman and Mariju is barely twenty-three. 'I hope they are well?'

'In perfect health, but I was happy for Mum and Dad to stay away. It's not uncommon for a father to dislike the man who steals his daughter's heart, is it?' She poses, legs wide, back swayed, to show off a slight bump under the black linen of her dress. Her large dark eyes are her mother's, but her confidence reminds Agata of her father.

'What's important is that you look after yourself,' says Agata.

'Of course. And Matteo.' The pretty face creases momentarily as she strokes the bump. 'Matteo,' she calls.

The four-year-old runs around the edge of the pool, followed by three of the van children. He is in bare feet, having kicked off his shiny shoes, and his shirt is untucked. Their arms stretch toward him, fearful he will fall into the pool, but he doesn't want to be caught and looks in little need of rescue.

'Don't worry,' says Agata. 'They'll protect him.'

Natale calls out, '*Stai attenti*!' as the little prince laughs and dips his toes in near the deep end.

'It was a business arrangement, you know.' Mariju turns to the group just as Figgi joins them. His expression offers no hint of his thoughts. He hands a glass of orange juice to Mariju.

The pregnant madonna shifts focus to Susan. 'You were paid well to protect us, weren't you? I mean, two million. Who wouldn't put themselves at risk for such a sum?' Mariju does not look like the kind of woman who would put herself at risk for a mere two million, but Susan says nothing and nods.

It strikes Agata that Susan's long shining hair is of a similar length to Mariju. And from behind, they have the same height and build: Alessandro's perfect foil.

Alessandro's hand in hers.

Agata's memory is like a paper cut, and she blinks. What happened to the summer when it was she who was the young, dark-haired girl by his side? Excusing herself, she walks to a trestle table loaded with enticing antipasti. She puts down her drink and pulls out a tissue. There are things she knows about Alessandro that no one else knows, and the secrets burn inside her.

Aware only of being the centre of attention, Mariju continues to chatter. 'My husband was drawn unwittingly into doing business with those criminals. He told me he would never be free until we exposed them.' She bends her head and carefully wipes a threatening tear with one polished nail. 'He was so brave.'

Agata catches the look on Figgi's face, but no one comments as Mariju's jewelled hand rests on her stomach.

'Don't distress yourself,' says Susan in the awkward pause.

'The family should be proud of him.' Mariju changes to sudden anger. 'He was misunderstood. You know he was,

Figgi. That's why I honoured the commitment to give the old Dutch holiday house to Natale and Renzo. And I want you all to know Alessandro was going to buy a castle for us to live in. Buriano, he called it. My husband promised me the moon, and he would have delivered, if not for those criminals.'

'Susan has donated all her money to our new charitable foundation in his name,' says Figgi.

Mariju pats the stomach again. 'My children are well provided for by Alessandro's portfolio.' Her nose tilts to the sky. 'I don't need Daddy's money, or anyone else's. Alessandro made a legal will, you know. He was like that. Thought of everything.'

Not everything, thinks Agata, aware of the limitations of Mariju's knowledge, but no one, not even her parents, will ever fill in the details. And somewhere in her heart, she wants to believe Mariju's version of Alessandro—if not for herself, then for his children.

Natale has given Matteo a toy wooden sword and shield. As the child approaches his mother with mock threatening behaviour, Mariju hands her glass to Susan and scoops him into her arms. The little boy protests, but Mariju kneels, keeping a firm hand, and demands a local photographer take a picture. Matteo makes a practised smile into the lens before squirming away to play with the other children.

Agata presses her lips together.

'Do you still feel angry at how he mistreated you in London?' whispers Figgi, who has moved to Agata's side.

'It wasn't me he treated badly. It was Luca. He and Alfie bullied Luca terribly. You remember? Luca was sent by your father to ensure the sale of the flat you all lived in during University. They treated him like a servant.' The criticisms are long overdue. 'Sorry, Figgi. It wasn't you.'

Figgi lays a hand on her shoulder and then moves away. He speaks to Susan, and they disappear into the house. Susan has put forward a detailed proposal for a migrant centre in the empty Miniera Hotel, all done under Figgi's careful supervision. Using the Foundation, he has obtained the promise of EU loans to refurbish Buriano in return for setting up a centre for unaccompanied minors who arrive at Italy's shores. In a rare show of unity, none of the locals have objected; the small, underweight children in the van have altered everyone's perspective. *Prima l'umanità.*

Vanessa stands nearby, staring at the view with a contemplative look. No longer in a work suit, she is sleek and sturdy in a dark blue sleeveless dress. Her straightened hair glistens at the shoulder, and bangles ripple at her wrist with each sip of wine. Agata approaches, and she turns with a wide smile.

'I was so pleased to accept Figgi's invitation to attend. I really wanted to meet you again, even though it's for a sad event. We've done so many Skype calls.'

These past months, Agata has survived on coffee, nursing Luca, and by working herself into the ground with long nighttime hours of meticulous preparation on dual language documentation. In a multitude of phone conversations and emails, she, too, thinks of Vanessa as a friend.

They squeeze hands. Vanessa is not into a European kiss. 'How's Luca?'

'Still very weak.'

Vanessa bites her lips. 'I thought he would die. That drug was lethal.'

Agata remembers the suicidal dash to *Soccorso Pronto*, the emergency room in Volterra and the crash team, pumping and fighting to revive him as his organs tinkered on the brink of shutting down.

'They say you don't realise how much you love someone until you're about to lose them.'

Vanessa murmurs her sorrow, and they stand a moment in the shade. Matteo struts, reminding Agata of her sons when they were little. Her throat tightens. In front of the kitchen doors, Figgi gives Susan a peck on the cheek before they collect more food.

'Are they an item?' A gurgle of laughter escapes Vanessa. 'What have I missed?'

'I'm not sure. They haven't said anything,' says Agata. 'Figgi has persuaded her to hand over all her money in return for setting up a child refugee centre in the Old Mines Hotel, and in theory, he will employ her to look after the place. He's secured EU loans to re-establish Buriano as a World Heritage site. The town is happy, because he's bringing work into the area. Turns out the enemy isn't the migrants after all.'

'I didn't have him pegged as a charitable sort. More a sophisticated Mafia type.'

Agata gives a lop-sided smile. 'I make no comment, except to say he's a typical Verdi. The family business has won the contracts for all the refurbishments, and they're tendering for a huge UN conference centre in Pisa.'

'Nice!'

'Figgi knows his way around bureaucracy,' says Agata.

'So Susan's not returning to England?'

'Apparently not. Figgi is sorting out her resident's status. She wants to help with the children and claims she wants to make a difference.'

'Make a difference?' Vanessa laughs. 'Haven't we all said that? People usually mean they're going vegetarian.'

Agata giggles. 'I know.' But then she becomes serious. 'I think Susan's terribly naive. I see my past self in her, but at least she's trying to do some good. Luca said, if we can learn to respect our differences, we are halfway to Heaven.'

'Not sure it's that simple.' Vanessa lights up a cigarette. 'But maybe I'm just an old cynic.'

'You are not old!'

The women laugh and finish their drinks. Ruby approaches, tail wagging. The dog has been introduced to the children, and they no longer fear her. She is a friendly person with four paws who desires only to eat lizards. To Agata, this is the first sign that the children are progressing toward improved mental health. Umberto has warned of the lasting effects of trauma, and The Red Cross has said it may take months to find relatives. Everything is a work in progress.

'By the way, we've been so busy collating information against the various names Baker gave us that I've never really had a chance to ask how you knew Alessandro Verdi.' Vanessa takes a drag and narrows her eyes.

Agata indicates they need a more private conversation. They grab another glass of wine and walk away to sit on an olive wood bench at the back of the house. She feels a sudden desire to confide in someone outside her Tuscan circle. 'Quarter of a century ago, Alessandro and I met in London, when I was a nanny for a rich family.'

'London, huh?' Vanessa is unaware of Agata's internal struggle. 'That reminds me, Baker's testimony will see a chunk of our corrupt officers go to jail. And now he's left England for his new life abroad. I'm not sure where he's gone.'

Agata tuts. 'When Umberto's son was traumatised by a policeman on the Tower stairs, I thought it was your sergeant, but of course it was Baker. It's a shame he goes free. He didn't have any qualms about threatening Edu.'

At his name, the boy looks up. He and Wathiqa are huddled some distance from them, backs to a stone wall, bottoms on the ground and knees up. Between them, they share a set of headphones and an iPad. One white wire trails from each of their ears.

Agata waves. 'They're watching X-Factor Italia.'

'Just like my teenage son. Kids! Same the world over!' Vanessa sips. 'Look at it this way: Baker stuck to our pact. I wasn't sure he would, but Wathiqa's name has been completely erased from the witness statements. So a lie is his redemption. Figaro and I agreed to blame the escaped driver for Crystal's death. That's easy, seeing as his prints were not on file. And the girl is free to make the best of her life. She's suffered enough.'

'Umberto D'Angelo is filing the paperwork to become Wathiqa's guardian,' says Agata. 'He knows more than anyone about that process, having done it for Edu. And the town have finally accepted that the Butcher is a good man, after all.'

'All's well that ends well?' says Vanessa.

'Except I'd love to get the top man in the Syndicate. Why do the evil go free?'

Vanessa twists to look at her. 'Are you talking about the man called Jett? We haven't been able to prove the existence of the mysterious Mr. Stillttiger. The bank code numbers were wrong, and the name doesn't exist. If it weren't for you, I wouldn't have figured out the anagram: Stillttiger spells Little Girls.' She tips the ash from her cigarette.

'Jett is actually a Geoffrey, but he's untouchable. I think Alessandro's intention was to send a warning to him. Leave me alone, and I'll feed false information to the authorities. He knew Jett was a dangerous enemy.'

'Unlike Karol Berzins. We've toppled him. His cyber footprint and Baker's evidence have definitely put him away. Interestingly, no one has come to his defence. Bloody class system.'

A tall, handsome young man walks over to them and offers a platter. 'Found you, Mamma,' Dino says, gently kissing Agata on the cheek, and she smiles, introducing him. He is her favoured son and always has been. Green-fingered Carlo is Luca's favourite, but these days the divisions are narrower, as both boys draw closer to their father.

Vanessa accepts the food with thanks, and Dino moves away to give Edu and Wathiqa something to eat. They exchange a joke about the song they're listening to, and then Dino moves back into the crowd milling along the patio.

Vanessa watches him go. 'Good-looking boy,' she says, 'but come on!' She crunches on the crust of a bruschetta. 'I interrupted you. What about Alessandro Verdi? I sense there is more.'

The dry valley is sand-coloured interspersed with pale olive trees and the red blooms of oleander bushes. Late summer is a time when nothing hides, and far in the distance deer step awkwardly across harvested fields, searching for food and water. She has been hiding truths for too many years, and her confession is long overdue.

Chapter Forty-Two

A newborn baby, a palazzo near Florence, and a sick nanny all contributed to an emergency in Sir John's household in the summer of 1987. Many Italians were employed for the upkeep of the summer residence, and one suggested Agata as a solution. Being the eldest of ten, she was an experienced minder of small, colicky babies. She also spoke stilted but proficient English. Two months turned into five years, with a chance for her to live and work in London. She signed the Official Secrets Act, a non-disclosure agreement, and told her own family half-truths. Yes, they were respectable. No, she was never out of sight of the children. In this way, she abandoned life on a farm and took to the city with no regrets.

If she had ever considered the local Verdi family wealthy, the life of Sir John's family opened her eyes. Their two homes in England resembled museums with furniture that could have been plundered from antiquity. Cleaners wore uniforms; the two Head Nannies wore a brown and white-collared affair, and she, as the under-nanny, wore a grey tunic. There were drivers in blue livery and cap, and several limousines for various occasions. The deliverymen never set foot in the front door, which was reserved for important men in suits.

An aura of privilege ran from the top floor nursery down to the basement kitchens. Agata was twenty and aware that the Prime Minister visited, but Sir wasn't in Parliament. One of the princes visited, but Sir wasn't part of the Royal household. So what did he do? He wasn't elected, but plain clothes men escorted him everywhere. It wasn't her business to know. Her job involved filling in gaps in the nannies' schedules. Some days she sat in the Daimler as a driver ferried her charges to and from their exclusive schools. Other days, she slept in a cot bed next to their rooms on the nursery floor. Everything was exciting.

By chance, she met Alessandro in a Knightsbridge pub in the summer of 1991. The Verdis had bought a small house in London to see the boys through University, and he lived with his cousin, as well as a close friend, Alfredo Mara. When she and he became lovers, there was no shortage of comfortable rooms in which their affair could blossom. They breathed the charmed life of those with sufficient money and youth and few cares. On her days off, they danced to Bryan Adams and shared ambitions. He was convinced the moon would bend to his will, and she believed him. She wanted to live a city life forever, and he supported her dreams.

But things changed when Alessandro met Jett.

Jett was the stepson. His socialite mother had little time for her eldest. His father had died, and Sir John sent the boy to Eton, discouraging visits to the family home. The nannies knew why. Every snowball had a pebble in the middle. Every ice cream he gave to the little ones was topped with dirt. As he grew older, the family cars developed sudden punctures in the absence of a driver. Not that anyone could prove anything.

Vanessa is listening intently. She has finished the bruschetta and smokes a second cigarette.

'One day I had a fight with him and I blacked his eye,' says Agata.

She laughs. 'You! You blacked his eye? How?'

'I'm the eldest of ten. I know how to deal with boys,' says Agata. 'It was easy. He was always groping the eldest girl. The nannies called him a pervert! I learned the true meaning of this word.'

'What did he do in return?'

'Threatened to have me sacked, but Sir John took my side and offered me a job.'

Vanessa looks impressed, sucking on a cigarette.

'If I had accepted, it would have changed my life.'

'But you turned him down? Why?'

Agata wasn't homesick. The thought of returning to her roots depressed her. Many of her friends had gone abroad or to the cities to find better paid work. Confiding her dilemma to Alessandro, she was shocked when he took Jett's side.

'He's not like that.'

'You know he is.'

'He told me you misunderstood him. He was a gentleman and didn't attack you back, so why complain?'

Her decision was swift. If Alessandro considered Jett's behaviour acceptable, she couldn't trust him, and if she couldn't trust him, she had to end their relationship.

Returning home, Agata learnt from Figgi about Alessan-

dro's misdemeanours and his illegal sale of the Mappamundi. It vindicated her choices, and with a reference provided by Sir John's wife, she obtained a job in a Florentine dress shop and began seeing Luca. But after her years in the thick of luxury, such a life lacked appeal. When Luca proposed, her parents encouraged her to accept. At least she could live in Florence.

Weeks before her wedding, Alessandro walked into the shop.

He said he had come back to claim her, and she glowed. Jett was in the wrong, and she was right, he said, and they kissed. At that moment, she forgave him for everything. This was love. He rented a hotel room overlooking the Ponte Vecchio, and they spent the night wrapped in each other's arms with murmured passions and promises. But she woke, flushed in the early morning, to find he'd left. The handwritten note claimed his visit was Jett's suggestion. Tell Agata, no girl leaves Alessandro Verdi; he leaves the girl. Last night had been a lie, he scrawled, a suitable revenge. This was Jett's influence.

Humiliated, she returned to the shop and Luca. No one had seen them together, and no one needed to be told. The marriage was an inevitability, and a honeymoon pregnancy led to a baby, born a month premature. Although you wouldn't have known from Dino's size.

But this second part of the story, Agata keeps to herself. She cannot speak of it.

'I loved Luca in a different way,' she says simply. 'I came back for him and chose Florence over London. Unfortunately, when Dino was born, our honeymoon baby, he was a wild child. Nothing like his father. I guess he reminded me of a young Alessandro. He reminded me of another time in my life.' She forces a laugh. 'Thankfully, my second child, Carlo, is exactly like Luca in everything.'

Vanessa sips, her eyes on the horizon. Agata wonders if she has said too much.

'So, you loved Luca, but maybe Alessandro more?' Vanessa offers at length. 'Many women like bad men.' She drains her glass.

Agata lips make a soft noise of denial, that denies nothing.

Vanessa smiles a knowing smile. 'I'm not one of those types who thinks: tell the whole truth and nothing but. You don't get to be my rank without a little negotiation along the way, and the truth is, we all break the rules sometimes. Like we did for Wathiqa. Everybody has secrets.' The detective leans close to her. 'But whoever I've wronged in life, I see it as payback for those who harmed me. So I make it a principle not to do guilt. There are too many bastards in the world running around free with blood on their hands.'

'You mean Salvini? He's banning the Italian Navy from rescuing migrant boats in the Mediterranean. They'll drown while he washes his hands of them.'

'Who's Salvini?' Vanessa frowns, then laughs. 'Oh! Your Prime Minister. No. I wasn't thinking of politics. But hey, let's keep in touch. You could invite me back to this magical land as your guest. My husband would die for this view.'

'Is that my ten Hail Marys? The price for misplaced love?'

Vanessa stands with a brief laugh. 'Come on. People like you and me might not save the world, but we've caught some traffickers, and protected some children from deviants, even if we've enriched the coffers of the Verdi family. We've done our bit.' She squeezes Agata's arm. 'Your husband seems like a good guy. I wish him a full recovery.'

Agata remembers something Luca used to say in the early days of their marriage: small justices. They couldn't stop corruption at high levels, but they could stop the muggers on the street. Italy didn't always get the government it wanted, but families could uphold simple values and protect their children. And anyway, Luca always said there was no enemy at the gate. Those medieval years were long gone. Now the truly evil and corrupt sit in bars with gold-plated credit cards and fast cars and yachts. The oligarchs, the tyrants, the unknown billionaires.

Vanessa picks her way across the grass to the patio area toward the throng. 'Why don't you come to London and stay with my family when Luca improves? Stuff Brexit!'

Agata wonders what it would be like to go back and walk the same streets. Put the past to bed. 'I'd like that,' she says. 'Even if England separates from the EU, there's no reason Italy and England should be enemies.'

'Spare us the politicians.' Vanessa brightens. 'We have Big Ben, Buckingham Palace, and tradition, and you have the medieval cities and *La Dolce Vita* and the food. It's a great friendship!'

'Ah, yes, the food. And the wine.' Never mind the bugs and the lethal grappa, thinks Agata. 'Maybe during a visit, we can put together a plan to catch the bigger bastards who slipped away.'

'Maybe,' says Vanessa, choosing another antipasti and another glass of wine.

Agata contemplates her life. Dino has promised to return for a while and help with the restoration of their home on weekends. Then he will be off to study for a degree in software programming. To Luca's delight, Carlo has said he will map out their land as a Tuscan organic farm. To this end, he has already contacted several American Universities that have reciprocal eco-projects. One of them has agreed to work with him.

Good things are happening, even if they're not in the news.

She makes a silent commitment to bury old ghosts and concentrate on present joys.

On the patio, the children play together in the sunshine, and for the moment, they are safe.

Afterword

Montecatini della Torre is based on the hillside town of Montecatini Val di Cecina, south of Pisa, Tuscany.

I lived in this town for two years, and when I first visited the Belforti Tower in 2017, (the inspiration for the Torre di Verdi) I thought what a fantastic location it would make for a Murder Mystery novel.

(https://www.torredeibelforti.com)

All this happened before COVID, but I remember with clarity, a land of great beauty, and also of change.

Discover it for yourself. Don't just go to Pisa, Florence, and Sienna, but take a small detour and enjoy a weekend in this magical town.

On the opposite ridge, you can see Volterra, the amazing Etruscan walled city that I viewed every morning from where I was staying. Take a drink at Il Buglione in the main piazza, on which La Pizzeria is based.

https://www.ilbuglione.it/ I loved this place, which is why this book is part dedicated to the owner, Stefania Falchi.

Go see the old Mining Museum—mentioned as La Miniera.

https://www.museodelleminieremontecatini.it/

(Don't get the location confused with Montecatini Terme, which is near Lucca.) Instead, discover Montecatini VC. It is a gem of a place, where no murders or mayhem have ever occurred, other than in my imagination.

I hope I have whetted your appetite.

Acknowledgements

I would like to thank my many Beta readers who advised on the writing of this novel, and those friends who encouraged my writing.

I am also indebted to Sarah Hart (hart.sarahea@gmail.com) for her work as Copy Editor, identifying where 'British-isms and American-isms' clashed; and to thank Victoria Kennar (vkproofreading@outlook.com) for her eagle eyed proofreading; and to thank David Prendergast (ebookscoversdesigns.com) for his wonderful help in creating the lovely cover of Montecatini.

And of course, I am indebted to you, the reader, for choosing to read this book.

https://amzn.eu/d/jggVsaH

This historical novel tells you about the hidden love affairs of Franklin Roosevelt and the women who surrounded and influenced this disabled president. Politics with a soft glove.

Please get in touch, and follow me on social media for information about the background to Montecatini and more novels to come.

Website: https://www.justinegilbertauthor.co.uk

On Instagram and X: @justinegilbertauthor

and on Facebook, Justine Gilbert in Whitstable, Kent, UK.